Buzzard Luck
And Other Outdoor Misadventures

By O. Victor Miller

Also by O. Victor Miller
The Tenderest Touch
One Man's Junk
Where Remedies Lie

Copyright © 2022 O. Victor Miller
All rights reserved.

Dedication

This book is lovingly dedicated to Tillie Jones Hicks, the Black saint who raised me and my sister. From a tenant farm outside Leary, Ga., she came to work for us when she was 18, when I was a year and a half, and Sister was an infant. Having no children of her own, she influenced our early childhood, sometimes more than our parents did. She gave us a childhood full of rich love and taught me something of the music of the English language spoken in the deep South. Through her eyes I saw the injustice of Jim Crow segregation, when to be human you had to break the law. From her I learned that immoral societies corrupt the souls of moral folks. All the days of my youth she sang Negro spirituals. At night she terrified us with visions of Hell fire and damnation. She frequently reminded me I was "slap full of the devil." Thanks to her, I delight in breaking rules. Without her love, it ain't no telling how bad I could've turned out. She gave us her lifetime of selfless loyalty and love.

Disclaimer

Stories get fat in the telling, or they die. Sometimes truth runs through them like a streak of lean. Facts are manipulated, added, changed and invented to make a story. Sometimes we've got to lie to tell a deeper truth. Paleolithic nomad scouts climbed the mountain ahead of the clan to come back and tell what lay on the other side. To goad them on, he had to paint a pretty picture around the campfire to urge them off their tired asses to go ahead on. Language was invented to help us stretch the truth.

Lying has honorable tradition. God lied to Adam when He told them the forbidden fruit would kill them. Cain lied to God about the whereabouts of Abel. Jacob lied to Isaac to steal Esau's birthright. And so on. Editors have called these stories *Viction* in keeping with my father's view that a good story may require "stretching" the truth, that a good storyteller shouldn't let true facts get in the way. In this I am my father's son. Sometimes I get carried away. Readers should, in the words of Coleridge, exercise "a willing suspension of disbelief." Just saying.

Acknowledgements

I measure my wealth by friends I've shared wilderness with. I thank my companions and hosts in outdoor misadventure who provided me places to enjoy, whether you meant to or not. Special thanks to O.K. Fletcher, Frank Wetherbee, "Big" and Dr. Henry Hart, Mary McNeil Collier, Dr. Michael Roberts, Catherine and Mitchell Mountcastle, Lee Geer, Sonny and Mack Able, Jim and Barbara Fritz, Cuzi Pez, Bill Pace, Bill Cooling, June White, Don Abrams, Billy Mac and EJ McAfee, Chip Hall, Mike Mooney, Joe Lawson, William R. Kicklighter, Gary and Corrine Flannigan, Clyde Edgerton, J.K. Jones, Janisse Ray, Jimmy Jacobs, Tom Seegmueller, Polly Dean, Bill Martin, Vic Sullivan, and Uncle Thad Huckabee. Forgive me if I made too much fun teasing y'all. Be assured I never wrote about nobody I didn't love, except a time or two. I've got a heap better friends than I deserve. Special thanks to my mentor and hunting buddy, Clyde Edgerton.

A college teacher in my own hometown, I spent 27 years with admirable colleagues and students. Some administrators appreciated my unscholarly publications, some didn't. Dr. Lynn Kennedy, my former humanities chairperson, encouraged me and came to my defense to her peril, earning my undying respect and love. Rosanna Almaee, director of the writing lab at Darton College, won my heart working her magic on my students. At Darton I made a few enemies and a mighty heap of friends. Thanks, friends.

My amazing editor and significant other, KK Snyder, put this book together. She edits most of what I write and nearly everything I do. She and my sister take turns feeding me, enabling me to be the sorry ass Southern male I've always been. Blame them.

I'm especially grateful to indigenous people of the U.S.,

Mexico, and North, South and Central America who befriended me and shared adventures, food and drink. I'm most indebted to my Kuna friends in the San Blas archipelago of Panama's Caribbean coast, especially the island village of Ukupsini. I thank you for your natural hospitality and for lending me your eyes to better see the interconnectedness of nature. In particular I thank Lucio Arozsemena, my Kuna first mate and sidekick in misadventure, and his remarkable wife, Luce, who accepted me into their hut and hearts. Thanks also to Mani, Luis, Domingo, Nadile, Gordo, Fabio, Tomi, Old Moo and Pescador Brown. Among these wonderful people I lived the richest two and half years of my life so far. I don't think I'll find better until I return. *Nuede.*

1

Introduction

In 1942, the year I was born, John O. Huckabee, Mama Jane's first cousin, was killed in England, on a motorcycle while leading an army convoy. The immeasurable grief of my great aunt and uncle created a vacuum they filled with me and my sister. In Daddy Oscar's words, they spoiled us rotten. It happened that John O. was an avid outdoorsman, who loved the woods and streams. I was heir to all his sports equipment, his guns, his bait casters, his boats, even his clothes. They made me into him, as best they could. I was encouraged to spend my days out of doors. Mama Jane wrote excuses from school for me to go hunting or fishing with Uncle Thad. Tillie kept my supper warm in the oven when I was out after sundown. John O. is one of the ghosts that haunt this house.

One of the greatest of my daddy's many legacies was to teach me to love a swamp at night. He taught me to catch bullfrogs, snakes, and alligators, to love a symphony of insects, peepers, bullfrogs, and the occasional roar of a bull gator claiming his turf. Daddy Oscar published his first book at 80, my age now. Without his colorful stories, I'd be hard pressed to write anything at all. He made folks laugh, himself the butt of the joke. Mama Jane tried to cultivate me and mostly failed. She was the last of the Southern ladies, a Colonial Dame in a matriarchal society.

Southerners know the magnetic fetch of land, to the homes we come home to whether we want to or not. Where our people are buried, where our dust settles, and our ashes are scattered. Here our people are, like them or not. I'm grateful to you who know me best as a son of a bitch but welcomed me home anyway. If I'd known I was coming back, I would've behaved better before I left. As it is, my quixotic sorties of misadventure have circled me like a buzzard home to roost in my childhood home on the Flint River in Radium Springs. Georgia, right smack where I started from four score years ago with nothing much to show for it. Here my sister, Marjorie "Sister" Miller Musgrove, takes care of me, providing a haunted home full of childhood ghosts and a riverbank to get drunk on with my dog. We are two old people living together who aren't married to each other, trapped by penury in a house still full of Mama Jane's antiques, blessed and cursed by mutual memories of childhood.

These stories are mostly culled from freelance articles published in *Gray's Sporting Journal* over a period of 25 years. Arranged by dates of publication, the collection provides a sort of autobiography of misadventure. During that time James R. Babb, Russ Lumpkin and Mike Floyd respectively have accepted and edited most of these stories. Others to thank are Jimmy Jacobs at *Georgia Sportsman,* Michael Brooks of *Albany Magazine,* and Quinn Cook and KK Snyder at *Southwest Georgia Living*. Nobody gets published without the help and intervention of editors. I've had some good ones, and I'm grateful.

Writers can't exist without readers. Words can't jump off the page without somewhere to land. With readers we share our deepest thoughts and perversions, stuff we wouldn't confess to spouses, shrinks, priests, pastors, or prostitutes—an intimacy like no other. So, if you are reading this, thanks.

3

Table of Contents

Torments of Hell	5
Hot Grits & Blue Yonder	12
Ludowici Squirrels	20
Genetic Integrity of Partridges	31
Dove Tactics	41
Bear Ballet	48
Real Men Don't Fly Fish	56
Gator Fleas, Shoalies and der Thunderkracken	65
There's No Shame in Missing a Bobwhite Quail	74
Dog Days	84
Clyde's Quail	93
Gun Dog	105
Crocodiles in Paradise	114
In the Bowels of the White Witch	126
The Wisdom of Solomon	136
Dog Snapper	148
Magdalena's Crocodile	158
Bad Thinking	172
Juice and Joy	184
Ideals	192
Fish Tale	200
The Devil's Game	209
A Fine Kettle of Fish	219
Pork	226
Hooterville	242
Quail, Dogs & Grandmothers	249
Buzzard Luck	259
Avarice	268
The Goodbye Bob	278
Circles Unbroken	286

The Torments of Hell

But all the woods about the place were full of black snakes, which would rise up like a human being and look one in the face, then glide away without doing any harm.
—Passamaquoddy Myth

Carl Sagan says our fear of snakes derives from primal memories of a dim evolutionary past, when arboreal ancestors snoozing among the branches were preyed upon in darkness by pythons and white oak runners. The same midbrain nostalgia accounts for our fear of falling, which waxes pale next to our fear of snakes. For most of us, the mere glimpse of a snake prompts a complex reaction between the hypothalamic and reticular systems, and we jump through our asses.

Tillie Hicks, the Black saint who raised me, never heard of Carl Sagan. She had a post-Edenic enmity of snakes that derived from the Bible. Tillie taught me that a coachwhip snake stood on its tail among the cornstalks and whistled when it spied you walking down the road. It lashed once and cut through high grass like a zipper on a nylon jacket. When it caught you, it tied you to a chinaberry tree and whipped you to death with its tail.

"It ain't no use to play dead neither. He run the end of his tail in your nose hole to see is you breathing. Then he go back to whipping you some more." God ordered coachwhips to bruise folks' heels, and they've been bound by God to do it since the coachwhip tempted our general progenitors with forbidden fruit.

"I'd run," I said.

"You cain't outrun no coarchwhip," Tillie answered.

"They bite they own tail and roll like a tire."

"You told me hoop snakes did that."

"A coarchwhip do, too."

Black snakes chased pregnant women to nurse on them. They weren't as fast as coachwhips because they didn't have to be. They loved mothers' milk and killed a heap of babies, strangling them by crawling down their throats to suck up milk in their bellies. But the original snake, around before babies or black snakes, was the coachwhip, and it was the main reason Black folks wandered around in large, loud groups, according to Tillie.

Tillie put the fear of God in me and Sister to make us manageable, but she believed everything she told us, working herself up and getting scared, too.

"Those children are petrified," Mother complained. "What have you done to petrify those children?"

"That the only way they behave."

Mother went along with anything Tillie invented to manage our deportment, since the mere thought of motherhood wore Mother to a frazzle. Her biggest fear for the first 18 years of my life was that Tillie would quit. Ours, too. We couldn't imagine life without Tillie. "Y'all doan behave, I moan quit" achieved a spontaneous moratorium on any mischief Sister and I could imagine. Tillie could out preach Cotton Mather on the torments of Hell, where coachwhip snakes mostly ran things. I guess I grew up with an unnatural indifference to rattlesnakes, which were nothing next to Tillie's coachwhips. I wore other mortal cautions threadbare worrying about coachwhips and Hell.

Tillie was also afraid of the Flint River, which flowed along the banks of our backyard. Her fear of the water may have derived from mythological affiliation with the River Jordan, which to cross over was synonymous with death, or it may have derived from the simple fact that Tillie couldn't swim; whichever, I knew my only safety from her wrath

7

lay in running to the riverbank and hiding in the primroses, where her fear of snakes and the Flint River protected me.

There were plenty of snakes on the riverbank, but I was less afraid of them than Tillie, who'd run us down and pinch us black and blue if we couldn't make it to the wild roses. Tillie, who had legs like an ostrich, was at least as fast as a coachwhip. Wide-eyed with sin, I'd hide among supralapsarian thorns. Petrified.

After I grew away from Tillie's mythic wisdom, my fear of reptiles equalized between coachwhips and rattlesnakes, which is to say that I became less afraid of the devil and a little more cautious of hemotoxic reptiles. Rattlesnakes regained their ability to set off complex reactions between my hypothalamic and reticular systems, and the first time I ever tried to milk a rattlesnake, I choked it. A freshman at Mercer University, I'd lied my way into a job teaching science at the Macon Junior Museum. The director, who'd left sociability and sanity in a Japanese POW camp, asked me to milk a little diamondback somebody had brought in. I studied the procedure in a book but faulting a membrane to cover the mouth of a beaker, I substituted the condom I optimistically carried in my wallet. (Children in those days didn't recognize prophylactics; the parents along the back wall didn't seem to recognize them either.) Stretched over the beaker, the nippled Trojan seemed inversely appropriate to "milking" since it resembled a formula bottle.

I caught the snake just behind its head, reckoning to hook its fangs through the latex and squeeze its jaws until amber poison pooled in the jar, but holding the reptile's head in one hand and the beaker in the other, I realized I didn't have enough hands.

The subtle bastard cranked its body and went after my thumb with fish-bone incisors squirting juice. I got rattled, perhaps from some primal memory of coachwhips. Wedging its body between my elbow and ribs, I tightened my grip behind the snake's head, which torqued and nodded as I lectured through gritted teeth and sphincter lips. The snake raised its tail and rattled, buzzing just below my ear, and I started coming unglued. I plugged the fangs into the Trojan, misaligning the snake's upper and lower jaws.

"Teacher! Teacher!" said a little girl on the front row.

I ignored her. I had my hands full. The snake became even more agitated, its body writhing in my armpit and its tail buzzing in my ear, but the child—bracing her raised hand with her other arm, which lay across her head, wasn't going to be put off. Now she was waving everything from the waist up. "Teacher," she cried, "the snake"s DAY-ud!"

"No, he's not," I countered. "Snakes relax after you milk them, and they fall asleep."

The adults against the back wall nodded in affirmation, and indeed the turgid rattlesnake had collapsed, slack as a stocking. I coiled it up in its cage, dismissed the class and buried it after the classroom had emptied.

"Where's our rattlesnake?" the museum director asked a few days later. "Must've got loose," I said. The secretary quit on the spot. The rest of the staff moved about gingerly for a while, their quick fingers pecking paperwork like egrets stabbing fish. I knew I was safe from having to milk another rattlesnake. The staff would never accept another one.

*

Years later I forgot about the head-torquing, body-cranking gyrations rattlesnakes can undertake. When deer hunting with sociology professor Fred Simmons, I saw a canebrake rattler crossing a red dirt road. I slammed on the brakes and expertly grabbed the reptile behind its head. I'd planned to take the snake home to teach the kids what not to play with, but the snake torqued loose and bit me on the ball of my thumb.

"Shit!" I said, my thumb peeking out of my fist like the

9

rosy spadix of a skunk cabbage. "Twenty percent of poisonous snakebites don't envenom," I informed Fred hopefully.

"Your thumb's already turning red," he observed.

"Open me one of them Budweisers. He only got me with one fang." I chugged the beer, sighting down the side of the can at my swelling appendage.

"Aren't you going to shoot that snake?"

"What good'll that do?" The snake tracked our conversation with its head.

"It might make you feel better if you die or lose your hand. Also, if you're not careful, you're going to step on him and get the other fang in you."

I pricked my thumb with my pocketknife and sucked it all the way to town. "Cutting is no longer recommended for snakebite," Professor Simmons said, "and take that thumb out of your mouth. I'm not driving through Albany with a 40-year-old man sucking his thumb."

"It hurts," I said.

"The opposable thumb," I reminded him, "is what separates man from the other animals."

"Opossums have opposable thumbs, too. They are also, by the way, immune to rattlesnake poison."

"Can't you drive faster?"

"Automobile accidents kill more people than snakebites," he said.

By the time we reached the emergency room, the end of my thumb was the size of a plum, and I was seeing enhanced colors, not only in my thumb but also in the world around me, which had turned sort of golden. The trees were turquoise, and Fred's face was a transfigurative white tinged with psychedelic orange.

Cash Corleone, ER surgeon on call, hooked up an IV and started pumping antivenin. Nine vials. "Young snakes are more potent," he explained.

"H'mmm, that sounds right," I said, remembering better

days. I don't know if my mystic calm was due to the proximity of the eternal or to the morphine Corleone pumped in with the antivenin, but the swelling finally went down, and the pain went away. I had to stay in ICU overnight and in the hospital another day after that because Corleon didn't know how rattlesnake poison and antivenin would react with my heart medication. Ten days later my face and hands swelled up like catchers' mitts. Serum sickness, Corleone said.

With me, it seems that snake trouble has roots in quests for non-Biblical knowledge, just as Tillie preached. When teaching Discovery, a summer program for youngsters, I draped an 85-pound python over my shoulders and staggered into a classroom full of kids, who shrieked in unison. The astonished constrictor instantly whipped a love knot around my neck. It took the zookeeper and two other Discovery instructors to wrestle the snake loose before my eyes popped out. I finally collapsed at my desk, wheezing.

"Do it again, teacher!" yelled the kids. "Do it again!"

The only other serious injury I've received from a snake was from a gentle white oak runner I took into a college composition class. What's education all about if not a confrontation with the faculties of reason? I put the snake on the floor to let the students observe it while I went to the blackboard to diagram the Jacobson organ, an olfactory sensor in the roof of the snake's mouth.

With my back to the classroom, I heard wild screams and turned to find pretty Amy Lovelace in one corner, running in place. The puzzled snake, having retreated to the same corner, was coiled before her in a great gray mound, flicking its tongue to catalog Amy's perfume and other confusing scents that exuded from her person. I scrambled to capture the snake, which bit me when Amy kicked it with her Keds. She also stomped some hairline fractures into my metacarpal before I could drag the snake out of range.

*

   All in all, even poisonous snakes do a lot more good than harm, and I almost never kill a rattlesnake or a moccasin, without which the woods and wetlands would fill up with rodents, tourists from Ohio and Styrofoam litter. Forty-three thousand Americans died in motor vehicle accidents last year, while poisonous snakes killed only 10. Firearms and hunting accidents accounted for 37,474 deaths, but a brace of rednecks will get drunk, throw loaded .30-06s in a rattletrap truck with bad brakes and speed to a hunting lease, where they'll stumble around worrying about rattlesnakes. If they step on a snake, it's because they're watching out for them in the trees, even though poisonous snakes can't climb. Snakebite is almost entirely restricted to people trying to kill snakes, catch them or milk them for a junior museum. They carry no communicable diseases, although the mainstay of their diet is rats, which caused the Black Death that killed three-quarters of the people in Europe and Asia during the 14th century.

   I wish there were more things in the world to make my heart gallop and pitter-patter, not fewer—especially now that women have become too dangerous to mess with. And it suits me fine if the swamps and wetlands fill slap up with rattlesnakes and cottonmouths and copperheads and king snakes and white oak runners. But coachwhips? Now, they're something else.

Hot Grits & Blue Yonder
For Mike Roberts - The doctor in the Duchess

The only thing more dangerous than a drunk in a pulpwood truck is a doctor in a Cesna. —Unknown

In a theology class at Mercer University during the 1960's, I was impressed by a quotation by Reinhold Nieburh in his famous book *Moral Man and Immoral Society*: "Man, unlike other creatures, is both gifted and cursed by an imagination which extends his appetites beyond the requirements of subsistence." I doubt I read the whole book, but that quotation has come home to rest regularly, haunting me all these years, because it accurately describes a fatal flaw of Southern males who lack the wisdom to know what's good for them and the patience to let well enough alone.

We covet the very things we should avoid. Like civil wars, high-strung bird dogs, and high-tone women who don't go to sleep after an argument. Our imagination extends a fear of falling into a mania for flight, so we neurotically invent angels and buy airplanes. We also attempt quixotically to alter the essential nature of things, dear things like hyperactive bird dogs, somnambulant women, and gravity—although everybody knows it's easier to accept and adjust to those things than to manage them. If there are appropriate maxims to these truths, they are as follows: If God wanted man to fly, he'd been issued wings; don't fall asleep if something's boiling on the stove; and seek the wisdom to accept things that can't be changed, truths which I hope the following parable illustrates.

13

*

"Sam is one hardheaded son-of-a-bitch," Frank Wetherbee explained as he buckled the shock collar to his new pointer's thick neck. "Which is why I have to turn his collar all the way up." My mastoids ached as I clenched my molars, trying to keep my mouth shut about hardheaded.

Early shock collars weren't as dependable as the ones you buy now. They didn't have all the bugs ironed out. A low-flying airplane or a hand-held walkie-talkie could set one off. This disfunction conditioned Sam to point birds with his tail between his legs, but I'm getting ahead of myself.

Frank got Sam from a friend who hunts from horseback in north Florida, where the flat open terrain allows him to sit his horse and watch dogs work for a country mile. He can stand up in his stirrups and see for another mile. Sam ranged too close for Florida and too far for Wetherbee, which illustrates the same flaw in judgement with which we choose our wives. We marry high strung women and try to settle them down or get us a slow gal and try to soup her up, leaping from one extreme to another instead of settling in comfortably on the middle ground. We don't really want what we think we want. And we almost never want what's best for us, a flaw that prompted Frank to get a dog who ran like a cheetah and then to try to make him hunt close.

Or take Wayland, a good old boy who sat around the T.V. with popcorn crumbs on his crotch, thumbing through the *Sports Illustrated* bathing suit issue. "Boy!" he said as his imagination extended his appetite beyond the requirements of subsistence, "I bet she could run the fat off my old heart." A month later I saw him walking out of a singles bar with his elbow locked around a teenage myocardial accident looking for a place to happen. A month after that they got married. One day she got to acting ugly, so he turned her over his knee. She pouted about it, which he thought was cute, until he went to sleep, and she threw boiling grits on his face. There's nothing you can do about hot grits but scream, that and speed around in your pickup truck with your face out the window. Molten lava is better than hot grits.

*

A doctor friend of mine, Streetman Vester, wanted more than anything in the world to fly an airplane. He took lessons for years without ever being able to solo, until finally his instructor told him to give up. Some people aren't meant to fly, and he was one of them. The instructor hated that he'd taken so much money from Streetman, and his conscience wouldn't let him to take any more.

Dr. Vester trudged sadly off the tarmac, his leather cap clenched in his fist, but before long he found an ultralight for sale. You don't need a license to fly an ultralight, a one-man apparatus that looks like a beach umbrella with an Elgin outboard motor. I know what he was thinking. If I can't handle a big airplane, I can start with a small one and work my way up—dangerous logic. It's like believing you can handle a small woman or beat up the little guy in a bar. Some very virile things, like viruses, come in small packages. Small women are handy at slinging hot grits or potash syrup after domestic arguments, and little guys can whip your ass before you know it, having collected plenty of experience as first draft choices in bar room brawls.

Dr. Vester bought the ultralight with a check about the same time Frank brought Sam up from Florida and started gearing him down to a dog he could walk behind. The good doctor found an Oldsmobile dealer with a hanger and a dirt strip in his backyard who was willing to put up with the doctor coming out every Saturday and Sunday to taxi back and forth along the airstrip.

So, he did. Streetman carried a handheld portable two-way

15

Motorola walkie-talkie to chat with his wife, to advise her of his progress, and to tell her when to have supper hot.

Two days every weekend he nearly drove the Oldsmobile dealer crazy with the noise, and the Oldsmobile dealer's wife crazy with red dust. He'd get the ultralight right up to takeoff speed, reach the end of the runway, shake his head, check in with the Mrs., taxi around and do the same thing again.

He'd beat his fist against his thighs, curse himself for cowardice while something inside him, some subterranean voice that's privy to the wisdom of the ages, whispered, "No, don't do it. Stay on the ground where you belong."

But late one Sunday afternoon just before dusk, he did do it. Not quite intentionally, but with malice aforethought, nonetheless. The takeoff was serendipitous, but not inconceivable, since Streetman had been trying to fly an airplane, any airplane, for most of his professional life and had paid out thousands of dollars to flight instructors. You mess with something long enough under the right conditions and you can achieve some small measure of accidental success. Enough monkeys pounding on enough typewriters long enough, still probably won't write *Paradise Lost*, but they might hack out a couple columns for *Albany Magazine*. Or like the 80-year-old lawyer's young wife said when she wound up pregnant: "You never know when an old gun's liable to go off."

Anyway, near the end of the strip, the throttle stuck or the doctor hit a bump he hadn't hit before, or a freak gust of head wind puffed him, or maybe his moxie surged, or some atrophied gland squirted hormones into his bloodstream.

Miraculously, the airplane bounced off the ground and the physician was airborne before he knew it. Since he'd never had any experience landing, he went ahead and flew.

"Wow," he said after he'd cleared his first row of planted pines, "This is-ah-great. I should have done this sooner."

After so many jerky stops, starts, and aborted missions, the lift-off was powerfully orgasmic. "Why, oh, why, did I wait so looong?"

*

Meanwhile, the same Sunday, back on Gravel Hill Farm, Frank and I had finally gotten Sam to range within eyesight, and we succeeded in witnessing an actual point. We'd been pretty sure all along that Sam pointed quail. It's just that we couldn't get close enough to see if any birds got up when he did. Sam, or a white speck that could have been Sam, was frozen into a crouched and classic rictus two hills over. We'd been jogging all afternoon like Maasai warriors, our shotguns at port arms.

As we closed in the last hundred yards, Frank raised his transmitter like the Statue of Liberty, reminding Sam he meant business. Like the doctor's takeoff, we'd worked long and hard to do what we were doing now. Both of us paused, wheezing like a couple of wind broke mules, forty yards from the patch of beggarweed where Sam pointed.

"Just look at that!" Frank gasped. "Ain't that the prettiest thing you've ever seen?"

Sam was frozen like a concrete dog, the sculpted muscles of his powerful shoulders rigid, his tail pointed toward the darkening sky, where the whisper of the breeze through the longleaf pines slowly gave way to a rising neurotic whine, too high-pitched for a regular airplane. We hardly noticed the aircraft was getting louder overhead. As we approached Sam to honor his point, the doctor's Motorola walkie-talkie set off Sam's shock collar. "Kiwi Base, this is Kiwi Bird," he broadcast over the little engine. "I'm airborne, do you read me? Airborne!"

To say Sam busted the covey would be an irresponsible understatement. He sprung up on his hind legs, spurting urine and bouncing around in the covey like a pogo stick with flapping ears—*AROOO, AROOOP*—as the electricity jazzed his blood. The birds flew, not up and out in any common direction to fan out and settle into huntable singles. They splashed centrifugally, like a lawn sprinkler, outward in all directions from the bouncing dog in wild and whirling flight, sloughing random feathers. Sam bounced like a kangaroo over the last hill of wiregrass and longleaf pines, his front paws never touching the ground. *AW, AW, AW, AW!*

Frank slapped the control transmitter with his open palm, then threw it down and began stomping it with his bootheel. "What the hell?" he said.

Sam disappeared over one horizon, the doctor's airplane over the other. Of course, I didn't know it was the doctor's airplane until later, just like I didn't know that his walkie-talkie set off Sam's collar.

"We sure broke that dog of pointing birds," I said. "Why didn't you shoot?"

"I threw down on that little airplane, but it ducked behind a tree. Why didn't you?"

"I was dodging quail."

Frank and I began hunting Sam, not with him–for him. We looked until dark.

*

Dr. Vestus soared like an eagle, freed from the corporeal tethers of gravity. He gazed proudly around, purveyor of all that his aquiline eyes could see, from one bruised horizon to another dimly bloodshot by the afterglow of the setting sun. So caught up was he in the miracle of flight, he failed to notice that night had fallen and he was flying around in the darkness somewhere near the Mitchell County line, without running lights or any specific notion of his whereabouts.

When the terrifying reality of his predicament suddenly dawned on him, he decided he'd better land that ultra-light before he ended up on the windshield of a 747. But where? He could distinguish only dark patches and darker patches on the ground. Finally, he mistook a very dark rectangle for a field and went for it, crashing his plane into a stand of planted pines. The crash didn't kill him, but it broke up his ultra-light and some bones.

*

Before the crash Frank and I were still searching for Sam, and we might never have found him without a flashlight if the ultralight hadn't circled back over, setting off the collar again. Of course, we couldn't see Streetman, but we could hear him screaming, "Mayday, MAYDAY, Mayday!" over the mosquito whine of his engine as he passed over, barely clearing the pine tops. Lost people tend to go in circles on land, at sea, or in the air.

"What's that fool doing up there flying around in the dark?" said Frank.

We heard Sam again and found him balled up by a lightered stump with his paws over his ears, his tongue dirty from dragging in the dirt. Frank dropped to his knees, fumbling the collar off just as the lost doctor circled one last time. *YAHHHH!* Frank screamed, flinging the shock collar into a tuft of broomsage, shaking his hands like he'd burned himself with boiling grits. Frank was bent double, his hands sandwiched between his knees. In the darkness I could discern his grimace because his clenched teeth were faintly glowing a luminescent green.

Then we heard a putter and a whack as Streetman crashed into the stand of planted pines about a mile away. "Serves him right," Frank said.

"Hadn't we better call somebody?"

"We can't call somebody 'til we get back to the car," he snarled. "Besides, like I said, it serves him right."

We headed back to the kennels, Sam limping gingerly behind us, high stepping as if he dreaded the idea of grounding himself. His whiskers stayed kinky, and the shock collar stayed in the broomsage.

Dr. Vester lurched around Phoebe Putney Hospital for a while on aluminum crutches, making his rounds with his legs wrapped in plaster. He took up radio-controlled model airplanes, which he can crash without bodily investment.

Frank considered bobbing Sam's tucked tail to disguise his lack of temerity. Whenever the poor dog crawls up on a covey of birds, he shimmies like he's stalking diamondback rattlesnakes, but he has slowed down by virtue of the fact that he pauses often to glance in trepidation skyward, proving that even a high-strung bird dog can get religion and develop the theological notion that something up there is sitting in judgement with a transmitter or a flaming sword.

Like the rest of us, Sam must live by his instincts, whether he likes it or not. He hunts because it's his nature, but he hunts as though he were also aware of that natural depravity incurred with the original sin, that prelapsarian fall when lions stopped lying with lambs and pointers started hunting birds they aren't allowed to eat.

Ludowici Squirrels

Hunting I reckon very good
To brace the nerves, and stir the blood... —Matthew Green

"Squirrels!" I say. "I can kill squirrels at my birdfeeder."

"Not Altamaha Back Swamp squirrels, you can't!" snaps the chief. Dougherty County Police Chief William R. Kicklighter is used to having his way. He pouts if you don't jump flat-footed on every idea he comes up with, articulating acute impatience with his favorite expletive, "My damn!"

"I ain't driving to the other side of Georgia to hunt rodents when I can shoot rats at the dump," I say.

His gastropodous lip creeps out. "Some of my best memories are hunting swamp squirrels during the Great Depression."

"Bullshit! You were five years old at the end of the Great Depression."

"It lasted longer in Long and McIntosh counties. Anyway, what else you got to do?" I tell him I stay home Thursdays to watch for the garbage truck.

"My damn!"

Then I tell him...what the hell. The chief is from Ludowici, Georgia, famous for tile production and speed traps. In the early '70s when Kicklighter was a GBI agent, then-Governor Jimmy Carter told him to get over here and clean up gambling, prostitution, and election fraud. Con men were fleecing Yankees along U.S. 17 in clip joints where you could gas up, buy pecan pralines and Confederate flags, get your alternator sabotaged and lose a few thousand dollars playing punch-board or razzle-dazzle. Con men worked in cahoots with corrupt law officials who bought power with hijacked trucking cargo.

Maybe these old Georgia boys were still pissed off about Sherman's firebreak to Savannah, but robbing Yankees was still against the law, even in coastal Georgia, and it was an embarrassment to Jimmy and Miss Lillian. "Nobody tried to outsmart the tourists," Kicklighter tells me. "They'd out-dumb them." A New Jersey couple would pull in, chuckling at a sign advertising Frash Bald Peenuts-*hee-hee*-and lose their nest egg to a slick hick in overalls with a ripe belly and a toothpick in his mouth. If they complained to the law, a deputy would lock them up for gambling. Melissa Fay Green covered all that in her wonderful book *Praying for Sheetrock*.

Ludowici, Jesup, Guardi and Darian are in the part of Georgia that looks like Georgia's supposed to. Flatwoods, swamps, blackwater rivers, coastal marsh, where the salt air blows wind shadows across the marsh grass and sculpts the twisted live oaks dripping Spanish moss. You pull up to a house, folks make you set your feet under the table, their way of banking against hard times. When they run out of luck, somebody they've fed before will feed them. Kicklighter is understandably anxious to return to his youth for a couple of days.

*

Crossing the piney woods of the coastal plains, I flash back to boyhood visits with Uncle Charlie Hinson in Hazlehurst. In those days the pine trunks were skinned in shapes like arrow fletching, the yellow meat scabbed over with waxy sap. I remember Uncle Charlie's timber boots hook-laced to his bald knees. Our privilege was to unlace his boots and tug them off when he came in from tending turpentine cups. I remember the blue dents in his marbled calf where rattlesnakes had popped him. "Aw, the buzzboys mostly stays out your way 'til you change your pattern," he'd say. "Then you find one ever 50 yards." Uncle Charlie would wiggle his freed toes, and we'd skedaddle backward. "Y'all come back over here after the first frost and hunt dare," he'd say in the way of goodbye as Sister and I piled into the back seat of the family Buick. "We'll hunt ever day but Sunday." He'd cut his eyes merrily at Mother. "We get drunk on Sunday."

"Turpentiners were a pretty tough lot in those days," Kicklighter affirms. "They'd boil the coffee 'til it floated an ax wedge, then spit to scald wild hogs that roamed through camp. But wait 'til you meet Hughes and Elton."

Horace Champion's cabin is cedar inside and cypress out, cut from swamp timber and made into boards by his cousin's portable sawmill. A gasoline generator cranks out surging electricity, and there's a tin roof to sleep under when it rains. When it doesn't rain, acorns drop—plap—or the wind scratches in the limbs with sweet static.

The tin expands and pings in the morning sun.

"This swamp has been owned and hunted by Champions since we run off the Indians," Horace says. Elbert, his son-in-law, stands alone by the fire, looking like he might be descended from one of the Indians they overlooked. If anybody's a match for a Ludowici squirrel, this man is. He routinely wades armpit deep in frigid swamp water, stalking bucks, bears and Russian boars.

Altamaha River Back Swamp squirrels, they warn me, are different. They don't scamper and play. They zip through the treetops like grizzly synapses, lashing neurotic tails and screaming like monkeys. To call them, Horace pares off a piece of palmetto stem, splits it and inserts a reed made from the blade. He blows it, and the squirrels come to the high-pitched squall like rats to a Pied Piper, maybe to attack.

23

Ludowici squirrels have no natural predators. Even bobcats and panthers have learned that more calories are invested to subdue one than the scrawny flesh renders, and a wounded Ludowici squirrel is reputed dangerous.

Variously bred hounds trickle centripetally from the outer dark to our bonfire: Walkers, blueticks, beagles, razorbacks and curs; shy dogs, lean bitches, boar dogs and gyps. "Somebody took drunk," Horace explains, "and turned the dogs out." We stand around swapping lies. An amateur boxer in his youth, the white haired Kicklighter walks on his toes, which means he can't hold still without shuffling and box-stepping. He told me once, "You get caught flat-footed, somebody'll knock you slap to next week." Inspecting a crime scene or hearing a lie, he waltzes to silent melodies. Or maybe to music installed intracranially 35 years ago by a Marine pug who caught him flat-footed.

We scratch, spit, grin and sip whiskey, listening to the hounds strike, trail, babble and bay—*bar-roop*—running through the night like brush fire. Man, if life gets any better than this, I'll be scared of dying.

*

I listen to stories of knife fights and killings; of the open range and livestock fenced out, not in; of spring roundups to castrate and mark hogs in the flat woods. Instead of branding, the feral animals' ears were notched, some rustled with such serial and diverse frequency as to have no ears at all. The infamous Sheriff Poppel claimed every hog in Long and McIntosh counties. "If you wanted to know whose hog it was," Horace explains, "you could look up under the tail. If there was a circle under there, it was one of the sheriff's hogs." Every hog with a meat asshole, it was said, belonged to the law.

We talk of cane grindings, syrup kettles, dip vats and turpentine stills; of stump whiskey; of banking sweet potatoes and cooking off cracklings; of lard, chitterlings and lye soap. Of screwworms that ate off the sides of deer's faces.

"When I was coming up, we fed the dogs sweet potatoes," Horace says. "They done aw right on it, but if you was behind one that farted, it turned you off the road."

"We was too poor to have dogs," Kicklighter says.

They turn in and chat from their Army sleeping bags and blankets, their voices transfigured into cartoon bubbles from the ends of olive-drab swaddling.

"You've eat chicken feet, ain't you, Bill?"

"No, I don't recall ever eating any chicken feed," answers Kicklighter, deaf from a lifetime of shotgun blasts like every middle-aged Southerner.

"Naw, chicken feet, not chicken feed."

"Oh sure, I've ate chicken feet plenty of times."

*

Around midnight I get up to go to the bathroom, then remember the generator's off and the toilet bowl iced over, so I go outside. I bump down the hallway where, as my eyes adjust, I see vapor plumes blowing like teakettles from Elbert's and Horace's sleeping bags, the ends I assume to be the heads. Their breath, maybe because of stump-whiskey fumes, glows blue in the moonbeams.

"While you're up," growls Kicklighter, "how about getting me another patch?"

"Patch?"

"Cover!"

I feel my way around the cabin until I find a stack of cotton quilts, peeling a couple from the pile. I hand one to the chief on the top bunk. He grunts in perfunctory appreciation as I burrow, shivering, back into my mound on the bottom bunk.

"You rattling the bed," says Kicklighter.

As soon as I'm tucked in good, he says, "My damn! I

dropped my patch. Hand it up here."

I lean out and pat the frosty floor, accidentally finding a bottom corner of my own patch and handing it up to Kicklighter, who snatches off all my covers.

"You ungrateful old bastard," I squall. "I get up to get you some cover, and you swipe mine."

"Turn a-loose," he bleats. "I got it."

"Let go, you got mine."

We saw the quilt until Kicklighter yanks me to a sitting position, then tumbles from the top bunk. We both crash to the floor, tangling into covers, invectives and flailing legs.

"My damn!"

"What is going on over yonder?" cries Horace. "Hey, we don't have no bullshit at the hunting camp!"

*

The next morning, I limp on the edges of my feet to keep my flat insteps from sticking to the frosty floor. Supper has solidified into frosty lard like pecan pralines from a Ludowici clip joint. Kicklighter rises, yawns and grabs his scattergun.

"Well, gentlemen, I believe I'll go down to the Back Swamp and kill us up a mess of cat squirrels," he says. Hunting vest ponderous with shotgun shells, he disappears into the tangled green wall at the edge of the swamp to stalk his quarry, and we sit on the porch listening to desultory gunfire that sounds like the tail end of the Tet Offensive. Finally, he staggers out with a dozen squirrels. Horace and I skin them while the chief, who says the excitement wore him slap out, takes a nap.

Horace whacks off the paws at wrists and ankles. He lops off heads and tails and neatly skins the truncated rodents, piling mousy scraps like merkins while hot oil pings in the fish cooker. When he flicks water in the pot, there's a crack like a .22 short. It's ready.

When squirrel flesh hits hot pig grease, it twitches and draws up, compressing sinew and fiber. We gig at the fizzing lumps with a barbecue fork, merely bobbing them in the fat, unable to skewer them with the tines. We hunt up some tongs.

At supper Kicklighter recounts the hunt. "I was shooting them out the top of a water oak with low-brass eights," he tells us. "They'd hit the ground running, so I swapped out to magnum fours and got to killing a few."

*

Horace is chewing, his temples working. There's a piece of purple meat left on his plate that looks like the corner torn off a motor mount. "You might ort to stuck with eights," Horace says. "When they carried that off, you should've let them go ahead on."

"Yes," nods Elbert, "I believe I'd pass on a squirrel who run off with a load of bird shot. Maybe downsize to number nines and cull down to the younger ones."

"Well, this squirrel's slap full of shot," says Kicklighter, spitting shards of gray metal onto his plate.

"That ain't shot," says Horace. "That's your fillings."

"My damn," says Kicklighter, tonguing a molar.

Camp food is simple and substantial. I learn to eat eggs scrambled with rice and sour cream mixed in grits. We eat fried sweet-potato chips, fried venison, fried squirrel, fried wild pork.

After two or three days, when I step off the porch into the dim sun, grease trickles from the corners of my mouth. I know when I get home I'll leave a rainbow slick in the bathtub, and my cardiologist will claim he can hear the fat sizzle as it drips upon my hot heart.

We run out of grits and molasses and drive to Brown's General Store, where I'm fascinated by strange tools hanging on the wall. There are hacks, saws, scrapers, hatchets, yokes, chains, cups, broadaxes and bull-tongue plows, brown with old rust. There's one medieval implement with iron spikes that looks like something left over from the Inquisition. Kicklighter calls it a weaning cap. I try to imagine fitting the devilish thing around a cow's udder without getting trampled in cow flop.

"Naw, it goes on the calf's head," Horace explains. "The cow kicks it walleyed when it tries to nurse."

"My damn!" says Kicklighter, shaking his head.

*

Early one afternoon Horace hauls me on a four-wheeler into a pristine tupelo and cypress swamp. I shinny 30 feet up a bay tree in my climbing stand. I don't see a deer, since the dogs have run them all to South Carolina. This stretch, he assures me, harbors no squirrels, but time stands still in this gloomy place. It's sweetly eerie to hunt all day in the cathedral hush without hearing a horn or an internal combustion engine, to escape all stratifications of labor. Here Horace doesn't man the graveyard shift for the pulpwood company that pollutes his beloved river, here Elbert doesn't work for his wife at Fort Stewart, here I don't grade English papers for apathetic teenagers and here Kicklighter doesn't give a damn for law and order. I blow vapor through my fists and watch wood-wrens puff against the cold.

At dusk Horace bounces back down the trail to pick me up, standing on the pegs. We ride down an abandoned logging road, mud splattering our shins like flat O.D. paint. Suddenly we stop. "Hogs," he whispers, dismounting and lifting his shotgun from the handlebar rack.

With shoulders hunched collar to cowlick, he tiptoes among the tupelos, carrying his gun like a suitcase, his other hand held out for balance, fingers splayed. He disappears into green tangle at the water's edge.

Squinting, I see concentric silver ripples and spot two

black boar hogs shaggy as bears. They slosh forward, bobbing for crawfish in hock-deep water, their trombone heads wagging and dipping as though connected by springs. Grunts leak out with each step—*runk, runk, runk.*

A cypress trunk grows a rusty limb as Horace's barrel eases from behind it. My heart stutters. I hold my breath. There's a thunderous blast and white smoke. One hog collapses. The other glares balefully and starts my way. I draw my feet up, squatting on the saddle, holding the handlebars with white knuckles. "Shoot, dammit, shoot!" Horace drops the second hog as peripheral buckshot boils the water. We load up the hogs and creep home, tires rubbing the insides of the fenders.

*

And now it's finally my turn to enter Back Swamp alone to pursue Ludowici squirrels. My moment of truth. I'm infected with congenital and archetypal blood lust, anxious to enter the catharsis of the kill. Kicklighter holds open my vest as Horace offers a ritualistic dollop of stump. "When you knock one down," he warns, "be careful walking up on him. A squirrel dies wide-eyed, so if his eyes are closed, watch out. He'll be playing possum to pull you in. If you ain't sure, shoot him again. If his eyes are open, touch your barrel to his eyeball. If he winks, shoot him again."

"What if he just twitches?"

"Shoot him again."

When I leave the cabin armed with a .22 Colt Woodsman, my hosts' jaws drop. "You better take Elbert to back you up," Horace advises.

"Not me," said Elbert. "I'm hunting hogs this morning. I ain't feeling up to no squirrels." Elbert's black eyes, framed in beard, blaze with wild temerity.

"Save a bullet for yourself," Kicklighter warns.

"That's a good one," I laugh, but nobody smiles.

29

"Don't let dark catch you down there neither," cautions Elbert, pointing toward Back Swamp with his thumb and tongue.

The red oak I'm sitting under soon begins twitching with life. Squirrels materialize, crawling through treetops like gunmetal maggots. I blast one, and it tumbles from a branch and lands in a squat in dry leaves. It's an old squirrel fringed in hoar; his frosty hackles bristling, he glares with demented onyx eyes, screaming like a power-steering pulley belt, leaving me unhinged, a limp .22 pistol in my hand. He starts toward me, hissing, arching his back and lashing his tail, his orange incisors dripping acid.

"Help!" I scream, steadying the Woodsman with both hands, realizing with horrible clarity that the squirrel is not mortally wounded, that I've merely barked him, blasted branch instead of rodent.

How I manage even to graze the squirrel with a second shot is beyond me. The barrel of my Woodsman vibrates like a tuning fork, but the bullet somehow plows a crimson furrow through the mousy velvet of his skull, invoking more power-steering pulley screams that clabber blood. I've seen squirrels scratch fleas with blurred haunches, a motion faster than the human eye can register. This rodent scrambles up me and catches my hair, running in place to scratch out my eyes, biting me on the bridge of the nose. It's amazing how far you can sling a cat squirrel when you're terrified.

*

"What happened to your face?" Horace asks back at the cabin.

"I don't know; it was quick. That's either where the squirrel mauled me or where I dove into the dammit-vines and cat's claw to get away."

Elbert dabs moonshine on my eyelids and the bridge of my nose, which looks like it's been stabbed twice with a screwdriver. "My damn!" Kicklighter says.

"I'd rather hunt hogs than squirrels," I confess after Elbert retrieves my abandoned pistol. Elbert's hog is hanging from the gambrel, dripping syrupy blood from its slotted nose.

"Aw, squirrels ain't so bad after you get the hang of it," grins Horace. "Maybe you can start out on chipmunks and bears and work your way up."

Genetic Integrity of Partridges

We know nothing about the impact of this practice [release of pen-raised birds] on the genetic integrity of wild quail. —George A. Hurst

*S*ome say it was a land swindle involving latter-day carpetbaggers and scalawags who bought up land dirt cheap after boll weevils and the Depression gnawed their way through Southwest Georgia, creating quail plantations and bogus notions of Southern gentility fostered by Yankee industrialists who'd read *Gone with the Wind.*

They called their acquisitions "plantations," although indigenous Southerners hadn't the faintest idea of the difference between a plantation and a big farm. Now the area has gained worldwide fame as the Quail Capital, and dozens of quail plantations mottle the Southwest Georgia map. Pilgrims in designer brier britches and bandana ascots deplane corporate jets to enjoy the scrotal heft of shotgun shells in an atmosphere of horseflesh, leather and gunpowder, riding behind gun dogs that stalk through wiregrass and longleaf pine. It's big business. Riverwalk Plantation alone pampers over 2,000 quail hunters a year who come here from all over the world in pursuit of the aristocrat of game birds.

Nothing fills lungs with clean air like wading through frosty wiregrass at dawn when the world is sprinkled with diamond dust amid fall's inflammation of hardwoods. The horses huff vapor. A liver spot pointer, his tongue bloody from dragging through cat's claw, is locked into rigor mortis on birds that zip around in the broomsedge before exploding into wild and rattling flight. Swamp quail corkscrew through the gallberries.

Birds take off like rabid bats launched from slingshots. Blam, blam!

"Hell's fire! I didn't cut a feather!"

"I didn't even get my damned safety off!"

Quail hunting is different from when I was a kid. Non-equestrian hunters may still ride the hunting wagon's comfortable seats, but a tractor or jeep has likely replaced the flop-eared jack and jenny, and plantation guests now inhale exhaust fumes instead of mule flatus.

When I was a kid, Ike (Eisenhower, for you young folks) came down to hunt quail on Blue Springs once in a while, but now celebrities as diverse as Chuck Norris and Mary Ann Mobley flock here in droves to shoot pen-raised quail over dogs that cost what Buicks used to.

Two years ago, General Schwarzkopf came to Campbell Farms just ahead of a group of Atlanta surgeons, one of whom was disappointed at missing a chance to meet the outspoken general.

"What do you want to meet him for?" a cardiovascular surgeon inquired of his partner. "What would we have to talk about with a general?"

"We've got plenty in common," answered the first doctor. "He's killed almost as many people as we have."

Another thing that's changed since my boyhood is they ain't near as many quail. The population is in dangerous decline, about a 70 percent decrease over the last 30 years, and despite what some may tell you, the problem has more to do with habitat than with predation. Quail ordinarily suffer somewhere around an 80 percent annual mortality, usually offset by reproduction. But successful reproduction demands food and the cover of edges and fencerows, the type provided by tenant farmers and the 40-acres-and-a-mule approach to agriculture that characterized the South after Reconstruction right into the 1960s. But that no longer describes Southern agriculture. You know times have changed when the Mellons' famous Pineland Plantation clearcut all the way to the Cooleewahee Creek to raise 243 acres of catfish, of which $500,000 worth swam off during a flood.

One dubious answer to the decline in wild birds and the increasing demands of quail hunters is pen-raised birds, "liberated quail," the shooting preserves call them. Although these birds are used practically everywhere, the best thing you can say about them is that any damned fool can hit one, which helps make celebrity hunts successful.

According to Tall Timbers Research Station, the average released bird lives 11 days. Of 159,000 "liberated" birds, only 1.2 percent survive a year. I've seen an entire covey of these birds recycled into hawk manure and owl pellets faster than a corporate jet could fly a hunting party down from Boston. I once saw a cold-trailing Llewellin setter lock down on coyote spoor next to a cone-topped metal feeder where a half-dozen birds had been released the day before. The bewildered hunters stood behind the dog at port arms, staring at the feathery turds as though they expected bobwhites to fly like phoenixes from poop. To airborne and landbound predators alike, the metallic clank of these feeders has a Pavlovian ring.

When putting out birds just ahead of a hunting party, it's best to windmill them, one in each hand, to get them dizzy enough to hold, but liberated quail are sometimes too trusting or indolent to fly, and the dogs snatch them before hunters have a chance to fire.

Without natural predators, wild quail would be as stupid as pen-raised birds. Foxes and hawks tend to kill tame quail and educate wild ones. Predators do more good than harm by keeping nest-destroying rodents in check and keeping game birds on their toes. They bust up coveys in spring to ensure dispersion and genetic integrity. We should all know by now that in matters of ecology one hand washes the other. My plantation friends like to take me quail hunting because I can shoot a box of shells without ever cutting a feather. Like other predators, I teach survival skills and bust up coveys, thereby perpetuating genetic integrity.

Even rattlesnakes, which eat lots of cotton rats and no quail eggs, are beneficial to wild quail habitat, at least until they hang a fang in your prize setter. I was hunting once with Putnam Fairweather and Jay Powell when I stepped in a stump hole and fell eye to eye with a coiled diamondback the size of Oprah Winfrey's thigh. I sprang to my feet as Putnam threw up his shotgun. "Wait!" I said. "Snakes do more good than harm to wild quail populations."

Rusty, Putnam's liver spot, was pointing the reptile and shaking like the proverbial dog defecating peach pits.

"You wanna step back?" Putnam queried.

"Wait, wait," I cried. "Let's catch the snake and use him to snake-proof bird dogs."

"Snake-proof dogs?" Jay, Putnam, Rusty and the rattlesnake all looked at me like I'd cracked my dog whistle.

"Sure, I'll get a vet to suture his mouth shut. Any dog that points him we'll juice with the shock collar."

Putnam's mouth made a perfect equilateral triangle beneath his salt-and-pepper mustache. His eyes squinted like hickory nut seams as he pondered whether I was a thoroughbred fool or just purely ignorant in matters of the moment. He shot the snake from the hip, spattering snake meat and broomsedge on my canvas britches.

"Putnam just dog-proofed your snake," Jay said, sucking a tooth.

I removed my boots and unlocked my toes, which had knuckled under and cramped with the blast. Then with my pocketknife I dissected salvageable portions of the reptile, removing a full-grown fox squirrel from an elongated membrane of stomach.

"See?" I said.

"See what?"

"Squirrel."

A pecan farmer, Putnam hates a squirrel, but he still wouldn't repent killing the diamondback. I butchered the reptile into steaks and accidentally fed them to my mother-in-law when they got mixed in with some dove breasts my sister cooked.

Landowners often ask me to shoot bobcats that trespass on their quail covers. I tell them I will, but I've never been able to. I tried once, aiming at a sleek bobcat with paisley gray fur, but just before I pulled the trigger the cat looked into my scope, and through the magnified pupils of those wild, wild eyes I saw into its soul. I'd have shot myself before I shot that cat, and I decided right then and there that if I ever kill animals in the name of quail conservation, I'll shoot the irresponsible blockheads who abandon puppies and pussycats on country roads to fend for themselves on quail eggs and chicks. One healthy bobcat is worth a long-bed pickup full of pen-raised quail and fickle pet owners, in my opinion.

Putnam says liberated quail infect wild birds with blackhead and other maladies that can spread to wild turkeys. They attract hawks to the area, causing a feeding frenzy of "predator/quail interaction" that overlaps into the wild bird population. He hates pen-raised birds and has never released one on Pebble Ridge.

I live across the Kinchafoonee Creek from Fowltown Farms. Billy Mac and E.J. McAfee, who have known me all our lives, think I poach their birds, but I don't. I accidentally roadkilled a plump partridge one morning on the way to work and ate her smothered in gravy. So savory was she that I will at least admit to coveting my neighbor's coveys. For all I know the word "covet" derived from "covey" sometime back in the days when my poaching progenitors were being chased across McAfee Grange in Scotland, keeping them on their toes and scattering bevies of potentially incestuous Millers.

  Billy Mac shares Putnam's aversion to birds raised in captivity, but he does feed his wild quail cracked corn and sorghum all year to make up for nutritional losses caused by insecticides. He provides plenty of cover, plants long lines of sweet sorghum and philosophically tolerates predators, except house cats, which he hates with the same passion Putnam harbors for rattlesnakes and squirrels. In a way, though, I love pen-raised quail. They keep bobcats sleek and rich Yankees happy. A happy Yankee is a good Yankee. Without happy Yankees there'd be no plantations and damn few wild quail.

  Putnam plants vetch, partridge peas, beggarweed and lespedeza, and harrows to encourage grass seed and insects. Both men are careful to leave plenty of cover when they burn. They realize that habitat is everything, or nearly so, and in the regimented and intelligent stewardship of land lies the answer to saving quail. The solutions seem to lie, as they so often do, in the ironic and paradoxical love that avid bird hunters have for a quarry they spend so much time trying to kill, something animal rights activists may not understand, although intelligent birdwatchers do. Songbirds need what bobwhites need.

*

  The kamikaze quail is a well-known phenomenon. Even among wild birds there'll be one that flies back through the shooters instead of flushing ahead of the dogs, a trend that by and large has been genetically successful. Kamikaze quail often live to reproduce, although shooters sometimes don't, and kamikaze chromosomes flourish among released birds. Seasoned guides who neglect grasping the back of their clients' belts during a covey rise often have stippled complexions.

37

I used to stand up on the dog box and try to swat kamikazes with a Prince Pro, until one day on a celebrity hunt when I was showing off my overhand for twin Hollywood soap opera starlets. I was impressed with these strange, bleached women with thousand-yard stares and spun-glass hairdos. From the dog box I had a view of creamy cleavage through semi-buttoned safari shirts, and the starlets' voluptuous smiles made me flutter with endorphins as though I were full of little quail birds trying to fly—a phenomenon perhaps rooted in a genetic integrity I imagined to be my own.

"Point!" yelled the hunt master, lifting his orange cap. One of the twins dismounted, loaded her shotgun and hurried to the frozen dogs, a German shorthair honoring a lemon spot. The dog master stepped forward to flush the birds with his flail. Amid the excitement of the covey rise and the blasts of firearms, one terrified kamikaze, having never heard a noise louder than the clank of a water pan, beelined within reach, but my eyes drifted from shuttlecock to mammary cleft, and before I could raise my racquet the little bobwhite lit on my head and clutched my scalp with pinprick talons: Suddenly I was gazing into the dual nostrils of a double-barreled Parker haloed in platinum bouffant. Just as she discharged both barrels I jumped from the wagon, the quail flapping its wings as though to carry us both to safety, and then it shat analgesic birdlime into my cowlick and burrowed in.

"You made me miss," she pouted, breaking her shotgun and ejecting two spent shells. "Why'd you move?"

*

The cheapest and safest way to hunt quail is to buy pen-raised birds for $3 apiece and release them one at a time from a pasteboard box, with economy making up for any loss of sport. The cost of running a medium-size quail plantation approximates U.S. foreign aid to one of those small countries that flesh out the United Nations' back benches. Individual sportsmen pay around $28 a minute to hunt wild quail, and it's worth it. You don't put a price on spiritual things like hunting wild quail or fishing with a fly rod?these are things we do to practice for the hereafter, which is why there's still a covey of birds on the fringe of every country graveyard?but for those who appreciate the poetry of the bottom line, here's an actual budget I snitched from an anonymous quail hunting plantation in west Dougherty County:

Quail-Hunting Budget Annual Cost

Land lease - $10/acre x 1,000 acres - $10,000
Hunting jeep w/boxes - $15,000 divided by 10 years - $1,500
Insurance, jeep, and hunting liability policy - $2,000
Gas/oil/maintenance on jeep - $400
4 dogs (trained) - $1,500 x 4 divided by 7 years - $857
Dog food and vet bill - 4 dogs x $1.30/day x 365 days - $1,898
Kennel cost/doghouse, fencing, septic tank - $5,000 divided by 15 years - $333
Shells, 1 case - $100
Hunting licenses - $20
Bird patches, feeders for quail, supplemental feed - $2,000
Hunting clothes and supplies - $400
Amortized shotgun cost and maintenance - $100
Electric collar, whistles, collars, ropes - $200
First-aid/snake-bite kit - $25

Total $19,833.47

Conclusions
Cost per bird at 300 quail/year - $66.11
Cost per hour of hunting - $220.37

Notes
1. Assumes 1,000 acres good land hunted every Saturday during the season.
2. Average kill of 20 wild quail per day.
3. Actual hunting time - 3 hours morning, 3 hours evening, 15-day season - 90 hours.

Cost of Wild Quail Supper for Six

1 box grits $.90
1 head lettuce $1.25
2 tomatoes $1
Salad dressing $1.50
Bread (French) $1.75
Sweet tea $2.00
Butter and garlic $1.50
2 quail per person x 6 guests $793.32
                             Total $803.22

I killed my first bobwhite on Funston Plantation (now Oakland) with my Uncle Thad Huckabee; I was shooting a Winchester Model 12 20-gauge pump that had belonged to his son John O., who died in England in 1942, the year I was born. My son killed his first bobwhite on Pebble Ridge with Putnam Fairweather using the same gun behind a dog named Bear. On Thanksgiving, my 12-year-old daughter, Maisy, hunted the same wiregrass behind Sam and Rusty but declined to fire the same gun. I haven't had much luck hunting with my daughters, but I love them anyway.

When I was Maisy's age, I spent every allowable fall and

winter weekend on the Champion Farm in Worth County, where I hunted quail with a Black kid of pure but unknown genetic integrity. Luke, an orphan without a last name, slept in a corncrib, and we were more or less the same age, although Luke didn't know exactly how old he was. Gator, the Black patriarch of the place, tried to age him once by looking into his mouth.

"He 'bout the same age as this boy here," Gator concluded after looking into my mouth.

On crisp winter mornings I'd crawl out of the featherbed and eat cathead biscuits cooked on a wood stove and filled with a thumbhole of cane syrup. After breakfast I'd go outside and slap the side of the corncrib, which rustled like Rice Krispies as Luke stirred. I'd pass a sticky biscuit into the darkness, and a thin Black hand would snatch it. Soon Luke's ankle and head would emerge from the squealing trapdoor, a sliver of cornhusk in his hair, and we'd hunt, leaving our tracks in a sparkling world, walking up sometimes 10 coveys of wild quail in a day. Without cutting a feather. Luke would tote my shells if he could wear my canvas jacket.

One day when we came in empty-handed at dusk, Mr. Jim Champion, the owner of that wonderful place, told me the difference between a plantation and a farm regardless of acreage.

"This here is a farm," he said. "The folks that pay the taxes live right here and work for a living."

Dove Tactics
(for Big Hart and Henry)

*And oft I heard the tender dove
In firry woodlands making moan.* —Tennyson

"That's a pretty good retriever you've got there," says Mark Slappey, a fellow guest on an F&W dove shoot near Cobb, Ga. "She's picked up six of my birds and five of Lee's."

"Well, let me give you a couple of doves then," I say. "I about got my mess."

Looks like I'm high man on the field again, without firing a shot. This is a pay hunt George McIntosh and his son Jarrett invited me on because I lied, telling them I was an outdoor sportswriter for a popular magazine.

"That's the busiest dog I believe I ever saw," says George, lumping his cheek with his tongue. "How many birds you got?"

"Oh, I don't know. Close to a dozen." Actually, I know exactly how many doves are in my game bag. I've learned to count carefully, since game warden Jeff Swift gave me a ticket last year for having 13, one bird over the bag limit. Swift said he believed me when I told him I hadn't killed any of the birds, that my dog retrieved other peoples', miscounting in her enthusiasm. As a matter of fact, I confessed, I'd gone into the field without any shotgun shells, having forgotten to buy any.

Jeff said: "I'm not giving you this ticket for killing 13 birds. I'm giving it to you for having 13 birds in your possession."

In court Judge John Salter said he believed me too,

but that he was going to fine me as an incentive to teach Geechee, my Boykin spaniel, to count better. "For the time being," he said, gathering his brow and hammering his gavel, "at least until Geechee gets more mathematically precise, I want you to get down there and help your dog count birds."

Training Geechee to retrieve other peoples' downed quarry occurred quite naturally, resulting from an accidental combination of my Boykin's blooded hyperactivity and my poor marksmanship. When she was a pup, she dutifully sat by my side while I blasted holes in the troposphere. Finally disgusted, she began snapping at my ankles and barking, compounding my ballistic inaccuracy. It's hard enough to lead and follow through a moving target without having to worry about tooth-tracks in your ankles and ass, which is how I happened upon my dove tactics. As soon as I discovered Geechee's willingness to retrieve other hunters' birds, I trained her to ignore my whistle and my arm-flapping as I ostensibly called her back. It's easier than you think to train your dog to pay absolutely no attention to command.

In the old days, my shell per bird ratio sounded like women's church league batting averages, but I changed all that, and since I've retired from dove hunting altogether, I'm willing to pass on a few Machiavellian secrets. Since training my dog to go after every bird on the field, and observing a few commonsense hunting tactics, I've increased my bird to shot ratio dramatically. Often, I bag three or more birds per shot, and I don't have to resort to shooting them from power lines either or wait for them to puddle up on the ground. Most days I get my limit without popping a cap.

Having a dog gives me a visible excuse for encroaching on the best stand on the field. Geechee can usually get to my neighbors' downed bird before my neighbor can. This gives me reason to invade his territory—I'm returning his bird. "That damn dog," I'll say. Sometimes I even pluck the bird for him.

If my neighbor's birds don't fall in range of my retriever, I can still usurp his position under the guise of searching out a cripple. Before approaching a fellow hunter, I unload my shotgun and reload with empty casings, for safety's sake and for reasons I'll soon divulge.

"Dead bird! Dead bird!" I call as I wander into a fellow hunter's field of fire, making elaborate hand signals. I politely offer to hunt any of his lost birds while I'm finding mine. There is always, by the way, a snaky area near a good dove stand because poisonous reptiles know the best places to gather for heavenly manna, but Geechee is immune to hemotoxin, having been snakebit on numerous occasions.

At this point I usually give my neighbor one of his own birds, a good investment if his spot is good enough to hang around for a while. I ask him, "You see where my cripple fell, friend?"

"I must've been facing the other way," he'll say.

I hang around and chit-chat until a bird flies over. "Your bird," I'll say, and he'll say, "Naw, go ahead."

We bicker amicably until the bird is directly overhead. Then we both throw up. It's easy to watch your neighbor out the corner of your eye and to synchronize. After he shoots, I eject an empty casing. "Dead bird," I yell to Geechee, who brings me the dove, of course. "Did you shoot too?" I ask my host as he reloads. "How about that! We must've shot at the exact same time. I didn't hear your gun go off. Gosh, this could be your bird. I'll bet it is!"

"Naw, keep the bird."

If my neighbor downs a double, I'm careful not to claim both birds, but I'll remove two empty shells from my double barrel, protesting that I couldn't have killed both birds, no way.

"Well, if you knock any down you can't find, just holler

and I'll come back over."

Sometimes surveillance is necessary, sometimes not.

With my binoculars I carefully tally the number of doves downed by surrounding hunters, noting cripples and lost birds. If I can find a bird that puts him over the limit, he'll insist I keep it. It's an easy thing for a dove hunter to give up a bird he's already counted lost, especially if the recovered bird mandates that he stop shooting and zip his shotgun case. One reason I like to see the Department of Natural Resources attending.

Well, you may interject, my problem isn't so much bagging dove as it is getting on a decent hunt to begin with— the ones with barbecue, pretty girls and flocks that darken the sky. So sometimes I just ride around the countryside until I happen upon a hunt that looks good enough to crash. I like to see a DNR truck, indicating that the field isn't baited. Also, dove hunters are less likely to shoot you and your dog if the law is there. Using my methods, I can fill my limit quickly and quit the field before potentially embarrassing post hunt socializing begins, but sometimes I stay for the barbecue, where I try to charm my way into next Saturday's hunt.

My tactics work best with people who don't know me, so lunchtime Saturday on opening day of dove season finds me cruising around in my pick-up looking for a gathering of dove shooters preparing to convoy to the country. I walk around introducing myself and offering soft drinks until I find out who the host is, gleaning simultaneously a half dozen names I can drop in order to establish legitimacy. I sometimes thank the host for allowing Sam (a guy I just met) to let me tag along, but more often than not I just join the procession. The cooler of iced down drinks also allows me to orbit the field offering refreshments while casing the best stands. The cost of the drinks is nominal when you consider I no longer buy shotgun shells.

45

    If anybody calls me on the legitimacy of my attendance, I slap my forehead, claiming I've joined the wrong hunt. "Damn my thick skull," I'll say, "you mean this ain't Bubba an' 'em's hunt?" If caught irrefutably red-handed, I'll wait for the December season and claim I've been born again, worthy once more of restoration into the society of men.
    Thus, it follows that another way to establish legitimacy among strangers is to say you're new in the area and the preacher invited you. There's always a preacher with a different notion of fellowship than cliquish dove hunters have. Nobody's likely to raise an eyebrow against a preacher using a dove shoot to recruit the fallen.
    "Preacher? What preacher?" an unpolished countryman once challenged.
    "The Baptist preacher, of course," I replied, figuring that's as safe a bet as there is in Dixie.
    "What?" snarled the roughneck, who turned out to be the Methodist clergyman. "He here too?"
    But one Sunday morning a fateful misadventure occurred that made me stop dove hunting altogether. Which is why I'm willing to publish my tactics.
    I should've sensed trouble when I saw the hunters wore Nikes instead of snake boots and had removed their dogs' collars. The hunters looked a little rough but, what the hell, the hunting brotherhood is a democratic tribe, transcending socio-economic stratification. There were plenty of doves feeding in the field. I'd verified it with a phone call the night before to a good old boy who could see the field from the deck of his doublewide. "They's so many doves on the power lines it's dimming the lights."
    Sure enough, when I get there before daylight guns are already blasting away. In the first light I see vortexes of doves reeling flurry like dust devils. Boy oh boy. The doves swarm the field angrily, falling beneath the distant gunfire, which sounds like a brushfire in a stand of bamboo.

Geechee vibrates with anticipation. I unleash her and she bounces around like a jackrabbit. Then I see a glint of a patent leather holster belt and a speeding four-wheeler trailing a plume of dark dust against the crimson sky.

Hunters quit the field, vanishing into peripheral fringe and planted pines. It's as though Officer Swift speeds toward the central pivot of a spinning turntable that centrifugally slings hunters off the field.

He skids to a stop, obscured for a moment in his own dust. "You!" he says, dismounting and producing a pad from his hip pocket.

"Hey, I wasn't shooting. Why, I didn't even bring any shotgun shells. My shotgun's plugged and I'm two birds under the limit."

"This ticket's for hunting over bait."

"Bait?"

"How d'you think these peanut hearts got in this corn field?"

I glance between my feet. The ground is covered with a variety of extraneous silage, including a fodder that looks like party mix.

Meanwhile Geechee realizes the windfall of an abandoned field. She begins sniffing out discarded evidence, trotting it over, dropping birds at our feet and wagging her stubby tail.

"Stay, Geechee!" I command. "Sit!"

Geechee trots off again, obediently ignorant, panting happily and winking over her shoulder.

"Those aren't my birds," I insist.

"That's your dog, ain't it? The same one you told Judge Salter you'd teach arithmetic. And it looks like these birds are in your possession since you're the only one hunting."

Geechee trots up, grinning around the fluttering bird in her mouth. "That makes 15, don't it?" says Swift.

"Look Jeff, I didn't know this field was baited. I don't even know whose land this is." I run Geechee down and snap a leash on her collar. She bares her canines and growls like an idling weed-whacker. It's hard to restrain a conscientious dog once she gets started, but I finally collar her and bring her back to the four-wheeler, tangling up in a tumbleweed of peanut vines.

   Officer Swift lifts his black cap with his thumb and index finger, scratching his bald spot with his pinkie. He watches the sky for an angel or a UFO. Then he licks the point of his pencil. "You say you're trespassing too?"

Bear Ballet

I see a bay-ur. Whay ur? Thay-ur. —Child's Poem

When Ace Darden invited me and Kicklighter to go bear hunting on the east rim of the Okefenokee, I wasn't too hot on the idea. I already had a bearskin rug, a grizzly I'd inherited from my dead friend Mike Roberts. I haven't gotten around to putting the rug on the floor. It hunkers in a Queen Anne chair with its paws on the dining room table. The canines and claws, fully capable of raking a fat man to the bone, act as my deterrent to hunting bear.

"C'moan," said Kicklighter, "you can bring your camera. Sell the pictures to some wildlife outfit."

"Well..."

Ace is a senior projects engineer for safety and the DNR Hunter Safety Instructor for 1997. He graduated from the Naval Academy and survived over 200 missions in Vietnam. "The missions were a matter of basic accounting," he grinned. "You just have to make sure your landings balance with your takeoffs." His co-pilot for the bear hunt was Jerry Corbin, retired Merck utilities department super, retired general in the Army National Guard. In Race Pond, Georgia, we were to hook up with Jackie Carter, a former Marine seriously wounded in Vietnam. I was in good, safe company, according to Marine Reserve Sergeant-Major and county police chief Bill Kicklighter, a hunting safety instructor himself. With this crowd I wasn't worried about getting shot or being thrown in jail.

When Indians killed a deer without asking forgiveness, they were smote with arthritis, but they were under no such obligation to bears, whose spirits could re-incorporate.

49

Bears evolved from a tribe that got tired of the grunt and sweat of scratching out a living and took to the wilderness to slurp honey and munch nuts. A bear was an anomaly to Indians, a four-legged critter that could stand upright on its feet like a man: big medicine. Bears defied categories, pushed the envelope.

   Georgia bear hunters are an anomaly, too. They enjoy only three weekends of bear hunting per year, six days, for which they buy permits, feed dogs, oil firearms and lease land. Ace's club, Trail Ridge, leases 9,000 acres, and there are lots of bear. The plentitude is attributable to good DNR game management and evidenced by electric fences around beehives. Sometimes you see a ravaged cornfield that looks like a backhoe went through, and once in a while a bear will take a fatted calf or decimate a chicken house. So, yeah, bears can be a nuisance if you need bicameral justification, although your right brain tells you one sleek, healthy bear is worth any number of calves, cornfields and chicken shacks.

*

   We left after midnight, and Kicklighter snored all the way to Waycross. When we got to the Crossroad Truck Stop at Race Pond, he suggested I toss my sleeping bag in the bed of his pickup and catch a couple hours of shuteye while he snoozed in the cab.

   "You too big to get comfortable in here," he explained.

   I tossed and turned, snuggling up to the spare tire, thinking of—well—bears.

   When my daughter was two and a half, she'd ride the back of my neck along the boardwalk through Chehaw Park Zoo, holding my hair. "Let's go see the bear, want to?"

   She never remembered from time to time how big the bear actually was. She could cover her storybook bears with her small hands, and the teddy bear she slept with was larger but toothless, with a little red tongue. As we rounded the final turn of the boardwalk, the bear loomed from memory to reality, standing there monolithic and omnipotent, maybe rubbing his shaggy rump on a tree. He'd look at her and growl, and she'd snatch out little handfuls of temple hair and wet the back of my neck. Every time.

"Let's hurry home now, Daddy. I gotta go potty."

The night I came home with Mike's grizzly, my 18-year-old stepdaughter was out for a little underage drinking with her girlfriends. I stuffed the bearskin in her canopy bed, tucking her comforter under its snarling chin. Around 2 a.m. she eased into the driveway with headlights off. I propped on one elbow and listened. Her key slipped quietly into the front door. The pine floors creaked beneath her stocking feet. She tiptoed into her bedroom and snapped on the light. "Maa-muhhh!" she cried, slinging a six-pack through the ceiling fan.

*

We gathered at the hunting club and started riding the roads, dog boxes loaded with yowling Plots, blue ticks, Walkers, black-and-tans—big dogs with loose skin and sad brown eyes. Shy dogs, tails between aitchbones, bred in blood and bone to chase the thing that can kill them the quickest. The hunters hung their heads out truck windows, looking for tracks, soft prints in the dust. Staying in touch with radios, they gauged size and estimated freshness before setting the dogs on a promising one to see if they'd take to it, strike and trail.

"You'd think something big as a bear would leave a remarkable track," I observed.

"They don't," said Ace. "When Indians tracked bears, the bear sometimes doubled back on them. The braves shinnied up saplings too small to support a bear."

"What if the bear just shook him out?" I asked. I pictured

an angry bruin steadily swatting a sapling that hummed like a tuning fork, a twittering Indian clutching the topknot and gritting his teeth.

"Life wasn't always easy for our aboriginal forebears," Ace concluded. Eventually our hunting party found faint impressions in the powdered road. Bear!

They stopped their 4x4s, squatted, studied a footprint, pointing, stirring the dust with sticks. These tracks seemed made by toy bears filled with helium—airy bears. I didn't believe quarter-ton bears could trudge so softly. Ace selected a suitable track, discussing its merits with other hunters over the crackling radios. They put the dogs down. *Aw-roo, aw-roo.*

Jackie led the drivers, who followed the yowling hounds. In safety vests, the rest of us spread out, crimson splotches along the yellow dirt road, ready to shoot at any bear that charged the line of scrimmage. Pickups sped back and forth in columns of swirling dust, antennas lashing, changing positions to head off the dogs, shifting the line.

A Datsun pickup with lacy doors skidded up in a cloud of dust. A bearded face filled the window as the truck tilted to the rocker panels. "Get fixed," he said. "This here's a good place for him to break through, right there through them buttonwoods."

The biceps hanging under the ursine head were the size and color of a cured Virginia ham.

"I better ride with you," I said. "Stand in the back, be a lookout, balance out your truck."

"Naw, I moan scoot over to extend the line. You can look out right here," he added ominously, scratching off in a sooty backfire, hunkering over to see through the windshield.

Three times the bear threatened my sector, and three times I cocked my quivering revolver. I could hear the dogs' timorous yips and the bear crashing through the scrub and gallberries. Dogs sound surer of themselves chasing coons, rabbits and deer. *A-roop. Eek. A-roop.* I glanced down the road to watch Kicklighter climb into the bed of his truck and steady his rifle across the cab. Beyond him Ace stood braced like the Ethan Allen minuteman, his sawed-off Marlin .444 braced against his thighs.

My camera forgotten, I cocked my pistol and glanced around for a sapling, which was about all there was—pine saplings, scrub oak and buttonwood. My .44 magnum, generally a comfort in dark valleys, wilted, the long black barrel drooping like a Halloween candle too close to the hearth. Optical illusion? I felt a simultaneous weakness of sinew and knees as my manhood diluted. If he comes out here, I thought, I'll dive in the ditch, ball up into an undetectable wad of Realtree, tell the others I ducked to give them a shot. I could see the treetops shaking as the bear yanked them out by the roots, and the hounds yipped and yiked as he swatted them like volleyballs, but again he turned away. Moments later I heard an angry roar and shots.

Jackie said bears tree in hardwood bottoms. This one climbed a tupelo and stood upright on a limb before Jackie shot him.

"He sounded like a refrigerator crashing down out of that tree," Kicklighter said.

A tandem file of grunting hunters dragged the bear out with chain chokers around its wrists. Paws like catcher's mitts appeared through the cat's claw, followed by the enormous black bear, a sunken orbital socket crusted with blood-blackened dust where the bullet had passed like a bumblebee through his eye. A chain choker stretched his long arm, as though he swam through the thorny vines. Bears belong in the reverent gloom of virgin hardwoods, forests where a transcendental web runs through raw nature back to something eternal. The Okefenokee is something like that, but the Georgia flatwoods, millions of acres around the rim, have been cut over and replaced with rows of planted pines. The bear was out of context here on the dirt road, incongruous in the hacked-out and turpentine land of gallberry bushes and bramble, like some Old Testament god banished to pseudo-wilderness. An anomaly.

  We lifted his pumpkin head for photographs, cutting off his protruding tongue and turning his good eye to render him lifelike in death. Even dead he was noble in his inert power and sleek black fur. We stood around him in a kind of hushed reverence that recalls the deadly dance of hunters and bears for 300 millennia. A communal thread among hunters, a dim revival of an atrophied sense of commitment our primal ancestors felt in full for a quarry fully capable of turning on them, swapping in one terrifying moment the roles of hunter and hunted, capable of mauling some serious ass, crushing thin skulls and shredding girded loins. You can't see a dead bear without being touched by that ironic love hunters and hounds feel for the thing they are bound and bred to bay and kill, without which there'd be no bears, no wilderness, pseudo or otherwise.

  A pretty lady in camo showed up with a little boy about the age Maisy was at Chehaw. He wouldn't get in the picture, no way. He must have heard about reanimating bears. The hunters must have too. When they loaded Jackie's bear on the tailgate, his truck squatting on haunches, air hissed from the bear's keg-sized lungs, and the hunters jumped back in a centrifugal scatter. I dropped my camera and scrambled backward up the bumper, hood and windshield of Kicklighter's truck, printing crescent heel marks and breaking off a wiper arm. The cab bent in with a thunk as the abandoned bear rolled off Jackie's tailgate. I was fixing to climb the radio antenna, it being the closest thing to a sapling.

  "My damn! Get down off my truck," yelled the chief, who

was himself on the far side of the ditch.

Jackie weighed in his bear at the check station at 355 pounds while the other drivers were divining with telemetry dogs scattered all over Charlton County. On the way back to Albany, I nudged Kicklighter, trying to quiet his snorting so I could hear the radio. He opened one eye, squinting the other, tilting his head to see under the bill of his county police ballcap.

"Is that the way they catch convicts? You know, with dogs, perimeters and all?" I asked.

He studied me. "Watch the road," he said.

*

Since the hunt I've suffered flare-ups of arthritis for not apologizing to a spike buck opening day. I've also been plagued by disturbing dreams. My wife says I ignited my arthritis sleeping in Kicklighter's truck and that the dreams were sparked by subliminal guilt from stuffing Mike's bear into my stepdaughter's bed. In the dream, I part the bushes and find myself face to face with a gigantic black bear. I draw my .44, which wilts like a plucked lily. I pirouette, running pell-mell in somnambulant leaps and airborne arabesques, the bear's honeyed breath dewing the backs of my ears. I'm enveloped in hairy arms. Harmless bullets drip from my flaccid revolver, and I'm forced into a pas de deux to the music of growls, snorts and smacking lips. We tango until the back of my neck is slurped concupiscently by a bearish tongue the size of a calf liver just before my head is engulfed in slobbering darkness, my face caged by yellow incisors. *Yahhh!*

"What is wrong with you?" yawns my fourth wife. "You bicycled all the covers into a wad and I'm cold."

"I'm moving the bear rug," I announce, "maybe to the basement. I'm a little worried about what our friends will think, you know, about us having a grizzly at our dining

room table and all."
"Well, move it if you want to, but your friends won't."
"Won't what?"
"Well, you know."
"What?"
"Think."

Real Men Don't Fly Fish

Many men go fishing all of their lives without knowing that it is not fish they are after. —Henry David Thoreau

For whatever reason, fly fishing is what the middle-aged yuppies are up to. This new breed of fisherman keeps his cell phone in his split-willow creel. He takes fish towels, fat-free pretzels and ice chests of Perrier on his excursions and wears fingerless nylon gloves to prevent sunspots. He has never eaten a mullet or a mudcat, and he speaks politely to his catch before releasing it.

Yuppies spare no expense when it comes to fancy fishing. They buy fishing rods that sell for what used cars used to, with gold-plated reels internally jeweled like Swiss watches. The line costs as much as the reels, so if you tangle one in your trolling motor, you're liable to go to bed with a sick headache. But this is only the fiscal surface. These guys wear $100 vests with silver hemostats and $9 toenail clippers hanging down. They buy laminated maple landing nets and wear fancy hats with penlights and clip-on magnifiers.

The fly fisherman's shelves are lined with Nick Lyons, Sparse Gray Hackles, Isaac Walton and videos of *The River Runs Through It.* His fly case is the masculine equivalent of a jewelry box stuffed with the exotic feathers of rare birds. He exalts in his wet flies, dry flies, streamers and nymphs.

Basic outfitting requires a tax-wise loan, but to compound extravagance, these idiots are involving their wives, who were too genteel to fish before Victoria's Secret started featuring chic fly fishing apparel. In my mind, when you take your wife fishing, you're swapping leisure for labor in the first place and courting bankruptcy to boot. But the most pitiful subspecies of the new fly fishermen is the upwardly mobile good old boy who actually knew how to catch a fish before these pale piscatologists invaded the Southland like fire ants and armadillos. These poor boys live on the cusp, trying to please upwardly mobile wives. Mutating from redneck to yuppy, they fish in better clothes than they work in and flick Woolly Buggers when they'd rather be running bush hooks for a flathead cat. They stand on the bank in new waders and Orvis vests, whacking the waters into froth, overdressed as boar hogs in Chantilly lace.

Albany veterinarian Dr. Henry Hart, a recent convert to fly fishing, espouses the theory that the sport's popularity comes from the subliminal excitement derived from probing dark canyons of the subconscious. Fish, like the symbolic fodder of dreams, are titillated to the surface with a limber rod, in a process that can be particularly edifying well into advanced maturity. Hart stays current in psychology because he has to housebreak neurotic poodles and keep peace among the gaggle of middle-aged musicians in Relapse, his rock 'n roll band. Incidentally, Dr. Hart attributes the universal phobia for reptiles and fears of falling to residual conditioning inherited from evolutionary ancestors who lived in trees, where they were safe from everything but arboreal snakes and the suck of gravity.

Jerry Benson, the new fly fishing guru in town, is one of those responsible for the fancy fishing rage. He offers a how-to class in fly-casting through Continuing Education at Darton College, and he welcomes women, who are lured to the sport by the expensive sportswear and upbeat china patterns in Fly South, his mail order catalogue.

Women cast fly line better than men do, which is another good reason to leave your wife at home. Finesse, Jerry says, accounts for that. Fly-casting is almost the only sport where you don't follow through with the stroke, so women are often less jaded by habit. It's a limp-wrist art executed between 2 o'clock and 10 o'clock, identical to flipping a stuffed olive with a cocktail fork. A female fly fisher looks like a bright waterbird in her billed hat and with one leg raised in the shape of a 4.

Jerry hasn't acquired a lot of places to fish yet, other than the Olympic-sized pool in the Darton College gym, so one day after class he invited me to a holding pond behind a housing project off Oakridge Drive. The lock is rusted off the chain link gate, so we entered easily where boggy banks fester with KFC boxes, car batteries, happy-meal toys and Styrofoam cups. Our footprints release flatulent and sulphurous gasses as we prepare to launch the boat. I thread fly-line through the snake guides and tie on a Matuka-Mylar streamer. The water, thick as paint and red as spaghetti sauce, coats my fly line, and I'm wondering how to get the stuff off.

"A friend turned me on to this spot," Jerry says. "Nobody fishes it. There's no telling what we'll catch."

He's right there. The holding pond is downstream of Riverside Cemetery, where 400 caskets popped up during the 1994 flood. Something very macabre could be bobbing around in this pond.

"There's plenty of structure to hold fish," he adds.

He's right again. For generations of intercity prosperity, residents have been tossing broken and stolen items over the chain link fence. Big Wheels, truck tires, automatic weapons and shopping carts can be seen jutting through the surface.

But Jerry wants to determine the emergence cycle of aquatic and terrestrial insects. He wants to fathom the entomology.

"You've got to match the hatch," he says, snatching at a cloud of airborne bugs and then pecking into the barrel of his clenched fist. "*Culex pipiens*, mosquitoes."

He holds up a minuscule dry fly that looks like it was tied

from eyelashes or nose hairs.

"Mosquitoes are swarming," he continues. "If they don't hit an adult female, I'll throw the nymph."

"You can tie mosquito nymph? I can't even see mosquito nymph," I note.

A Hudson hubcap is embedded in rusty mud. Jerry poles over to it with the blade of his canoe paddle, lifts it and passes it to me. Through my bifocals, I can barely discern tiny wiggletails kicking around like spirochetes.

"You can tie those?" I ask. "Well, actually a heart surgeon buddy of mine ties the nymphs, using loupes, the optics doctors wear to suture blood vessels. If you can sew an artery, you can tie mosquito nymph," he answers.

Thoracic surgeons are natural fly fishermen. They can tie microscopic bait, pronounce the scientific names of insects and afford the equipment. Dr. Tony Hoots, it's said, can tie a gnat.

Since yuppies tend to take up fly tying too, you better not take your cockatoo to Westover Animal Hospital unless you want it returned with bald spots, with some of the plumage going into Henry's tackle box. Most fly fishermen are health care professionals—gynecologists, dentists, nurses, chiropractors and vets. If you get snagged by a barbless hook, you don't even have to leave the trout stream for the ER. There's usually a podiatrist or brain surgeon at each elbow.

"You going to pitch a dry fly?" I ask Jerry.

"Yeah, you go deep."

I can't go very deep, l think. The water is hub high on a corroded tricycle about eight feet out from shore.

My first cast lands like a mound of angel hair pasta, but I lash the tip of my rod until I straighten some of it out.

"Too much declination on the back cast," advises Jerry. "Cast to that half-submerged tire. Tires are good fish attractors."

I sling a haymaker and begin stripping line. Suddenly I feel a tug.

"I've got one on!" I screech.

"Don't horse him," Jerry cautions, with paternal pride though he's half my age. "You've got a light tippet."

"Get the net ready!"

"No, work him over here. I'll lip him," Jerry says.

Jerry puts his rod down, grasping the gunnels. He leans over, adjusting his polarized sunglasses to see through the petroleum slick.

"What do you reckon it is?" I ask.

"I don't know but I saw a white flash. It's some kind of tube-shaped fish that swells when you tug him and contracts when you give him slack. He's hooked in the upper lip, though, I can see the fly."

Jerry reaches through the iridescent film and lifts my catch. "What have we here?"

"A condom!"

"What the heck?" Jerry's eyes widen.

"I don't know. A Trojan, maybe?"

"Ugh!" He flings it back. It burps an air bubble, ripples once and sinks out of sight—catch-and-release. I worry that Jerry is going to rub off his epidermis raw with the fish towel. An opaque film adheres to his forearm like elbow-length latex gloves, but he is determined that student not outdo teacher. He'll not be skunked by beginner's luck. He picks up his fly rod and assails the water until he gets a strike from perhaps the only animate object in the pond—a living fossil. It resists sluggishly, but at least it's an actual fish, or a distant progenitor of one. He tugs it through a glob of algae alongside the boat. This time we use the landing net. The pop-eyed thing is coated with yellow mucus. It has a whiskered, Edward G. Robinson mouth. Unwilling to touch it, I lift the tippet, hoisting the head as I chop the neck with the paddle. The thing Jerry has caught groans and croaks, flaring scabrous gills and coughing gouts of dark blood. Chancres along its side look like they could have been made by the suction of tentacles. Maybe something else lives in the pond.

"What have you got there?" I inquire.

"Looks like a walking catfish."

"I thought they became extinct during the Pleistocene."

"Maybe not. They gulp air and supplement oxygen intake with their swim bladder. They may be the only thing that can live in a pond as polluted as this one. This one would've crawled off to a cleaner spot if it hadn't been for that fence."

"Maybe that's why they put fences around holding ponds in the first place, to keep them stocked."

I remove Jerry's fly, discovering hemostats are good for removing hooks from fish you can't stand the idea of touching, the stuff bad dreams are made of. We contemplate the fish for a while before shoveling it over the side with an oar.

"You got to get used to fishing in ponds like this one," I tell Jerry. "It's all we'll have when the Republicans get through with environmental legislation."

I slap a mosquito on my forearm. "Hot damn!" I scream as it stings me like a hot needle.

"You swatted my fly," says Jerry. "See if you can work it out without bending the gape."

*

"Let's go somewhere a little more natural," my fly fishing mentor suggests the next day.

Putnam Fairwether, another of Jerry's students, gets us invited to Cottonmouth Pond outside Pelham. Cottonmouth Pond, far more natural than the holding pond off Oakridge, is a pretty lake surrounded by azaleas, weeping willows, stumps, alligators and snakes.

"Three can't flyfish from the same skiff," Jerry announces as we launch our fishing craft. "I think you're ready for the old belly boat, Vic. Putnam and I'll fish from the skiff, where I'll provide pointers."

"Let Putnam, have the belly boat," I offered. A belly boat is a $295 innertube with a crotch strap. You use it with $170 neoprene waders and wading shoes that range from $75 to $115. Of course, over the shoes you wear swim fins you can order for $130. About the time you get outfitted, a belly boat is about the same price as a bass boat without the trailer.

Jerry hasn't brought his neoprene waders. Without waders, sitting in a belly boat is like wearing a wet diaper. My white legs dangle in duckweed and among God knows what reptiles. I kick to the far bank, listen to the "MY RUMP" of bullfrogs and watch Jerry and Putnam, about 50 yards away, false-casting like windshield wipers.

Finally, I quit coveting a dry place in the boat and start actually having fun. I start catching red-belly bream hand over fist, wearing them out and threading them on a stringer trailing behind me.

I make a roll cast I'm real proud of. The leader unfolds beneath a willow overhang, and my rubber spider splats against a dark log before dropping penultimately upon still waters, waiting for a bluegill to suck it in. The spider lies in the center of centrifugal ripples on the chrome surface, flexing its rubber legs. Good action. I've been saving money, buying my flies at The Gag Shops, adding hooks to Halloween arachnids with suction cups you lick and stick on window panes. Wow, this is the life! But the "log," disturbed by the fly line that just lashed its flanks, moves, sighs and plops into the water. I immediately recognize the former log as a snake about the size of my leg. A cottonmouth moccasin, for which the pond was named, has entered the water and submerged beneath the onyx surface.

Appropriately terrified, I kick away from the bank with considerable torque. Cottonmouth moccasins can't bite underwater, I tell myself, immediately realizing the lie. They eat fish. Moccasins specialize in biting underwater. Fish! I remember I'm trailing a stringer like a stalk of bananas. I think about casting off the stringer to reduce drag—catch-and-release —but as I pass Jerry and Putnam see Jerry's rod bend double then snap. "Dang! " he cries. "An alligator just snapped my fly rod!"

"Do what?"

"An alligator took my Marabou streamer and ruined my new rod."

I feel my glands contract, squirting adrenalin into my vascular system, mainlining, as my haunches shift into overdrive.

"Don't worry!" Jerry says. "It's a Redington with a lifetime warranty."

I'm leaving a blunt wake and a rooster tail, but a slight change of direction wraps the slimy stringer of fish around my naked leg. A dorsal fin pricks my calf and I know I'm snakebit at the very least. It's a delicate balance to commune with nature without becoming a link in the food chain.

"Look at him go!" yells Putnam.

My fins spanking whitewater. The next thing I know I'm on the opposite shore standing on wobbling legs by the truck while a rottweiler gallops up snarling and holding me at bay.

"From where we were," Jerry says when they pull in, "you looked like a ballerina with an inflatable tutu, except for all that arm-flapping."

I inspect my catch. Several bluegills have bite-sized crescents missing from their tails. Something in my subconscious has been nipping away.

"I keep having this dream," I confess to my veterinarian when I take my dog in for parvo shots, "that alligators snap off my legs, my belly boat gets top heavy, and I flip over and drown."

Doctor Hart is wearing a shirt with kitty cats all over it and a baseball hat studded with dry flies. He pinches his chin.

"The reason you're scared of alligators is you feel guilty about something. You running around on your wife?"

"No."

"Well, you're up to something. You don't have to tell me about it, but you may need to take up some socially uplifting hobby. I recommend fly fishing—very soothing psychologically."

Gator Fleas, Shoalies and der Thunderkracken

If I'm not going to catch anything, then I'd rather not catch anything on flies. —Bob Lawless

𝓕or my fifty-third birthday I received a bevy of luminescent wet flies with long rubber legs. They arrived with the following note, which I assumed to be a critical backlash to an article I wrote called "Real Men Don't Fly Fish" in the June issue of *Albany Magazine:*

To: Mr. O. Vic Miller

HAPPY BIRTHDAY!
  You are now in possession of five experimental flies expected to revolutionize the entire fishing industry. As far as we know, there are no other flies like these anywhere in the world. The secret lies in the unusual material used in shaping the abdomen of the flies. This material was recently purchased for 75 cents from a vending machine in a filling station bathroom on Hwy 17, Walterboro, S.C.
  If these flies are as phenomenal as indicated in our tests, you may order this material from Glow-in-the-Dark Condom Co. located at P.O. Box 23, Avondale, Georgia. Enclosed is a sample of the material to tide you over while waiting for your order.
  Directions: Expose flies to light 60 seconds before casting. The glowing bugs are irresistible to all species of fresh and saltwater fish.

Good fishing from Hall Tackle Company.

Hall Tackle Company, it turns out, is Chip Hall, the only married guy I know who has his fly vise attached to the kitchen counter and his peacock herl and grizzly hackles strewn over the breakfast bar. Eat supper over there and you're liable to find African goat hair in your gazpacho.

Chip can tie anything from crab lice to sand fleas. Sometimes he gets carried away and fabricates insects eaten by neither bird nor fish. Like the hung-up love bugs that splat your windshield. He's a fanatic, stopping his jeep for every roadkill to harvest hair or feathers. His wife, Betsy, puts up with him marginally and is always willing to get him out of the house, so Chip is allowed to go fishing night or day. On rainy days he amuses himself by drinking bourbon and tying houseflies that fool Betsy into swinging at them with a swatter. He sits on his barstool watching her, wearing a magnifier that distorts his eyes.

Anyway, this story has another setting, the Flint River rapids off the first-hole fairway of the Radium Springs Golf Course. Before John Yoeman went off to medical school last summer, he and I took fishing and scuba excursions early afternoons while the sun was still high, shining in golden shafts beneath the fast-water rapids below Radium Dam. There, the rushing water cuts deeply between Goat Island and the green limestone banks, through channels dredged a few hundred years ago for river barges, past a shoreline piled with fossiliferous rocks. In calmer places you can weight yourself down and catfish along the bottom, fanning the sand with your hands to uncover arrowheads and camel teeth, whalebones and sharks' teeth, chert artifacts the color of caramel. One summer I found a straight-sided Coke bottle manufactured in Albany before 1912, according to John Temp Phillips, a collector. There's lots of wonderful junk in the Flint River.

Late summer when the water table drops and artesian springs make up a higher ratio of river water, the Flint turns jade. If you dive the deep holes with a flashlight, you can come face to face with monstrous flathead catfish, and in the springs, where layers of cold water blanket the limestone bottom, big stripers—some weighing 50 pounds, circle like gray ghosts, their eyes the size of golf balls. Shoal bass haunt the rapids, wonderful fish that fight like rainbows on amphetamines, grown strong from life in fast water.

  I buckled on a scuba tank and two weight belts and catfished near the upstream mouth of the deep channel beneath the first hole, exploring the crevasses, crawling hand over fist over the limestone boulders along the bottom of the trough while John went downstream, where he hooked and landed a mullet on a topwater plug.

  Milford Crowe, a nobody, says this is a lie, but it's not. Milford says there are no mullet in the Flint, but he's wrong. Russell Martin says he'd hate to take either side in a contest of veracity between me and Milford, but as of this moment my opinion is in print, which gives me a leg up on Milford, in my opinion.

  Anyway, John caught the mullet while I was hanging on for dear life to the corner of a limestone boulder, flapping like a flag some 20 feet beneath the surface, trying not to get sucked into the pipeline trench cut for antebellum barges. I was careful not to turn my profile to the rushing water, which had the power to smear my lips and rip off my mask. Getting tired, I wished I'd entered quieter water to look for treasure. Suddenly the corner of the boulder broke off and I washed loose, tumbling down the flume, my scuba tank clanging against limestone and flint.

  I couldn't fight the current, and I was too weighted down with lead to swim, so I tucked and rolled, protecting my head with my forearms as I shot the flume, whizzing along the amber lunar landscape. I knew I'd wash the length of the first-hole fairway. Then I'd crawl to quieter water, surface and yell for John to come downstream and get me. I had plenty of air to just go with the flow, so I relaxed and concentrated on dodging rocks until I was swarmed by shoal bass, some really big ones, which kept up with me as I tumbled and boinked off rocks. I decided to come back here someday to fish.

*

"It was the craziest thing I ever saw," I told everybody who'd listen. "Those bass followed me the length of the first-hole fairway, some three hundred yards."

"You damn fool," Chip said, "you were knocking gator fleas loose from the bottom and the shoal bass were feeding on them. You were chumming them up."

"Gator fleas?"

"Yeah, the larval stage of the dobsonfly: hellgrammites. Shoal bass love them."

"All we got to do," I told Chip during my next trip to his kitchen, "is drag a logging chain behind the johnboat to chum up the shoalies." The chain, I figured, would serve the double purpose of slowing us down in the fast water and breaking loose hellgrammites. They ought to hit a fly, I figured, tied so it looked like a hellgrammite.

"They ought to hit a fly tied to look like anything," Chip said, "especially if it glows in the dark."

"Can you tie hellgrammites?" I asked. His eyes focused out about 200 yards beyond the refrigerator, and he nodded once, fiddling through some peacock herl on the counter.

"He can tie anything," Betsy affirmed.

*

As soon as the water level got right, we fastened a chain to the carrying handle of the johnboat and hooked up the trailer, making a single pit stop to shave some white belly hairs off a flattened possum. We put in at the Marine ditch and motored south, passing Radium Dam where I'd squandered the principal and interest of my childhood. Frank Middleton, Carlos Phillips, the Musgrove brothers and I started diving in the Flint during the late 1950s, and I never quite got it out of my system. We figure there's something addictive in the chemicals that wash in there from industry and agriculture.

Before that, Joe Lord, who was married to Marvin's and Shirley's mamma, fished every afternoon beneath the Romanesque stone arches of Radium Dam, where the cold blue water from the springs splashed like lace over the floodgates and marbled into the brown river. I can see Joe now in his khaki shirt and trousers, a permanent fixture in the shade among the cypress knees, catching shellcrackers and eels from the mottled water, eels born faraway in the wide Sargasso Sea, they say.

Joe always tolerated our splashing, shouting and rock skipping with a stoic acceptance nonexistent among modern adults. He never got a bite when we were around, but on Wednesday afternoons he'd even allow Buster Vansant and Bobby Franck to hang around. At dusk he'd roll up his bamboo poles, mount them on the brackets above the windows of his green 1947 Dodge and chug by us on the dirt road as we walked home to supper.

The Flint is the most beautiful river in the world once you overlook city flotsam and get far enough downstream from the rusty exudates that leach into the water from the old dump near the Oakridge Bridge. Stay away from the drainage ditch at the civic center, too. A hard rain gully washes enough litter, bottles, cans and general crap into the river to enable a biblical stroll across its surface. I'm scared to dive near Merck, too, where fishermen have told me that fumes escaping from the discharge pipe have sometimes made their eyes water.

Merck has its discharge sampled regularly, and a description of it sounds like Evian spring water, but I steer clear of there anyway, discomforted by the knowledge that the samplers are on the Merck payroll, a setup that could be termed vulpine security. Once I snorkeled a mile downstream and collected a crusty white rime on the top of my head like a skullcap. I had a lock of hair chipped off and analyzed. The Health Department chemist just shook his head, holding out supine palms and rolling his eyes toward heaven.

Radical environmentalists warn that pollutants have caused rivers to actually combust into flames. They say that the right mixture of contaminates has the power to disfigure divers, citing the example of Benny Waldorph, who scubas the river as regularly as I do. I don't think Benny's appearance is due to pollutants. I've known him since high school, and he has always looked pretty much like he does now, unless the river can be named culpable for turning his whiskers gray.

*

The only problem with the chain, besides the mind-shattering clatter and a vague feeling that it might be unsportsmanlike if not outright illegal, was that we were chumming up the shoal bass behind us, creating a feeding frenzy beyond our casting range. "We need two boats," I observed as happy bass frolicked in our wake, "one for the chumming and one to fish." Our retarded progress down the roaring rapids made us feel as though we were going backwards. We cast flies into braided water where I'd once found a flint knife.

Suddenly the sky darkened, and we were shrouded in thick shadow. Above us loomed a puffy cloud shaped and colored like the bruised buttocks of a Sumo wrestler, cleft darkly through the center.

"That's a pretty bad looking cloud," said Chip. "Smell that rain!"

"That's ozone. Fish bite better in a barometric low just

before a storm."

"We're liable to get wet."

"Since when did you start worrying about getting wet?"

Veins of heat lightning illuminated the cloven cloud, pink as a peach. Flatulent thunder followed, as though we were threatened by the fiery bowels of some sky deity. Then we became enveloped in strange phenomena. When Chip cast his fly line, it remained horizontally suspended in the charged air over the water, the tippet actually rising above the leader, his dobsonfly hovering as though it had come to life.

Our eyes met in disbelief. Had Chip finally tied a dobsonfly larva accurately enough to bridge the Platonic chasm between real and ideal? Had he created the soul of dobson, fabricated from dun hackles and self-illuminating condom and fine gold wire? Had Chip's creation animated itself? We both felt a tingle, which we misinterpreted as spiritual ecstasy derived from a witnessed miracle. As we marveled with unhinged jaws, the airborne hellgrammite snapped like a firecracker in a curl of white smoke, and I realized that we were feeling the charged air of celestial electricity polarizing between the tip of Chip's graphite Orvis and straight through my metal boat to the last link of the chain that grounded us, electrically speaking, to the rocky bottom of the Flint River.

Positive streamers waved, strokes and return strokes of Saint Elmo's fire.

Chip said the subsequent surge of current rolled my lips into a hideous rictus that bared my teeth, which glowed luminescent green like the hellgrammites he'd tied from glow-in-the-dark condoms. He also said he saw and heard the spark of galvanic electricity that synapsed the gap between fillings in my upper and lower molars, melting the amalgam and leaving smoking cavities the diameter of my dentist's drill.

"Yaaaaah!" I cried, blowing smoke. My feet began to boogie on their own as my gluteus maxima twitched like frog legs in lemon juice.

The sudden charge, he testified, did wonderful things to my neck hackles, which bristled, fizzed and kinked like steel wool touched off with a match. My thick eyebrows, he said, absolutely backlashed.

The only thing that kept us from frying like grasshoppers was our providential drift over a hole deeper than the length of the chain, which fell plumb without reaching the bottom, although the spark gap did shock two flathead catfish belly-up to the surface.

"That was close," Chip said. "Take me to shore; I don't want to be late for church."

"It's Saturday."

"Maybe we can find a synagogue."

I cranked my Johnson and hauled in the logging chain, which still tingled my hands. We sped upstream, careening through river rocks, hellbent on reaching the neutrally charged landing as the slanting rain chased us up the channel. The river birch and cypress knees flickered like pickets, and Chip's jowls flapped in the wind. I mumbled Bible verses as the tip of my tongue explored warm molars.

We passed the first-hole rapids at Radium Country Club and Radium Dam, where the deluge caught up with us. Through the gray rain I could almost make out Joe Lord in his khakis, as though the close encounter had zapped me back to my childhood.

The same lacy water poured over the mossy floodgates, and the same scab-bark sycamores and tortured cypress trunks leaned over the stippled chop.

I blamed our close call on Chip's hubris of tying flies that were too damn real. It's not nice to play God or screw with Mother Nature. Just look what happened to chain-shackled Prometheus and prideful Victor Frankenstein, who set out to vitalize inanimate objects. Scientists tell us that, some four billion years ago, a 50,000-degree lightning bolt nuked some organic soup and provoked the nutrients to set about evolving human meat, so it seems appropriate that a higher power took Her best shot at Chip and missed, sending a high-voltage hint for me to continue tying flies that look like dust balls under the sofa and to watch out who I fish with during afternoon thundershowers.

There's No Shame in Missing a Bobwhite Quail

I joy when the quails come. —Caliban

"No matter what any woman says," I explain, "hunting puts a man back in touch with his blood. Your mother may think killing is cruel or superfluous now that food comes wrapped in cellophane, but a man has to keep his killer instincts honed, else he loses his basic humanity."

Jeremy's single mother isn't thrilled about letting her son cut middle school to hone his killer instincts hunting quail, but the boy nags that he'll be spending the day with a certified teacher. "Certifiable," Mom sighs, signing the permission slip. Her reluctance steels my resolve to initiate the boy to the male virtues involving the hunt.

Clyde, my neutered Boykin spaniel, is in the boy's lap, head out the window, cheeks flapping.

"Mothers," Jeremy says as we drive past Stonebridge Country Club on our way to Wynfield Plantation. "You can't live with them, and you can't live without them."

Like most avid hunters, I hate golf and detest golf courses, desert lawns that waste water and leech toxic fertilizers into depleted aquifers. I take a moment to express my ecological prejudices to Jeremy, pointing out the impropriety of importing exotic flora into the indigene. "Look at that, palm trees growing alongside chinaberries! What does that tell you?"

"Palm trees need oceans to disperse the coconuts?" the boy ventures. He's smart, the primary reason I took him on as a protégé. That and 10 is the age when boys should start hunting, since girls won't have anything to do with them and they can't drink whiskey. As a 56-year-old, I can relate to Jeremy mano a mano on the issues of spirits and representatives of the female persuasion.

"Well then, you see why coconut palms don't belong in South Georgia, but the real problem is grass. That's where civilization took the wrong fork. Hunters were transformed into shaggy shepherds who passed their time ambling over meadows, swatting goat turds with a shepherd's crook. That's what started us down the road to decline, and that's why people think like sheep. Man has been watching over sheep and doing God knows what else with them for thousands of years. Here's an example. Look how the masses turned against smokers—ostracizing them, banning them from public places, taxing them to death, scapegoating them. Shepherds are worse than sheep," I declare. "Shepherds follow sheep around!"

"I don't smoke," says Jeremy.

"Well, neither do I," I point out, "but that's not the issue. It's grass I'm talking about. Grass!"

"Mama said tell you to take your Ritalin," Jeremy advises, "when you go to talking funny."

*

Medication was suggested by psychologist Mick Cardone for attention deficit disorder, news to me after five decades of believing I was sharp as a laser. "People who have ADD as bad as you do rarely amount to much," Dr. Cardone explained.

"I have a graduate degree in literature," I reminded him, "and I've been teaching college English at Darton for twenty-six years."

"That's my point," he said.

I asked him to recommend disability accommodations, a private secretary to keep me on task. I envisioned a leather skirt and high boots, compulsive neatness, somebody pretty enough for me to pay attention to. Dr. Cardone suggested golf, chess, or needlepoint to improve my concentration. "Golf is symptomatic of the sickness of ungulate conformity," I informed him.

"Maybe Ritalin will help you to focus."

It does. Medicated, I point pretty girls like a bird dog and run my mouth incessantly.

"I'm trying to cut back on Ritalin," I tell Jeremy. "I may've had a couple extra milligrams too much today already, but you might as well face the facts, son: America has been transformed into a nation of shepherds. And it's not just a countryside garnished with surreal green sod and triangular pennants. The sprawling urban cityscapes fester with miniature golf courses—plastic apes, giraffes and dinosaurs—moronic microcosms of indolence glorified by Scottish shepherds. The US of A is a mecca of half-baked and eclectic ideas fleshed out prematurely by a rampant technology."

"I like Putt-Putt," insists Jeremy.

"Well, it's the grass that's really offensive, with its entourage of mowers, weedwhackers, edgers—gadgets in service to the world's blandest weed: Grass!"

*

We pull into Wynfield Plantation's mile-long entrance fringed with rye grass, then enter the main lodge, where a 6 x 7 elk the size of a tyrannosaurus hangs over the fireplace.

"I killed that buck at a waterhole on the back side of the place," Bill Bowles, the general manager, tells Jeremy. "Shot him between the eyes with a .22 short and folded him like a taco."

Jeremy grins.

"Welcome to Wynfield," Bill says. He shows us a safety video and gives Jeremy a gun handling lesson while I eat

M&Ms and peruse a promotional pamphlet, discovering complimentary golf privileges at Stonebridge are available for hunters who get tired of briers. Then he takes us to the sporting clays range, where he teaches Jeremy to hit moving targets. The boy tries a 28-gauge over-and-under, then swaps it for a youth model 20 with a shorter stock.

"It's a poor carpenter who blames his tools," I tell the boy.

Soon Jeremy is dusting clay targets. "He's a natural," says Bill. "Want to give it a try, Mr. Miller?"

"Naw, let Jeremy practice. I've shot plenty of clay birds in my day."

"Come on, Mr. Miller, be a sport. We've got to wait on the other writer, anyway. Susan Paul's hunting with us."

Susan Paul! Hot damn! Besides being the steamiest romance writer in Dixie, Susan herself is the stuff prurient dreams are made of—seductive, intelligent, statuesque. Her latest novel, *Till Death Do Us Part*, is great material to cuddle up with if you can't score the genuine article, and *Surrena's Choice* comes out in French this January. Now that promises to be a titillating opus, don't it?

Jeremy straddles a fallen pine, watching the sporting clays dip and hover through thermals as Ken Forrester, guide and dog handler, sends them sailing and I miss them. "Watch that log, Jeremy," warns Bill. "Don't let it throw you. I've seen it buck a man clean across the firebreak."

eremy tightens his knees, then grins.

*

I start shooting better, chipping about every third target, until Susan shows up in a canvas and leather shooting outfit and lace-up boots. Her blue eyes are deep enough to give you vertigo, but I stabilize myself by focusing on the highest fastened button on her overleavened blouse. Men say they don't take women hunting because women can't shoot worth a damn. The real truth is men can't shoot worth a damn with women watching. Susan herself shoots like a Viet Cong sniper.

The M&Ms have made me jittery, so I pop another Ritalin. When I lean over to police a spent shell, silver splinters fracture my vision. "Birds fly a lot faster than clay pigeons," I tell Jeremy. "I've spent my whole life shooting the genuine article, and I can't artificially override my instinctive lead for mere fun and games."

"Nice course," Susan tells Bill, tossing her frosted hair. "I understand Marty Fisher designed it. I'm glad you keep it up. Lots of clubs let their ranges get snaky."

"We need to sign on Susan as taskmaster," Bill grins, "whip us into shape, keep the plantation from reverting to a chaos of untamed nature."

"There's nothing wrong with good stewardship," Susan reminds him prettily. "Don't you agree, Mr. Miller?"

"The stewardship nemesis is grass," I point out, blinking. "It appeared back in the Tertiary and changed man's life forever. Grass can be grazed, its leaves endlessly nibbled without killing it. Indeed, the more grass is cropped or mowed the better it grows."

"Grass?"

"Grass allowed man to domesticate and herd animals instead of hunting them."

Jeremy's eyes are rolling; he's heard all this before. "We lost our sanguinary integrity when he started following livestock around, swatting goat turds with shepherd's crooks, which, by the way, is the origin of golf. I think it's insane when people cut down perfectly good trees to nurture a weed they have to cut back noisily every Sunday morning."

"Uh, good point, Mr. Miller," says Susan, her bottomless blue eyes staring about a foot and a half over my head.

"I'd rather see a world tangled in kudzu than sodden with grass."

79

"I think I'm ready to go quail hunting now," says Jeremy, "try my hand at the genuine article."

"Well, let's go!" cry Bill and Ken.

*

Cap and Dixie lock down, rigid as concrete lawn dogs. Ken takes Jeremy's shoulders and guides him to the point. Susan loads her over-and-under and tags along.

"Pick out one bird and kill it," Ken tells Jeremy. "Take your time."

Bill and I stay in the jeep. "Remember your first bird?" I ask him.

"Sure. I shot it over a pointer named Dixie, and I've named dogs Dixie ever since."

"When I was about that boy's age, I killed my first quail with this gun right here." I hold up my model 12 Winchester. "I remember the moment as clearly as I remember the color of my fourth wife's eyes."

The Winchester is shorter now. Dirt daubers built a summer nest in the barrel, and it split like a banana peel when I fired at a dove, tattooing my cheeks and eyelids with blue powder burns. Jack Daniel Garrett sawed off the split end with a hacksaw, providentially offsetting geriatric ocularity with a wider shot pattern. The last time Catherine Mountcastle invited me to Blue Springs Plantation, I killed four quail when the covey rise startled me into firing accidentally from the hip—a long time ago.

Jeremy steps up. Susan stands by, hanging on one shapely hip. Ken flails the brush, and quail blast out of the broom sedge like shrapnel. Susan fires twice and two birds tumble. Most of the covey is out of range before Jeremy collects himself to shoot at "the lingerer," that evolutionary misfit that survives to perpetuate genes by waiting until all the hunters' guns are empty. This procrastinating little bastard takes off like a whoopee cushion, but Jeremy gets off a shot—kapow—and the bird sails leisurely to the base of a persimmon tree 75 yards away.

I climb down from the jeep to console the boy. "That's why we call it hunting instead of killing, son. Any number of variables can intercede," I tell him. "There's no shame in missing a bobwhite quail."

"He hit that bird," says Ken Forrester.

"Why, sure he did," I say, winking at the guide. Ken sends the dogs over to the persimmon tree where they find a cock with a broken wing.

"Your turn, Mr. Miller," Susan offers. A wisp of pearly smoke rises from her chambers as she breaks the gun and bends over for the ejected hulls. My heart flushes, fluttering in my rib cage like a trapped partridge. Silver minnows swim before my eyes.

The dogs retrieve her double.

"Let Jeremy hunt. I've killed plenty of quail in my day."

After the boy downs two more birds, I decide it's a good time to pull him aside again for a lesson on the psychological subtleties of guns.

"Shooting is about sport, not power."

"I know that."

"Well, some hunters on the fringe confuse their firearms with sexual potency, on a subliminal level of course. The weapon becomes a negative phallus, displacing procreation with destruction. You'll understand a lot better when you're older."

"Do what?"

"Don't ever get your tallywacker mixed up with your scattergun," I advise.

"Sick!" says Jeremy.

"And make the first shot count."

"OK, but I've only got a single-shot gun."

"Well then, you see why the first shot is important."

"What are you guys whispering about?" calls Susan.

"Come on, let's find another covey before sunset."

We mount up and move at a fast idle as Dixie and Cap zigzag over softly rolling hills of wiregrass, broomsedge and longleaf pine. "This is as much fun as you can have with your clothes on," I tell Jeremy.

"That's a good one," says Ken. "Point!"

The dogs are locked down solid, Cap backing Dixie. Susan insists I take this bird, most likely a single from the covey we just jumped.

"I'll flush," she says. "Let's go." She exchanges her over-and-under for Ken's flail, and we approach the point; I smell perfume and gunpowder and hear the cat's claw scratching her trousers. From the corner of my eye, I see her britches stretch across her behind as she bends to slash the brush, and I instantaneously fantasize antidotes for a midlife disordered by the distractions of attention deficit.

"Notice how we do this, Jeremy," I call over my shoulder. The silver minnows have fattened into tadpoles now, hunting a penetrable egg.

The single rattles into the sky. I shoulder the pump. *Blam, blam, blam.* The kick sends more silver sparks swirling into my vision, like a Roman candle instead of a sawed-off 20-gauge. The bird turns on his afterburner, like they do, corkscrewing over a rise, which may be why they call it flushing. My retriever, Clyde, cocks his head.

"Look at him go!" cries Jeremy.

I hold out my gun in disbelief at the optical illusion inspired, perhaps, by excitement and medicinal overdose. The dwarfed barrel seems to be melting, wilting at least.

"Does this gun look bent to you?" I ask Ken.

He closes one eye and sights down a gun not much longer than a bugle—choked like a bugle, too. "You know, I think you might be right," he answers. Ken's job is to agree absolutely with anything a client says or does as long as it doesn't endanger a dog.

"Well, I hit him, but that's a lot of green."

"They sho is," Ken says.

"I couldn't have missed that bird. I had it dead on him all three times."

"I think you hit him," says Ken.

"You didn't cut a feather," smiles Susan.

"Dead bird, Clyde. Dead, Dixie! Dead, Cap!" I shout. The dogs go about their business of sniffing and pissing. Clyde yawns and flops back down in the floorboards, curling to lick himself. I lay the Winchester in the gun rack, where it sags.

"Sometimes they fly dead," I inform Jeremy, "like chickens with their heads chopped off. Pure reflex. He fell just over that rise like the first quail you shot."

"That's where he set down all right," agrees Ken.

"Dead bird, Clyde! Hunt dead." The Boykin looks up, then resumes licking.

Clyde's attitude has deteriorated since I had him fixed.

"Nothing goes to waste in nature," I explain to Jeremy. "The hawks will get him, or the raccoons."

"They will, he ain't careful," says Ken Forrester. "Oh, I mean his carcass. You know what I mean."

"Yessir."

"Of course, my model 12 has been damaged. The barrel blew up on me a while back...or did I tell you that?"

"It's a poor carpenter who blames his tools," Jeremy reminds me.

Dixie finds my bird, but miraculously it flies away. I don't expect to have to shoot a dead bird again, so naturally I'm unprepared, missing it twice with Susan's over-and- under as it takes off like a Bronx cheer.

"Some reflexes!" Ken marvels as the bird wings 300 yards to angle into a cypress bottom. "We best let that bird go before he kills one of my dogs."

I shake my head. "It just isn't like me to miss singles," I

insist. "Nothing like this has ever happened before. Maybe it's the medication." Now my brain is spewing silver sparks like an arc welder.

"That's why they call it hunting," says the boy. "There's no shame in missing a bobwhite quail."

The jeep pulls up. Susan, enthroned in the high seat, shimmers in a busy molecular aurora against the twilight sky. The dying breeze whispers in the longleaf pines, and my occluded heart taps music. There's nothing like quail hunting to put a man back in touch with his blood.

Dog Days

The more I learn about people the more I like my dog.
  —Mark Twain

"*I*f you're so intent on keeping that dog," snapped my fourth wife, "take him to the vet and get him fixed."
  Named for hunting buddy Clyde Edgerton, the canine Clyde replaced Geeche, my first Boykin spaniel, who wound up her mortal coils trying to retrieve a bull gator from the Wakulla River. With Geeche gone I'd struggled to honor my contemporary wife's wishes that we live without dogs for a while. But to me hunting without a dog is just shooting live targets, a selfish and mindless thing. A single season of dog deprivation led me to bring home another Boykin, plucked from the dugs of a purebred bitch and tucked into my shirt belly, replacing his mother's scent with my own. Clyde reached adolescence like a human counterpart, big-footed and clumsy, a little on the randy side if judged chauvinistically but with plenty of promise and a well-tuned nose. We went everywhere together, even to my English classes at the college. Students helped train him to wet-retrieve in the president's goldfish pond.
  "Fixed?"
  Both wife and stepdaughter resented Clyde. Maybe because I hadn't asked permission to get him; maybe because in Clyde's attempts to bond with them he plundered the dirty clothes and ate their panties.
  "You know what I mean. Get him neutered, castrated, emasculated. It's embarrassing."
  I know a guy, Seaward Corey, who pisses in his dogs' food to center them. Maybe it works, but the regimentation

lacks respect, in my opinion, inviting indecent exposure accusations from urban neighbors who don't keep abreast of bonding methods. I'd feel guilty as a kidnapper if a dog loved me for pissing in his food. Besides, this female flair-up, I knew without being told, wasn't about panties. Clyde must've dry-hunched somebody's leg, a Junior League sustainer or maybe a Colonial Dame. But what's a dog supposed to do to say Hidy? You can't abuse a puppy's dignity with neurotic, trivial acts like begging, speaking or lifting a paw.

"He attacked Miss Sissy Crouch from the Charity League Debutante Selection Committee," she confessed. "And I was mortified."

"Attacked?"

"He clasped her leg and nearly knocked her down."

"He was glad to see her. He's a friendly dog."

"I thought I'd lie down and die," she declared. That's what she meant by mortified.

I ventured an opinion about what Clyde would've done to her corpse if she had.

"You're as disgusting as he is."

"Maybe we need to get me fixed."

"I'm past my last nerve with all this. It's him or me."

"Him or you what? You thinking about getting yourself and MC spayed? Maybe ask Dr. Hart for a family discount?"

I should've learned not to diffuse gender conflicts with levity. Men and women don't see dogs the same way. A dog without a sweater and rhinestone collar is useless to women, or at least the women I've married. "Honey," I added, "please don't take this personally, but at my age I need a retriever more than a wife. Let's strive for a meeting of minds."

"He's gross!" interjected my stepdaughter, the presumed object of Sissy's visit.

Miss Sissy was gauging my stepdaughter's debutante potential, checking her out for the right stuff. Maybe man's best friend had just saved me a few thousand bucks plus an insufferable evening in a rented tux.

My stepdaughter, taking after her mother, was aghast, but it wasn't Clyde's fault his pee-wee ran out like lipstick when he was glad to see somebody. It was merely his nature, and aside from that the once hyperactive little puppy was showing a heap of promise as a retriever, and I was reluctant to risk adulterating his temerity. Spaniels have to be aggressive to handle the jobs Labs do. Already he'd hunt anything a big dog would. And while it was true he was bad to hump a leg, he'd also bring back any dove or quail you feathered enough to slow down.

He could catch a bonus bobwhite on the ground while flushing the covey or snatch a single out of the air before you could punch your safety off. He'd drag prey too big to carry. Anything too big to drag he'd jump on, barking and humping till you got there. Already he was famous among bowhunters, who'd sometimes call me in the middle of the night to put Clyde on a blood trail, which he'd follow until daybreak from pure libido. You could locate your quarry in the dark by the concupiscent commotion.

Find your boar or deer in the broomsedge divined by the upstroke dawning of bobtail behind. Clyde barked and barked in the accumulated ecstasy of venery.

On the other front, his proposed emasculation became a recurring topic at our house, and my subconscious knees drifted together each time the subject was broached. It just isn't right to fight Mother Nature. My fourth wife could no more be blamed for her urge to sweep maleness under the rug than Clyde could be faulted for his irrepressible prurience. At a certain point, mature women conclude that maleness is superfluous. This drives middle-aged men nuts because they suspect middle-aged women are right.

And so, they seek refuge in the arms of their daughters' contemporaries, who haven't figured out superfluity yet. They drive sporty cars and leave the top three buttons of their sport shirts open to display gold chains nestled in graying chest hair. They comb wings of gossamer hair over balding crowns. Or they migrate outdoors with their dogs to hunt quail and other quarry that won't land them in San Quinton.

It turned out that Miss Sissy hadn't come by the house for my stepdaughter after all, but for me. Apparently, her selection was a done deal. Miss Sissy wanted me to take lessons from Mr. Mervin Callahan, who'd teach me enough temporary poise to get me through an upper-crust puberty ritual without reflecting negatively on the proceedings.

Miss Sissy, stoning a double on the covey rise, also wanted me to speak at a DAR luncheon, where she'd neglected her duties as program chairperson to devote more time to scrutinizing the presentability of debutantes and their parents' position on the social registry.

I have no idea how Miss Sissy found me afield and Clyde home unless I was fishing in a belly-boat or a kayak too small to hold us both, but my womenfolk assured her I'd keep my appointment with Mervin Callahan, and that I'd cancel my noon class for the honor of speaking to the DAR—though they all agreed it might be best to meet and confirm, if for no other reason than to preserve the appearance of freewill.

Miss Sissy called on me at my office, standing by the open door as erect as a fighting cock. I was leaning back in a swivel chair with my feet on my desk eating an egg salad and ketchup sandwich, taking a break from teaching bonehead English to boys in ballcaps and Shakespeare to pretty country girls who end sentences with prepositions.

"Come in, Miss Sissy," I burbled. She did, complete with white gloves, parasol, and hoisted eyebrows. She spoke in an archaic dialect heard only in antebellum pockets of the Deep South and nowhere else. She elevated her lower mandible high enough to stress the ligaments of a scrawny neck, closed her eyes, and spoke with a precise grammatical infallibility.

"Professah Millah, uh Vic, understandin' you to be a distinguished gentleman of lettahs, we wondah if you might exact time from your busy schedule to comment on the new dahrection of Southern literature since the death of Margaret Mitchell. I'm an avid birdwatcher, don't you know, as are a number of the girls." Miss Sissy at 87 was one of the younger girls in the DAR.

I tilted back in my swivel chair, one cheek lumped with egg salad and light bread. "Do what?" I asked, not quite grasping the airy connection between *Gone with the Wind* and cataloging avian species.

Miss Sissy was sufficiently well bred to ignore Clyde, who'd sprung out from under my desk and clamped her leg like a fireman sliding down a pole. He hunched her atrophied calf with wide mouth joy, huffing like a choo-choo train, topaz eyes rolling, tongue wagging, the very picture of doggy ecstasy. I've got to admit Miss Sissy showed a lot of class, displaying only a barely perceptible quiver of jowl as she cracked Clyde's skull with her parasol.

"I declare, your puppy has run my hose!"

"That's just his way of saying hello, but that's not a run, ma'am. It's..."

It was time to call the vet, is what it was: Dr. Henry Hart, who promised the only difference I'd notice was that visitors wouldn't limp in circles with a dog wrapped around their shins. I, on the other hand, was afraid other dogs might notice Clyde's testicular deficiency and snub him, maybe piss on him or treat him like a middle-aged husband. But I was also getting mounting pressure (no pun) from my division chair, a neurotic reading specialist promoted way past her competency, to leave Clyde home. Hearing Clyde's clicking toenails down her hallowed halls drove her to distraction and memoranda. Pets were against the rules, and rules were rules. Right? Wrong! Never remind any Southerner, black or white, who grew up under the embarrassment of Jim Crow about the sanctity of rules. Under Jim Crow it was immoral to obey the law.

Still, besieged on multiple fronts, I finally hauled Clyde to Dr. Hart.

"Counseling sessions are available for better adjustment," he hastened to inform me when I confessed my misgivings.

"Listen, I'm not paying to have a bird dog psychoanlyzed."

"I'm talking about you."

"Hmmm."

Dr. Hart said he could replace Clyde's extracted testicles with prosthetic implants normally used for a condition called cryptorchism. "The other doggies won't suspect a thing," he promised, but I was no more willing to pay Henry to install false balls in Clyde than I was to have him psychoanalyzed.

Cathy, Dr. Hart's lab assistant, poked her head into the doggie OR. "Dr. Hart, Mrs. Miller called up to see if you can't give her a package deal and fix them both."

He grinned. "If Mr. Miller had got himself fixed thirty years ago, he'd be a millionaire."

"Yeah," Cathy snarled, "instead of settling up with all them ex-wives."

"Hmm."

Cathy clearly had no ambition of becoming the fifth Mrs. Miller.

I lifted Clyde, quivering, up onto the operating table. He looked up at me with trusting topaz eyes. Dr. Hart gave him an injection in the paw and placed a plastic gas cup with an accordion hose over his muzzle. Cathy hugged my struggling pal, his toenails scratching stainless steel.

"Careful, Cathy. This is when they'll bite you," Dr. Hart warned. "When they're in the twilight zone, they're not responsible."

Suddenly Clyde collapsed in her arms, his eyes dead as marbles, limp tongue folded on the cold tabletop. Cathy grinned demurely as she shaved Clyde's little scrotum and painted it with Betadine. Dr. Hart adjusted his light and bent over his grim work. He made a quick incision that opened like a small white eye beneath the point of his scalpel. His surgically gloved fingers squeezed the underside of Clyde's little bag and a cottony testicle popped out—blip— like a cocktail onion.

A lump the size of Clyde's gonad formed in my throat. I swallowed. "What's that noodle looking thing you're clamping off?" I choked.

"That's the whole shooting match rolled into one, the whole nine yards—the blood supply, the vas deferens, the spermatic duct and the gubernaculum or scrotal ligament." Dr. Hart lifted Clyde's left gubernaculum with the blade of his scissors. "Goodbye puppyhood, goodbye romance."

"Goodbye and good riddance," cackled Cathy, her brass eyes pinning me wriggling on the wall.

Henry clipped Clyde's noodle and tossed the severed testicle irreverently toward the dispenser. It hit the rim, bounced and rolled wetly beneath the autoclave. Cathy grinned, and my own scrotal ligament contracted my vintage landing gear into my abdominal cavity.

"Watch Mr. Miller," warned Cathy. "He's fixing to swoon!"

I entered a swirling pool of vertigo, holding the edge of the table above an inky abyss. Waves of nausea sloshed behind my eyes. I sank into a dark chasm spangled with floating lights.

"You want to put him in a chair... chair... chair?" a distant voice inquired. "No, drag him over by the autoclave. Prop him against the wall until I finish closing up here," said a sepulchral Dr. Hart. "He might fall out of the chair and sue me... sue me... sue me."

"His tongue's hanging out like his dog's, only whiter... whiter... whiter."

I felt myself drifting, or being tugged, through the cold dark. "Make sure he doesn't swallow his tongue," he advised.

"How?"

"Clamp it, but don't let him bite you. Semiconscious, he's not responsible."

"He bites me, I ain't responsible neither."

Seconds later, I suppose, I woke up screaming, a cold duckbill clamp pinching my tongue. I came to with Cathy squatted over me, plumbing my tongue with tongs, wearing the same bemused expression she wore when Dr. Hart lobbed Clyde's family jewels at the trash receptacle. Still flourishing a scalpel, he bent over and gazed into my contracted pupils. In an irresponsible, illogical flash I envisioned myself being fixed.

"Argggggah." I screamed. "Nawl!" Bicycling, I tried to kick Cathy back. "Not me! Not me!" I rolled over to all fours, retching, the duckbill clamps on my tongue wagging pendulously.

"God! What's he been eating?" Cathy brayed, a nasal sound made by raising the upper lip higher than the dictates of labial anatomy.

"Internal exsanguinations?" inquires the vet.

"Must've been. Surely he couldn't of ate nothing that gross!"

"By God!" Dr. Hart mused. "The fertilized eggs from some reptile?" As I floated upward toward a wrinkled pewter surface, Clyde's frozen eyes fixed me most constantly, no longer trusting, darker now than the usual lucent topaz.

I knew he'd never see me or the world the same way ever again, though he'd be free to hunt unambiguously with the pure delight of predation without hormonal distractions or social compromise. In a way I envied him. I envied him a lot.

Clyde's Quail

Thou wast not born for death, immortal bird! No hungry generations tread thee down. —Keats

Among the mutant kith and kin of partridge there is the rare quail, a maverick bobwhite—a swamp-bred SOB of unprincipled demeanor and dastardly disregard for propriety—an outlaw that squirts nitroglycerine mist and cock-rockets at rattling velocities through scrub and scuppernong, zipping out of range before most mortals can shoulder a scattergun or launch a sneeze.

These evolutionary throwbacks disperse among conventional highland coveys to mystify hunters and puzzle dogs. They get up wild, inspiring quail of milder manner to fly away with them. Or they hold stubbornly until stepped over, exploding into flight beneath horses who then throw their riders. They ensconce themselves behind single stems of broomsedge on bare ground where a skipper couldn't hide, and they'll stay there until it thunders unless a dog with more nose than common sense paws the mere idea of quail into corporeality.

On other occasions, having remained motionless and invisible through bizarre attempts to flush them, they rattle insolently away at the clack of unloading chamber or the click of safety. They flush up trouser legs of dismounted hunters, startling them into shooting their fellows. These mutants, though insinuated covertly into conventional coveys, comprise a subspecies distinguishable from other bobwhites by eccentricity of flight and by wild beady eyes that never close, even in death. Airborne, they defy aerodynamics, executing 90-degree changes of direction at full speed.

Dead or alive they emit an acrid musk associated with poisonous reptiles and lockups for the violently insane.

*

North Carolina novelist Clyde Edgerton visits Blue Springs Plantation the last weekend of quail season to miss birds with me and to commune with the spirit of a favorite uncle who took him hunting in the Florida flatwoods, teaching him to shoot before the air force ruined him. I've seen Clyde, after missing scores of conventional bobwhites, shoot and kill a maverick single that nobody else could hit with a firehose spraying cyanide. Were his wing-shooting to be judged solely by his predatory bond with these aberrations, or if there were no other quail in Georgia, he'd win the laurels of marksmanship he covets. I've tried to figure out how he hits these birds while missing all others.

At first it seemed that the archetypal encounter of killer and prey somehow ignited a spark in the primal sludge of Clyde's brainpan, supercharging mediocre reflexes, transforming him briefly into an automatonic epitome of predation, but now my explanations have modified metaphysically. Faster than the retina registers light, his weathered Browning barks deadly. The maverick quail tumbles into a pinwheel of feathers, graveyard dead before hitting the ground. It's as though the favorite uncle steps out of the hereafter to possess Clyde and discharge the old Browning, leaving his befuddled nephew with a smoking gun, drop-jawed and weak in the hinges. A dog fetches the quail. The man, chewing the inside of his cheek, studies it like manna dropped from a low cloud.

"Nice shot, Clyde!"

"Do what?"

*

95

A matched brace of somnambulant mules with hooded eyes jerks our wagon along an established course behind the cadre, horses, and dogs along the high ridge over the Flint River 40 yards behind Old Sam, the undisputed patriarch and high priest of Blue Springs, so sure of place he never looks anywhere but straight ahead, his black horse prancing steadily along the established course. Sam's cataracts have finally blinded him, and he's quit using his eyes to see a world that barely sees him, the grand old man dark as rich bottomland, so black he and his horse would disappear into shadows without the orange cap and Day-Glow trim.

I sit the padded leather seats of the dog wagon with Clyde and the stately Catherine, our hostess. We chat and listen to Old Sam sing to deep-chested pointers that charge through wiregrass sucking up scent while Freddie, a stocky centurion outrider, gallops the flanks, retrieving wide-ranging dogs.

A covey gets up wild some 75 yards out from the nearest dog, as it always has, a horizontal whirlwind off the longleaf and wiregrass ridge along the Flint River. They fan out into the Lonesome, as deep and inhospitable a swamp as there is in Georgia—a place immune to spring burning, a place where even the sun won't give you the time of day.

"What spooked those birds?" Clyde wants to know.

"They spook they own self," says Catboy, who drives the wagon.

"That swamp looks like a place my uncle took me," Clyde reflects.

"Cain nobody hunt them birds," says Catboy. "They don't hold for no body, man or dog. They flies off yonner to the brambles. Some says they not even quails. Us and nobody else don't hunt them things."

"Nobody?" I press.

Catboy smiles, wagging his gray head at the folly of the

notion. "Come up, mule!" The covey of Lonesome Ridge is composed absolutely of maverick individuals.

Cohabitating with cottonmouths and pooling genes in an ecology red in tooth and talon, they reverted to a type more reptilian than avian, thriving in heavy predation like the Wild West desperadoes who fled the law to set up shop in the Okeefenokee. I know all this, but I keep my mouth shut: Catherine doesn't need to know I'd poached Blue Springs from my home upriver before she was born. Alton Jones, an industrialist friend of Ike's, owned the place then. Sam used to chase me off this ridge to my hideout in the Lonesome, where I sulked like some teenage James Dean more sinned against than sinning, watching Ike's procession snake the ridge. Jones got killed in a private plane shuttling a suitcase full of cash to Biscayne Bay for Nixon's 1960 run against JFK. So it goes.

This mutant covey was here back then, so wild I could smell them without a dog. They haunted the thorny perimeters of Lonesome Swamp, retaining optimal leanness of around a dozen birds through, I surmise, cannibalism.

From my leaky skiff I jumped wood ducks through morning mist and shot squirrels from high branches. There were few deer in South Georgia in those days, but I hunted them anyway. The only bucks I ever saw roamed this riverbank, bolting out of range like the covey that just got up wild, flashing ass toward the Lonesome, where my younger self poached with impunity since no adult ventured into the gothic dark to patrol or post signs.

"Seems like you could trap them, breed some wild into release birds," I try.

"There ain't no release birds on Blue Springs."

"Well, it seems like somebody could."

"They tear up the traps."

The mutants aren't worth eating anyway. Reverting to their Jurassic ancestors, they have flatly helmed breasts hard as motor mounts plumed with sinewy feathers edged in black, suggesting an evolution from thick plates or scales. But specific anatomical data, together with recipes for subduing the purple flesh into edibility, are largely speculative due to the rarity of dissectible specimens. It's rumored they squirm during plucking. Old Sam advises covering the pot when cooking them, "or they jump out the grease like a bullfrog."

Catboy says, "Don't nobody have no business messing with them birds." Freddy insists his mama didn't raise no kids to eat frogs.

"I know that's right," says Eddie Lee.

The Lonesome was my adolescent utopia where kingmakers, game wardens, and presidents didn't tread, and the mutants, undiminished by shotshell or natural predators, had no manners at all. After sundown I'd hide my skiff on the east side and hitchhike home in the days when teenagers with guns could catch rides. Even women would stop for a boy holding up a thumb, a cat squirrel, and a scattergun. But just when you decide nothing in a perfect world can ever change, everything's about to.

Clyde and I came of age with the rest of our generation, rushing headlong into ill-fated marriages, drugs, and idiotic wars while the pale ghost of my innocence stayed to wander the Lonesome. Now I can't figure out if I'm the bastard son of the young nimrod in the thicket or he's the gallberry youngun' of a jaded me. After the army corrupted my marksmanship and graduate school ruined my brains, I returned home to teach where I had roots, where I'd hunted when the paint on my world was still tacky.

Until the maverick covey flushed wild, I hadn't considered revisiting Lonesome Swamp, either out of fear of what I might find or of what I might not. The swamp remained the spiritual home I couldn't come back to. Now, I'm starting to think it's the only place I'll find a quail psychopathic enough for Clyde to hit.

The mules whoa when the liver-tick freezes in a bicolor patch, the lemon backing.

Sam's bright cap levitates, magically announcing the point. Clyde and I climb down. Wink, Catherine's current beau, dismounts his mare. He tugs a stubby 12-gauge from the saddle scabbard, joining us behind the dogs. Catherine's swain, shirtless beneath black leather motorcycle vest, seems as incongruous to plantation quail shooting as his sawed-off shotgun. Catherine, a proficient wing shot, stays in the wagon, too genteel a hostess to pick up her Beretta and humble us with doubles. I never shoot well around Catherine anyway, her broad-shouldered serenity a fatal distraction to my follow through. If Wink knew the least of my prurient musings, he'd turn his riot gun on me. He must sense I'm too old and indigent to vie for her affections.

"I know that's right!" I overhear in a conversational snatch from Eddie Lee, who holds Wink's horse.

We approach the point, walking past the rigid pointer and the dog more quietly disposed, Freddy between us, stropping the lespedeza. I move in behind Clyde, closing one eye. The covey disperses like shrapnel. He picks his bird and shoots a yard wide, feathering a snowy hog plum. All morning Clyde and I have missed birds liberally without condolence, admonition, or encouragement from the stoic Sam. We've missed them with unflinching consistency. Clyde's timing is off, of course. A former jet pilot, he reviews each miss.

"I couldn't get on his six o'clock," he concludes in dogfight jargon.

We recently discovered we occupied Cold War Korea at the same time—I, a shivering grunt in a frosty observation post in the DMZ while he ripped through even colder air overhead. Today he uses his whole body to follow through, vectoring in air speed and drift. To hit quail consistently he needs to be chasing them in an F-4 Phantom.

The military didn't do my shooting any good, either. Off duty I begged a riot gun like Wink's from the MPs to go tiptoeing through old mine fields, kicking up pheasants, flinching with every quick noise. Even today a rattling single flushing from cover sounds like a Bouncing Betty to me.

"I just can't figure out what's wrong," Clyde complains.

"Hmm," says Freddy, returning to his feet from hitting the dirt. Clyde's crablike maneuvers to get on his bird's six o'clock make Freddy nervous. They don't bother me, as I dance along behind him holding his belt. We grin and tip our hats as happy birds sail fully plumed over the next rise, into the next glade and across the timeless river.

Without Wink backing us with the sawed-off pump we wouldn't have enough birds for thin soup. He picks up two cocks as Clyde and I trudge back to the wagon. Clyde wedges his inherited Sweet Sixteen back into the velvet-lined gun box. The blocky breech is worn silver by two lifetimes of shooting as is my Winchester beside it, a model 12 owned by John 0. Huckabee, a cousin killed in 1942, the year I was born. In the South, ghosts still account for the deeper mysteries. Like living Southerners, they stay home or return there to acquire a venue of familiar dirt. Clyde, far from North Carolina, brings one sole poltergeist to handle the Browning and make inconceivable shots on impossible birds.

Aside from Catherine and Uncle Sam, our marksmanship suffers other distractions from the past we don't express to the cadre, who've heard every thin excuse that can come out of a human mouth. Catboy, who skinned Noah's mules down Ararat, claims the most far-fetched alibis come from General Norman Schwarzkopf, a sometimes guest.

"I know that's right," agrees Eddie Lee, but Old Sam says, "Mista Ike the champion in that department."

I realize the wagon's padded seats and genteel conversation create an ambience contrary to Clyde's predatory instincts. The hypnotic squeak of harness and hame lulls the hunter spirit, dilutes endorphins that tighten leaders connecting a man to venery. We need to be stumbling through cat's claw and dammit vine, wheezing, breaking a sweat, keeping one eye peeled for diamondbacks, feeling the squirt of adrenaline when a rattling palmetto slaps a leg. After the morning hunt we'll forgo cordials and cucumber sandwiches at the big house to return to the Lonesome where the mutant singles flew. I want to see Clyde and his departed uncle engage those lawless sons of bitches mano a mano in a swamp so wild you'd have to be crazy to see it as beautiful. But Oh Lord it is beautiful. At least it was to me 50 years ago.

Sam, disinclined to lend a kennel dog, finds two pathetic mutts from beneath a dogtrot porch: one a pointer mix with dangling black teats and terminal mange, the other a genetic mishap involving spaniels, caul-eyed, thunderstruck, neurotic. Gyp and Rufus, Sam calls them, insisting they ain't none of his.

"You're giving us a gun-shy retriever?" I ask the grand old man.

"Moan loan you one a gun don't bother," answers the unapologetic patriarch. "He thunderstruck like I told you, but he ain't gun shy." Sam glances blindly at a perfect sky. "One lightning flash call him home up under this porch."

"What about the bitch?"

"She get caught up with that scratching, she make do for you gentlemens." Sam has the sweetest, disarming smile, healthy pink gums unencumbered by teeth and framed in darkest ebony. Gyp coils for leverage, a blurred paw raising a flurry of dandruff. Both dogs have taken long hard looks at life and deemed it unfit for further investment.

The maverick covey, already reassembled on the backbone of Lonesome Ridge by the time we get there, takes off like a cyclone of rabid bats when I set the jeep's hand brake.

"There they go!" Clyde hoots. They dip into the bottom, banking at impossible angles, disappearing into a living green tapestry of thorn and vine. I've seen the forebears of these birds materialize into blurred missiles from naked cover where not one stem of vegetation grew, erupting from infernal fissures in the earth that slam shut behind them. They rolled and tumbled evasively in midair without being hit, sometimes without even being shot at. They were totally aerobatic, rocketing from dead stalls to Mach speeds in wildly perpendicular directions. Now with 50 generations of inbred savagery spiking their bloodlines, I couldn't hit one with a heat-seeking missile, but if anybody can kill one of these berserk vampires, I decide, Clyde's dead uncle can.

"You watch 'em down?" the nephew wants to know.

"No, but I know where they went."

A shallow knoll rises from the spongy earth between a fork in the old riverbed, or it used to. A stand of yaupon holly, *ilex vomitoria*, evidences Creek habitation during the 1830s, when a redneck general with presidential aspirations was busy chasing Indians out of Georgia. Inland Creeks transplanted the asi from banks of coastal rivers for their black drink ceremony. Clyde's singles, unthreatened since I was a dumb kid with a 20- gauge, would hold in that yaupon, though they might flush screaming into our faces with flexed talons.

"You'll get one shot," I advise. "No use taking more shells than the ones in your gun. I'm not even taking a gun." I leave my Winchester with its previous owner and Gyp, who refuses to abandon the jeep. There'll be plenty of haints in the Lonesome without John 0. Huckabee. The threadbare

Gyp answers my call to duty with puckered eyes, arched earflaps, and canted scalp. She settles into an intensive scratch that lifts a puff of dermal chafe into the winnowing breeze. We couldn't drag Gyp's frayed hide into the Lonesome on a plow line with Catboy's mules.

"This is it!" Clyde grins, regaining his warrior spirit and loading three high-brass fours into the Browning. My belt loop cinches the spaniel's matted throat as I drag him tongue and toenails down the ridge. At the impenetrable briar perimeter we drop to our knees and crawl through a tunnel made by wildcats. The terrified Rufus halts abruptly, and I nearly cold-nose him. I prod him on with a lightered knot, his cropped tail pressed under a shaggy aitchbone

"He's winding them," I tell Clyde.

We enter the cold miasma where the bottom opens into old growth, high limbs groining a cathedral canopy of perfect gloom. The absence of sunlight chokes out virtually all ground cover but saw palmetto. We rise to tiptoe Indian file with Clyde on point and the mortified Rufus guarding our rear, slinking beneath tremendous water oaks and bone-white sycamore toward the heart of Lonesome Swamp. Foul gas farts from spongy footsteps in fetid peat. The spaniel elevates his nose to sweeter breezes leaking through the high dome of limb and tendril green.

Through tortured cypress knees as tall as healthy men, we slosh and wade in wide lost circles, unable to find the stand of yaupon or an exit. Landmarks barely remembered from youth have rotted back into the timeless Lonesome. Finally, we stumble upon watery footprints. Some damned kids have poached our birds, I almost hiss. These tracks are ours, Clyde notes. Rufus affirms with a sniff.

Escaping the Lonesome will be more of a challenge than entering it. Every low and prickly exit trail is identical to the one we entered, except they cul-de-sac in black-tipped thorn. The only way out is to find the river, swim across, and hitchhike to a phone, but Clyde will drown before he'll leave the Browning, and even if we somehow ford the Flint, nobody's mama is going to stop for two soggy old farts with a Sweet Sixteen and a thunderstruck dog. We'll have to blast our way back through the wall of briars with three high-brass fours.

A demonic screech followed by a chilling scream neither feline nor avian rips through the dank and dismal silence. Clyde freezes midway through a cautious step. The back of his neck and ears blanch as I rear-end him. The Browning discharges, blasting an obscene pink wound in a sagging live oak limb, reverberations slamming back on us and rolling around in the high dome of the canopy. Clyde picks up the spent hull, leaving his safety off.

"What was that?"

"Don't worry, I don't think it was a quail."

Suddenly, very close at my heels: a two-noted assembly call of naked brakes against rusty drums. Chilled through my marrow, I spin around, expecting Rufus to be gone. Incredibly, he's frozen into a palsied point, his mismatched eyes rolling uniformly white. I kick the empty space before his nose, where footprints fill with water, but no bird flies. I've seen these quail kicked bald without getting up, but here there's nothing.

Before the dog is nothing. Upon our sodden tracks there's nothing, only lacy shards of greenish light and dancing shadows. Whatever Rufus points is camouflaged absolutely. I stare into the void before the shivering dog's dry nose. At last I discern, mere inches from Rufus, a single onyx bead that compressed scrutiny reveals as an eye. I leap back.

"Shoot it, Clyde!"

"I can't see it!" Clyde raises his upper lip, blue eyes wagging from me back to fragments of pale light windblown through the canopy like tiny lunar moths orbiting a baleful orb.

"Shoot six inches in front of the dog's nose," I squeak. "Shoot the smell!"

He does. Whump! A deep black trench eradicates Lepidoptera, blasting clots of muck like shrapnel from a claymore mine. From the blitzkrieg of flying slush a pyrotechnic pinwheel erupts into the air, shedding diamond splinters from blurred wings faster than a hummingbird's. Mesmerized, I feel melting knees give way when a second blast licks its tongue into the corners of the twilight, an apocalyptic explosion intensified by echo and repercussion following too hard upon the first for an earthly Browning to eject and chamber ammunition. I sit down hard, casting twin intaglio orbs of ass into the frigid sludge as Clyde's quail vanishes into a sunburst that fades like dying sparks into the gloom.

It's useless to look for a dead bird even if Rufus could be bullied into hunting it, but I search the bare black turf where a mortal bird subject to gravity would've fallen. I overturn soggy layers of decomposed leaves with the edge of my boot and scrape around capillary roots without real expectations of retrieving a dead quail Not of This Earth in the first place. Still, through force of lifetime habits I search for some shred of evidence, a lone pinfeather or a fleck of ruby blood. Nothing. With the first rumble of distant thunder, we hear the plaintive howl from the lonely bitch on Lonesome Ridge. Rufus bolts toward her and we follow.

"Nice shot, Clyde."

"Do what?"

Gun Dog

The more I learn about people, the more I like my dog.
—Mark Twain

I've had hunting dogs all my life, English, Llewellin and Irish setters, beagles, Weimaraners, labs, and Boykin spaniels. The best gun dog I ever had was a Boykin named Clyde Edgerton, the namesake of the North Carolina novelist and a quail hunting buddy of mine. Generally speaking, it's better to have a good dog named after you than a kid, who's liable to grow up to disappoint you. I now have a Boykin named Bailey White after my good friend the Georgia writer. It's only friends that I highly esteem who become namesakes for my gun dogs.

When Clyde was just a puppy, I took him into a swampy bottom to let him find a deer I'd shot and marked down. From that day on he became a cracker jack at trailing wounded deer, especially those lost to archery hunters. He'd find the deer, humping away as you dragged it out. Then he'd jump into the bed of a truck and hump it there. People would call me at night to bring Clyde to trail lost whitetails. One of the guests at Blue Springs Plantation shot a trophy buck that ran off. The next morning the mistress of the plantation and I rode around in a jeep, sending Clyde into the swamp bottoms and hedge rows where we thought a wounded deer might go. Finally, we gave up. We sat on a hill talking until I saw movement out of the corner of my eye. Clydes little bobtail rising and falling in the broomsedge at the top of the hill. "Yonder's your buck," I told Catherine. We drove over to Clyde, who was dry humping the dead deer, panting and grinning ear to ear.

Clyde was my second Boykin spaniel. My first one,

Geechee, was killed and eaten by a Florida alligator. My fourth wife asked me to wait a while before getting another dog, but I was so distraught over losing Geechee, I acquired Clyde anyway. I guess I decided I could do without a wife better than I could do without a dog. I know that sounds crazy, but that's the way I was thinking at the time. I hasten to add that all four of my wives were exemplary women, commonly flawed only by their taste in husbands. I don't blame them a bit for being unable to live with me. Sometimes I even have trouble living with myself, but I never had any trouble getting along with Clyde. He loved to hunt, would bounce in place when he saw anybody dressed in camouflage or toting a shotgun, and he'd hunt anything. He'd hide when I hid, Clyde would, and stalk when I stalked. When he was a puppy stumbling over himself, I taught him to fetch a rolled-up boot sock tossed down the hall of my Airstream travel trailer, where we lived on a friend of mine's hunting land and hid out when trouble brewed and my fourth marriage started going south.

I took the puppy from his mother and put him inside my shirt and carried him everywhere I went, to bond with him and make him brave. I even carried him to the classroom, where I taught English at a community college in Southwest Georgia. Clyde was a hit with the students. He wandered beneath their desks chewing their shoelaces. That ain't the only thing he chewed. He was bad to get ahold of computer wires in the language lab, where I went on Saturdays to write fiction. I tried to keep an eye on Clyde.

If he made a puddle or a poop, I cleaned it up before I left, but a few administrators had it in for him. They claimed he was a nuisance and a distraction, imagine that!

The students on campus treated him like a mascot, throwing tennis balls he acquired from the tennis courts and golf balls from the putting green. They taught him to wet retrieve in the president's fountain and goldfish pool. He'd dive to the bottom to fetch the golf balls. He was a pretty puppy, a dark chocolate with curly ears with tawny highlights and amethyst eyes, so cute the physical education department accepted him as a natural hazard, tolerating him more than they would've an ugly dog, but the suits in the Administration Building lacked humor. They wanted Clyde gone. It was clear none of them had ever owned a gun dog.

Clyde generally went to sleep in the leg well of the desks both in my office and in the language lab. One Monday morning when I came in to teach my eight o'clock class, there was crime tape across the entrance doors of the Humanities Building. Police, press, students and teachers were crowded outside. No one was allowed to enter until the detectives examined the crime scene. A pervert, they said, had broken in the computer lab and chewed the crotch out of an embroidered foam rubber cushion in Miss Purdy's, the lab director's chair. Miss Purdy was in hysterical tears, being consoled. The chairperson of the Humanities division arrived just before I did. She asked if anyone had asked Vic Miller about it. "I don't think Mr. Miller would gnaw the crotch out of Miss Purdy's seat cushion," she said. "but he sometimes comes in on weekends. Maybe he observed something that will give the detectives a clue." When the culprit was revealed, I was advised again that pets were not allowed on campus. "Clyde's not a pet," I countered. "He's a gun dog. And what about the snakes I bring to writing class as subjects for student essays?" I usually brought king snakes and white oak runners, but I had on occasion used a python and a diamondback rattlesnake. I'd found that even the most apathetic student would start putting words on paper when a snake was loose in the classroom and the door was locked. Adrenalin was a good muse.

"We can't do anything about the snakes," the suits decided, since they were covered by academic freedom statutes. I guess it goes without saying I was tenured at the time and as difficult to manage as Clyde. We both had a hard time sitting still.

As Clyde matured, he developed the trait some puritanical folks found discomfiting. He'd show strangers he was excited to see them by humping their legs. He didn't discriminate. He was glad to see everybody, including suits in the administration building, who were accustomed to being taken seriously. It's hard to maintain composure with a humping dog latched on to your leg.

Dr. Henry Hart, my veterinarian and hunting pal, castrated Clyde while I assisted. It was hoped this would curb the poor pup's concupiscence. My wife suggested Henry fix me at the same time. She may've been joking, but that was the way she was thinking at the time. In retrospect, I agree that without glandular distractions I might've amounted to something. For several days after the procedure Clyde remained in shock, frightened, timid and shy. He hunkered down with his bobtail between his legs, refusing to smile. I gave him time to recover, rolling his tennis ball short distances, petting him and reassuring him, and after a week or so, recover he did. The only lasting behavioral change was an increased obsession for fetching balls. He wanted to please folks more than ever. I guess he thought if he wasn't a good dog, he'd get himself castrated again. He became fixated. He'd find any object that could be tossed, carry it to any stranger and whine piteously until it was picked up and thrown. Castration didn't alter his method of greeting visitors one bit. He'd still hump the leg of any visitor, Seventh-day Adventist, Colonial Dame, or the girl next door, but his welcome now was altogether without prurience. His greetings were manifestations of pure and unmitigated delight, a doggy dance no more erotic than a platonic hug from a matronly aunt. A eunuch now, Clyde was pure of heart, though the wife still was not appeased. "Can't you teach him to just shake hands," she said. I thought such trivial tricks were beneath a gun dog's dignity. It wasn't beneath his dignity, however, to roll in something dead, a common characteristic of hunting dogs the world over.

If Clyde had a fault, it was his excessive enthusiasm. Boy, did that dog love to hunt. Show him a shotgun and he'd bounce in place until you told him to kennel up into the back of the truck. Taken to the woods, he was the happiest little dog you ever saw. He hunted dove and quail with equal vigor, smiling the whole time. He wouldn't hold a point, but he'd act birdy before he pounced flatfooted into a covey, and he hunted close enough to give me a shot at the flushed birds. At times, especially if a pen raised quail flushed up, he'd jump up and snatch a bird out of the air before I had time to get my safety off. I had to be careful not to shoot low flying birds when he sprung into my field of fire. Whenever we could, we steered clear of pen-raised quail. *Whatzit, whoa Clyde.*

On a dove field it was hard to make him wait until I shot a before taking off after a bird that flew over. He'd set out after any bird I feathered and some I missed clean. He'd follow it to the woods on the far side of the field. Most times he ran off he'd return with a bird. If not mine, he'd bring one someone else feathered or shot down. Once he brought back a bird that put me one over the limit, and the game warden gave me a ticket. I tried to blame Clyde's arithmetic. I told the judge that my dog was young and couldn't count yet. He fined me anyway, insisting that I teach my dog to count. "No," he amended. "Next time you need to get down there with Clyde and help him count your birds."

One afternoon I was headed home after my classes. Clyde was in his favorite place in the back of the truck, his head into the wind, jaws flapping. We passed a dove shoot we weren't invited on and, unseen by me, Clyde jumped out of the truck bed and joined the hunt. When I got home,

I noticed he wasn't with me. I backtracked, found my dog hobbled at the edge of the dove field. "You come for Clyde?" a hunter inquired. "Yes," I answered, "but how'd you know his name? "We all know Clyde," he said. "Who the hell are you?"

Spring break of Clyde's second year we set out in my jon boat down the Chattahoochee and the Apalachicola for a four-day trip to the Gulf. Nights Clyde slept beneath my jungle hammock on the swampy banks. I kept a campfire going all night to discourage alligators. I still hadn't gotten over Geechee. When we got back, things at home weren't getting any better. My wife had decided, with Dame Van Winkle, that Clyde's and my side of the house was the outside. I moved my Airstream to a friend's hunting lease. We had no running water, so I showered and shaved every morning before class at the YMCA.

At the end of spring quarter, Clyde and I took off for the Appalachian Mountains of Georgia and North Carolina to fish for trout and to start a novel about a man who heads for Appalachia after getting kicked out of his house. On the way out of town, we pulled into a Wal-Mart, where I bought a pup tent and camping supplies. We stayed in campgrounds throughout the Appalachians, recharging my laptop in outdoor electrical outlets. I'd throw Clyde's tennis ball off an overlook. Sometimes it took him the better part of an hour to fetch it. I'd read or write on my laptop until he came back with the ball. He loved to fetch from whitewater rapids, once following it by washing over a twenty-foot waterfall. Clyde disappeared into the hydraulic and was gone an alarmingly long time, but he swam out. After he fetched his ball, we sat together beneath the waterfall listening to the babble and murmur of voices from under the rocks. There was nowhere you could throw his ball he wouldn't try to fetch it.

He'd even stalk trout with me, slinking along the bank.

111

When I hooked one, he'd jump into the water to retrieve it, something I'd have rather he didn't do, but something I couldn't break him of without endangering his ebullient spirit. One night we got lost in the Nantahala Wilderness, where Eric Rudolph, the Olympic Park Bomber, was hiding out. I had fallen into a gully covered in blackberry wands. By the time I cut my way out with my pocketknife it was dark, and I was hopelessly lost. Clyde may've been able to lead me out, but he didn't know we were lost. I had a single rainbow trout in my vest, which I cut into thin strips to eat raw. Clyde licked my scratches but turned up his nose at the delicacy and it didn't take much of it to satisfy my hunger for raw trout, which would've been better with salt and lemon juice. It was a chilly night in those mountains after the sun went down. I covered us both with poplar leaves against the dew and we spooned together until dawn, when I was able to find our way out. By this time there was no question that we had bonded.

After we'd been in the North Carolina Smokies about a month, Clyde the writer was notified by the Dougherty County sheriff that a missing person report had been filed on me. Did he know of my whereabouts? "It's hard to say," said the novelist, avoiding the question. But when he learned I'd been rambling around in the mountains trying to write a novel from a pup tent, he and Mary Hood, another imminent novelist, used their influence and donated money to secure me a fellowship at a writing retreat I'll call Brainbridge. A private cabin on top of a mountain and vegetarian meals were provided. I wasn't sure I could thrive on a vegetarian diet, and I know Clyde couldn't. We were both carnivorous productions who saw no reason to hunt or fish unless you ate what you killed. Clyde would've lifted a leg to a Caesar salad. Or worse. There was an orange cat on the screen porch when we arrived. Clyde shared his food and they got along fine after the cat slapped him for trying to say hello. The next morning, I was writing great guns when a Volvo slinging gravel came up the steep hill to our cabin—the facilitator.

Call him Irv. "Oh Mr. Miller," said Irv, "Iím so sorry but we don't allow pets at Brainbridge." Clyde was really glad to see Irv. He stood on his hind legs, wrapping his paws around Irv's chinos, tail blurring, eyes rolling, tongue wagging. Except for the cat, Clyde hadn't greeted a stranger for quite a while.

"If you mean Clyde, he's not a pet," I said. "He's a gun dog, but there was a cat on the back porch when we got here."

"Oh no," he said, "there are no animals at Brainbridge—allergies, don't you know."

"Well, you don't have to worry about that. Clyde doesn't have any allergies, and neither do I."

"I'm so sorry, but you're going to have to board your little doggie for your tenure at Brainbridge. Down doggie," he said forcing a smile.

"*Board* him?"

Yes, there's a veterinarian clinic in town that will be happy to take him in," he smiled. I looked at him until he turned away.

"I'll discuss it with Clyde and let you know something before supper this evening." At the time Clyde had never known a fence, a leash or a bitch—a female dog, that is.

Clyde followed Irv out to his Volvo, anointing a tire. Irv rode his brakes as he slid back down the hill, gravel pinging the undercarriage. I wrote until noon, shared a can of Vienna sausages with Clyde and drove to the reception center to check out. "Did you come to a conclusion about your little doggie?"

"Yessir," I said, tossing the key on his desk. "We decided to leave. We know y'all are vegetarians and all, so we ate that damn cat."

"Oh, Mr. Miller!" he said.

I hated it that my friends had gone to all the trouble and expense of getting me accepted at Brainbridge. I regretted leaving in less than 24 hours, but I just couldn't bring myself to abandon Clyde in our quest for freedom. We'd begun this odyssey together, I know it sounds crazy, but that's just how I was feeling at the time.

So, we took off again. When we came home for fall quarter and hunting season, the locks on my front door had been changed. That's how my wife was feeling at that point in time.

Clyde died in his prime. He never had time to disappoint me. We were in Louisville, Kentucky, visiting my second ex-wife in a country club subdivision when Clyde chased a squirrel across the street and was hit and run over by a teenager in his mother's station wagon. I scooped up his broken little body, and he bit the ball of my thumb. I was so distraught I didn't pull my hand away. I let him bite me again and again in the agony of his death throes. By the time we got him to a vet, his bright, amethyst eyes had rolled back in his head, his death mask grin revealed gray bloodless gums.

The most willing dog I'd ever owned was dead. He died the same year as both my parents, the same year my fourth marriage died. I lost my parents, my dog, my home and my job all in the same year. I mourned them all, minus the marriage and the job. Such was the double-edged sword of liberty. I didn't know what to do or where to go, so I acquired a sailboat and took off for the Caribbean. I know it sounds crazy, but that's just how I was feeling at the time.

Crocodiles in Paradise

Whoever fights monsters should see to it that in the process he does not become a monster. —Nietzsche

"Tell them sure, I'll shoot their crocodile." Lucio, my Kuna sidekick, translates from Tule to Spanish a petition from the village *sahila*, the chiefs. They want me to kill the renegade crocodile we saw in the Xiomara Grimaldo River at the foot of Uanega, the mountain village of the dead. What's a crocodile anyway but an alligator with an attitude?

"He is the one who swims to the island at night eating our dogs, who hides in darkness beneath the dock where the trade boats come," Lucio explains. The swinging sahila lie in hammocks, dangling from arterial threads between center posts of the dim congreso lodge. Smoking tobacco and solving problems the women haven't already taken care of, the sahila represent the living heart of the community. At any given time, odds are at least one of them is awake.

"And he attacks Demesio," Lucio adds a misdemeanor footnote, "destroy his property and bite his legs."

I've heard the story of Demesio's outhouse, suspended over the sea on rickety pilings and attached to shore by a plank bridge. After imbibing excessive quantities of fermented cane juice at his niece's *chicha fuerte*, a puberty celebration occasioned by her first period, Demesio rushed late at night to answer nature, which lurked beneath his privy in the form of a nine-foot crocodile that struck from below, splintering the outhouse and seizing bare legs hobbled at the ankles by trousers. Somehow Demesio tore himself and his pantaloons from the terrible jaws and scrambled away. For compensation, the crocodile ate the dock. Neighbors cheered from the moonlit doorways of thatch huts, presumably for the crocodile.

The sahila worry that the crocodile may also eat children, who comprise 70 percent of the tiny island's 3,000 souls and are harder to inventory than the dogs, which are used to catch iguana and tied with string outside the huts. Kids roam dirt streets under tribal rather than parental supervision, eating and sleeping wherever hunger and nightfall find them. In an island community where the number one health problem is malnutrition, Ukupseni boasts the world's skinniest dogs, subsisting on the mere rumor of iguana scraps. Though better fed than the dogs, iguanas have minimal caloric value, and miniscule amounts of iguana protein escape the *tulemasi*—the traditional stew of rice, coconut and plantains.

Kuna dogs survive on whatever nutrition they can derive from air. The emaciated South Georgia mongrel whipped up under the porch with a fishing pole is a butterball of obesity next to an iguana dog. Weakened by starvation, a pack of Kuna hounds is sometimes unable to subdue one lizard. It will take a heap of hounds to feed the crocodile that Lucio, Anna and I saw swimming in the Xiomara Grimaldo, the one the sahila want me to kill. Of course, I'd never go after the crocodile without approval from the congreso. You clear everything with the sahila if you're a gringo on a sailboat anchored off an island village in Kuna Yala. For all I knew, crocodiles were sacred, something to sacrifice dogs and outhouses to.

Anna, a Danish volunteer who came to the San Blas Archipelago on Panama's Caribbean coast to promote eco-tourism, is hot for jungle adventure. The sahila gave her to me because they don't know what else to do with a pretty, milk-white 20-year-old girl with hair the color of a carrot. Under my wing, they reasoned, her stay would be more, uh, educational. With the highest per capita incidence of albinism in the world, the sahila don't want the fair Anna messing around in the Kuna gene pool.

Suddenly a squat Indian with an oversized head leaps from a rough-hewn bench, shaking an angry fist and screaming invectives as his companions yawn and grin.

"Demesio," whispers Lucio.

*

So, Anna, Lucio and I had attended a burial on Uanega, the mountain where the Kuna entomb their hammocked dead, and were returning to my dinghy at the mouth of the river when she spied the crocodile and wondered what it was.

I told her: a fat crocodile with a nine-foot body the color of slate, warted with carbuncles the size of golf balls. To get this big he had to be slap full of Kuna dogs.

"Why doesn't he attack us?" Anna asked, a little disappointed.

"I don't know a lot about crocodiles," I shrugged. "Maybe he's holding out for a puppy or an outhouse." Some Kuna kids were swimming upstream. If the croc had a sweet tooth for Indians, he'd get one of them.

Without a ripple the croc submerged tail first into the whiskey-colored river, out of sight and predictability. Anna and Lucio crept toward the dinghy. Crocodiles, they say, can run on land like racehorses for short distances, whoever *they* is. I know a gator can scat. Still, I eased closer.

The big reptile cruised the bottom of the narrow river, head disappearing into a tangle of mangrove roots. I ordered Anna, an apprentice after all, to move in for a better look.

The croc's thick tail bristled with tall spikes. "The better for whacking a fair maiden into the river," I whispered, "where he waits with cocked jaws." My voice hushed like a Cub Scout master's around the campfire. "Then he rolls,"

I widened my eyes, "spinning her like spaghetti, dragging her to his den, where she rots, tenderizing among the dog skulls and long bones of distressed damsels."

My monologue, delivered in plain view of an actual crocodile, scared the hell out of Anna. She hugged herself to subdue tremors. The croc, sensing her presence, began to rise, at which point we both trotted to the dinghy.

"He'll make mighty fine tule masi," I informed Lucio, "if croc meat's anything like gator tail."

Lucio made a face like a rabbi served a plate of chitterlings. "Eat him?" A reptilian hiss issued from his throat. The Kuna do not eat crocodile or snake.

"Are you going to kill it then?" Anna wanted to know.

"I might."

"Why? To eat?"

"That, and us American exiles in paradise have to chase something to keep our sap up, Danish girls being too dangerous."

"What's sap?"

"Life's juices—blood, for example."

"And...?"

"That too."

"Maybe I will come with you," she considered, "if it's safe."

"Sure, I'll tie you to a tree and you can weep piteously. When the croc claims you, I'll bust his *cula* with a 12-gauge dum-dum."

"What's a dum-dum? I know what a cula is."

I bit my lip. Anna wasn't going to be much help unless I really did use her to bait up the crocodile. "A rifled slug for a shotgun."

"So, you have killed lots of these crocodiles then?" she asked.

"Naw, this is the first one I've ever seen, but how much harder can it be than a gator? Which you got to aim at with one eye and look out for the DNR with the other. Unless the croc in question is heavily armed, this expedition should be a walk in the park." Pride is a deadly sin.

"What is this DNR?" asked Anna.

"Game warden."

"Do we have them here?"

"We have sahila here."

The jungle path from the oxbow where we left the dinghy passes through a rough garden the medicine men, or *curanderos*, started laying out beside the river to lure botanists to Ukupseni to study jungle medicine—the curandero's contribution to eco-tourism. The project was abandoned when someone pointed out that Bab Dumad, The Great Father, spread the earth with useful plants he sired off Mother Earth to prepare the world for the coming of the Kuna. A comprehensive medicinal garden therefore would contain all vegetation. Selection implies uselessness for the remainder, thus a heretical contradiction of a perfect creation. The Earth, to a curandero, is a veritable garden with no such thing as weeds. The airing of this theological bombshell left the botanical experiment abandoned to the jungle and in the protective custody of a maverick crocodile, which patrols the river between the land of the living and the city of the dead.

*

Responding to the sahila's request, I return to my sloop, Kestyll, drawing a 12- gauge pump and a loaded .44 magnum from a locker. I hunt up a couple of dum-dums and two three-inch magnum 00 bucks. "This ought to do it," I tell Lucio. "I'll pack this pistol in case we get in close. We'll shoot him at base of the skull, short the circuit between jaws and tail, keeping him from biting us and rolling. The only harm he can do after that is claw ruts in your ass or slap it off the frame with his tail."

119

Lucio nods. He'll wait in the Uanega, uphill from the crocodile, which has already taken on mythic powers, a dragon between a cemetery and a garden. Engaging and killing the crocodile in his lair will instate me as an archetypal hero, impressing a Danish girl, saving an entire village from terror and starvation—well, hunger at least, if I add crocodile as a protein supplement to the Kuna's iguana and banana diet.

The next afternoon I dinghy to the village to pick up Lucio and his friend Mani, who show up with another Indian and a lame mongrel bitch named Achu, simply "dog." The pitiful mutt can barely open her eyes and is thin as a rake, emaciated even by Kuna standards. The plan is, we'll rope her to a tree to lure the crocodile in range of my shotgun. I have to agree to buy her in the event our best-laid plans take a fatal turn. The fickle Anna, scratching a mosquito bite, decides to stay home, perkily built distressed damsel replaced by a somnambulant bitch with wagging dugs.

I make jungle sounds—*err-EEE-ah*—flushing white birds as we enter the winding labyrinth of mangrove tunnels to the mouth of the Xiomara Grimaldo River, hardly more than a creek running its mazy motions through an abandoned garden in the shadow of the high mountain of Kuna Dead.

We reach the oxbow where we first saw the crocodile, secure the dinghy and tether Achu to a coconut palm. My cohorts retreat to the high ground of Uanega while I scoot up a palm trunk in my climbing deer stand. With the disappearance of her owner, Achu limps in sad circles around the tree, shortening her leash and barking asthmatically, each wind-broke yawp ending with a squeak and rattle.

I grow impatient on my own cramped haunches, but I'm careful not to wiggle around and loosen the scrotal coconuts that hang like a sword of Damocles above my head. The recoil from a three-inch magnum could unbuckle one and deliver me brained and comatose in the company and predicament of Achu. The higher I am, the more likely it seems.

As the dusk thickens, it occurs to me that the crocodile, rushing in like a racehorse from the twilight at an awkward angle, could devour poor Achu before I could get off a decent shot. I'm not sentimentally attached to the pitiful thing, but her replacement price is exorbitant, and she is, after all, the closest thing I have to a maiden in distress.

So, I come down from the tree, and now with a better view of the bank I see a long, green log, crocodilian if I use my imagination, one I don't recall seeing earlier but too large to be a crocodile, I decide. Plus, Achu's steady bark has not raised an alarmed octave at the questionable shape. I turn on my headlamp and walk past the dog, resisting a fleeting urge to pet her.

Stalking past Achu, I ease toward the suspicious log, which to my horror has disappeared, leaving in the mud a flat trail where a belly wide as a tobacco sled has slid in or out of the river, the deep claw prints on either side filling with water. "Uh-oh!" My feet launch into a high-stepping circular jig, my shotgun jerking from shadow to shadow, headlamp strobing palm trunks, mangrove roots and jungle vines.

Achu cocks her head. Her wheezy barking stops. I calm down, my blood laced with chemically emboldening adrenaline. I step from the crater of footprints I've tamped into the spongy soil, ashamed for even a mongrel dog to witness my panic, thankful the Kuna have repaired to the cemetery, thankful Anna stayed in her hut to do her nails.

My headlamp ignites a bright red eye floating on the water 10 yards from the vanished green log. I creep closer, point my shotgun at the glowing eye and blast a hole the size of a beach ball into the river. Raining water stipples the surface, which erupts tumultuously into a subsequent eruption of lacy whitewater as though the shotgun primed some serious subaquatic ordnance.

A warty, conical head rises from the boiling water, followed by an interminable length of reptile—a pinecone the size of a Pontiac that Bab Dumad had cut out with a pair of pinking shears while practicing primordial creation. A thing that could have lived among the dinosaurs and did.

Bristling teeth overlap powerful slapping jaws as the crocodile stands on its tail. My heart hammers home the insight that crocodiles are to alligators what cottonmouths are to red wigglers, tarantulas to ladybugs.

Achu's sparse hackles ciliate on split ends. She breaks loose, scatting through the unweeded garden and crossing the river with hardly a splash, yiking around Cemetery Mountain and into the gross jungle valley below, her yikes fading quickly in the distance. The thrashing wall of water subsides, and the monster disappears into swirling mud at the bottom of the chest-deep river.

My Indian companions magically appear. "¿Que pasa?"

"I've killed him, *an daim misa*, but he went to the bottom."

"We come back tomorrow then. Maybe he float up."

But by now my blood is a-fizz with a toxic stew of emboldening adrenaline and mind-numbing testosterone. I'm braver than I've ever been, committed to bringing to this stretch of the Panamanian coast both uninterrupted peace in the overhanging outhouses and a dietary evolution. I decide to swim down like Beowulf and pull his dead ass up. The Indians grab my arms and hold me effortlessly in place, the way they restrain a widow who tries to take the obligatory leap into her husband's open grave.

But wait. What's this? Intermittent spurts of effervescent water rising from the dark river followed by parting waters as the monster charges up the far bank, making for the jungle. Whoa!

I yank the .44 from its holster, aiming for the spot where

the thick spiked neck meets the long lean head. *Boom!* The shot reverberates through the jungle, setting off a chatter of sleeping monkeys. The crocodile shudders and slides lifelessly back into the black water.

"*Esso!*" yell my friends. "*Esso!*"

We shake hands all around. I get a couple of slaps on the shoulder, and I'm feeling pretty good for a man whose heart is hissing against his eardrums from where it's lodged in his throat. I've killed the croc, spared the dog and made an impressive shot with the .44, which I holster, handing Lucio the Remington pump.

I wade across the Xiomara Grimaldo to the shallow spot where the crocodile lies submerged, subdued and dead.

Although I can't quite see him, I identify a splotch of white that must be the ragged bullet hole that stopped his clock. I know exactly where the ruined head lies. My first crocodile! Wow! I'll just reach down, grab him around the neck, maybe wag him around a little for drama and then drag him back across the river. He'll weigh a couple hundred pounds out of the water, maybe three. Wow!

The throat is soft, cool as a beanbag, with high hard pyramidal plates behind. I lift his head, surprisingly heavy, to inspect the results of my marksmanship—a long open crack from between the rough knobs of the eyes down the top of his bill, the whitish blossom at the base of its skull. Just where I aimed. The Kuna are slack-jawed with disbelief.

Suddenly the croc spins violently, the initial torque ripping him from my grasp, barking my palms, jamming my thumb and knocking my legs from under me. The rough scales snag my clothes, gnawing me under as gear-toothed hide spins like a sprocket. The last frame of my vision, before my head disappears beneath the black water, is of the third Indian, a converted Christian, crossing himself. My headlamp lashes in the broiling white foam, turning it pink with crocodile blood, which I and the Indians assume is mine and that my final resting place will be the river that runs through an unfinished garden by the mountain of the dead, Uanega, entombed in the sour belly of a maverick crocodile.

But suddenly, as though dreaming, I'm on the other side of the river, standing with the Indians, yelling for help around a mouthful of mud. My arrival to bank from riverbed must have been too rapid for registry by human senses, for neither I nor the Indians remember witnessing that incredible transportation, but I am at the Christian Kuna's elbow before he finishes the last arm of his benediction, frog-eyed and dripping, my headlamp around my neck. It is as if nothing has happened, the still water undisturbed. But again, on the other side of the river come the telltale spurts that precipitated the croc's last advance. I pour the water from the muzzle of the .44 and stand ready. Again, the crocodile shoulders up the embankment. Again, I shoot it.

Again, it slides back into the water, this time with its bobbing head visibly breaking the surface. I wade over. He lashes. I shoot him again, and then again, and he moves, and I shoot again until finally he quits wiggling. We drag him to the dinghy and heave him in, a full quarter of his tail hanging over the side like an inverted two-man saw.

*

Two hundred wild villagers turn out at the trade dock and public square for our return. I'm astounded. Youthful hunters unload the croc and jog its earthly remains through the village, its great head and spiked tail wagging stiffly as we are chanted into tribal fame and mobbed by sports fans anxious to touch the shotgun and pistol that have slain the dread dragon. I can't get anywhere near the crocodile, which is kicked and jumped upon, dragged through the dirt, its teeth kicked loose and pried out by screwdrivers. I'm afraid the abuse will spoil the meat.

Lucio yells a few angry words in Tule, and the crowd parts as a half dozen Indians jog the crocodile over to an upturned dugout canoe and lay him spread eagle. We skin out the beast, which shrinks from the size of a Pontiac to a little over nine feet. The crowd thins to a few dozen spectators who hang around to watch the butchering in the dim lights from the community generator. Now is the time. To demonstrate it was indisputably comestible, I cut off a pearly ort of tail meat, hold it up for all to see and then pop it into my mouth. With a knowing smile, I start chewing as the Indians look on in disbelief, some masticating sympathetically and nodding their heads. I chew. The smile leaves my eyes as my gorge rises. The meat in my mouth tastes like some nameless carrion washed up by a red tide. Still, I chew. The indestructible sinew, resisting all efforts to break it down, actually begins to grow larger, threatening finally to bloat into an indefatigable wad, sabotaging my dietary innovations and making me a laughingstock of the very audience I'm out to woo. With a series of heroic gulps, I swallow, my Adam's apple pumping like a piston. I spread open hands to prove I'm not palming anything, maintaining my smile, which quivers like a bowstring held too long.

*

Well, it's over, I decide the next day. Now I can rest on solid laurels, Great White Hunter, savior of children and dogs, preserver of outhouses, killer of renegade crocodiles. The hide has been sent to the sahila for examination. I strut through the village robed in the glitter of new status, wearing a necklace of crocodile teeth nested like thin eggs in chest hair fretted with silver threads. *An daim maisa.* I killed the crocodile. Even the ace bandage that wraps my sprained thumb has become a badge of honor touched with awe by hunters and children, who never need to know how scared I was in the black water beneath the spinning crocodile. They feel no loss that the meat, so carefully trimmed and packaged, has spoiled overnight in a freezer that ran out of propane. Mum hunting pals, their heroism implicated with mine, won't reveal my manifest terror. The Danish girl, not having been there, can't bear witness to my palpable fear. Achu, who beat us back to the village dragging 30 feet of thorn-frayed rope, hasn't said a word. And if I didn't emerge from dark baptismal waters into the blinding self-revelation due those who confront their personal chimera, then neither did I wind up in the actual bowels of a crocodile—reason enough for smugness if not joy.

But a note of sadness has leeched through, starting as the Kuna jogged the beast's long corpse through the village, its great head wagging the metronome of chants and footfall. Then when the conquered reptile five times older than humanity was dumped on its back in the dirt street, children bouncing on its wide cameo belly with the triumphant energy of youth, a heavier melancholy flooded me that I knew wasn't going to go away—the ironic epiphany that comes with age to hunters who start to love the living prey more than killing it. Maybe I shouldn't have eaten the crocodile's raw flesh.

Maybe I'm just getting old, too old to hunt renegade crocodiles and try to impress 20-year-old Danish girls.

I feel a firm tug on my elbow. A messenger from the congreso has brought a decision, presumably new honors to be bestowed by the sahila. "I have news," he reports. "An Ustupu fisherman say now there is a bigger crocodile in the Ukupseni River than the one you kill. The sahila say maybe it is this crocodile that comes at night to our village. Now you must tell them when do you going to kill him?"

In the Bowels of the White Witch

My mother was a fish. —Calaban

"They cry when you keel them, and the meat is white and very savory," our guide, Macario Contreras, assures me.

"Armadillos?"

"*Si.*"

"You eat them?"

"Of course. We have always eat them, although it is sad to keel him and witness his tears."

"I heard they carry leprosy."

"No, no, they are small animals. They doan carry nothing but the shell on their back, their cascara. With long tongues they lick up the water and the ants. A burro is perhaps what you have in mind, a beast of burden. This is an armadillo."

"*Lepra.* They carry lepra."

"¿Como lepra? Who says these?"

"Hotz told me!" I shout over the wind. "My doctor!"

"What does a gringo doctor know about armadillos? *Mierda del Toro,*" he says. "Bool sheet. My people eat the armadillo for two thousand years, maybe ten thousand. Nobody never have lepra until Cortés carry it here in his sheeps."

"Cortés had sheep? Ovejas?"

"No man, he come from España in his sheeps. You are university professors?" he asks dubiously. "¿Maestros?"

"Si," I tell him. Macario and I are hanging on for dear life in the bed of a red Ford pickup batting ass through a cloud forest in the Eastern Sierra Madres, our T-shirts popping like flags. Two visiting University of Georgia System teachers, Anna Schachner and Dot Davis, are crammed into the cab with Paco, our driver, and Ramundo Cordova, our

Latin American literature mentor. When I hijacked his students and headed for the cloud forest, Ramundo acquiesced and came along, thinking maybe he could teach the women something. The World Council sent us UGA professors to Xalapa to exchange ideas and pave the way for faculty and student exchanges with the Universidad de Veracruzana in Xalapa, but today I'm headed for Río de Pescados, where there are supposed to be trout. I've toted my fly rod in a PVC pipe the size of a bazooka past paranoid flight attendants and customs officials all the way from Atlanta. I'm determined to snag a *trucha* by hook, gill net, gig or hand grenade.

The *gringas* slap the dash to trumpet, guitar and violin on the blasting radio. We are flat hauling ass through the volcanic mountains between Coatepec and Jalcomulco in the state of Vera Cruz, trailing black smoke and mariachi, hissing along a road that looks like it's been bombed. I peek through the back window. The speedometer needle is freewheeling spastically like a clock hand in a time warp. An iguana zips across the threadbare asphalt, and Paco swerves to hit it, dodging a pothole the size of a hot tub and slamming me into the load rails. The Virgin Guadalupe and a plastic Jesus sway and shiver on the rearview mirror. Paco knows heaven is better than Mexico and is trying to get us killed.

On the horizon I see the snowcapped volcano Orizaba, the highest peak in Mexico. Forty years ago, before Mexico City congregated the foulest vapors on the planet, I used to view the snowcapped volcanoes—Orizaba, Popocatepetl and Iztaccíhuatl—from my apartment on the Mexico-Toluca Highway. I climbed the smoky Popocatepetl twice, guiding school-chum Johann Bleicher the second time, losing the trail, getting us lost, stranded and nearly killed on an icy slope. Afraid to descend, we clung to frozen rocks with alpine axes and spikes slammed into the sun-glazed ice.

Eye-to-eye with soaring buzzards, we cussed, prayed and cried for our mothers as the moaning wind stung our faces.

"Are you sure there are trout in the river?" I fish for an encouraging word. "*Hombre*, the river is fool of trouts!" he screams. "And there are iguana, very savory with white flesh."

"You eat iguana? What's iguana taste like?"

"Very savory. Iguana is much like armadillo. I will keel one for you with a rock."

"I want trout," I say, "trucha."

"*Claro*," says Macario. "We will find trucha also. They call this place Fish River for good reason."

A fated armadillo crosses the road near the entrance of a coffee and mango plantation, where a crowd of campesinos in traditional white clothing and new sombreros stand waiting. It's rumored that the president of the republic will pass, and the campesinos have been given new hats and the afternoon off to stand there and wave. The Ford's front bumper punts the armadillo into the crowd like a soccer ball. The cracked shell sprays a crimson spiral nebula, bounces and rolls. Paco flashes a golden grin through the back window, and the truck swerves dangerously toward the mangos. An old man walks over in his huaraches, picks up the shell-possum, shakes it and grins. We sail past police with M-16s and pump shotguns. A couple of helicopters squat in a pasture. Paco hardly slows down for the checkpoint, although he blows his horn and waves, shrouding the cops in mariachi and exhaust. I wonder if the sombreros will have to be returned after the presidential motorcade or if the campesinos will get to keep them. They'll keep the armadillo.

At Jalcomulco we walk the cobblestone streets to a swinging bridge that looks like a snaggletooth xylophone. The loose boards clack as we step gingerly over dizzying gaps. Ninety feet beneath us, a river the color of chocolate milk foams over raging rapids. The bridge sways. I know I'd never set foot on this rattletrap if I weren't sandwiched single file between people I've talked into coming. The emerald mountains and the craggy gorge look like a scene from *Romancing the Stone*.

"*Romancing the Stone* was filmed here," says Ramundo.

"You're pretty set on this fishing thing, aren't you?" Anna inquires, her white knuckles around a cable.

"Come hell or high water!" I grin, bending my knees to stop the rattling.

"Well, there's your water," she nods. The monsoon rains have gushed down the mountains, drowning a skinny cow that bobs with lolling tongue in a whirlpool. A redheaded buzzard rests on the bloated rib cage.

The steep, muddy footpath strewn with donkey dung and pumice ascends the volcanic mountains. Stepping aside for Indian women who descend with baskets or washtubs balanced on their heads, we pass scattered pre-Hispanic ruins. We climb until my lungs and legs burn, finally reaching a cliff where we see a tiny whitewater raft disappear into a beige flume of Río Pescado. A kayak tosses like a wood chip behind it.

"The water is obscured by much rain," explains Macario. "We must climb high into the mountains where the big trout will rise to our hooks in the clear water."

A bright green blur zips across the path. "Iguana," whispers our guide. "We will keel the next one with a rock."

"Rock! You couldn't hit that sucker with a riot gun."

"The flesh is very savory."

"Rare, too, I bet."

The dust settles into the Sanskrit tracks as I wonder if a real iguana was really there. The streak I saw was faster than a scalded roadrunner, faster than a neon laser.

"*Muy raro*," he agrees. "You must stone them very precisely."

Anna, Dot and Ramundo seem grateful for the pause I view as temporary salvation. They glisten, I sweat. I'm wheezing in the thin air.

We follow the edge of the canyon, descending into the steep cloud forest. Above us are platform contraptions and cables through the treetops. I can't imagine any primate crazy enough to brachiate through the high canopy on a hand-held wire. A Tarzan on a pendulous vine would travel in slow motion compared to whoever tears ass through this forest.

"Want to try it?" offers Macario.

"I sure don't. I want to cast a nymph into Fish River."

"*Hecho*," he says, pointing to a thin silver ribbon in the distance, wiggling between the cleavage of two volcanic hills bristling with jungle green. "There is only to walk down there and harvest the trouts and iguanas." He rubs his palms together and licks his lips. "*Muy sabrosa*," he adds.

On the vertical footpath, my weak thighs cramp. My lungs rattle like an Arizona newspaper. With proximity the silver river tarnishes to pewter then turns to the characteristic chocolate of a Mexican river after a monsoon. This isn't the pristine whitewater river I've seen in tourist brochures and dreams. But by God I'm fixing to get down there and fish it if I have to tuck and roll.

Where the river forks we ford waist deep, higher on the women, bracing our downstream side with staffs whacked by Macario's machete. We hold tightly to each other in a daisy chain, fearful of getting swept away in a deluge of *creme de cacao*. Dot and Anna drench their T-shirts, and our Mexican hosts politely avert their eyes. The far fork, Macario asserts, is where trucha gather in great numbers. I forget my exhaustion and scramble over dry rocks and sand to a low waterfall, where I tie on a *mosca flamboya* created by daemon Aztecs on mescaline.

Bolero style, Macario whirls a handline weighted with

pebbles, slinging a hellgrammite into the turbid foam. I flagellate the caramel froth in the frenzied spirit of the fly's hellish artisan, but it is, of course, Macario who catches the only fish, a mudcat about the size of an enchilada.

"Pesgato," he says. "Very savory."
"Do they cry when you catch them?"
"¿Quién sabe?" he answers. "Who knows?"

*

As afternoon shadows stretch across the riverbed, I start dreading the return up the mountain, am in fact afraid of it. Already I know that Dot and Anna, basking on boulders to dry their shirts, are in better shape than I am. They'll wait for me at the top of inclines, offering condescending hands and kind smiles, maybe watch curiously as I writhe with infarcted heart on pumice and donkey dung. I decide to return to Jalcomulco by river, downhill and one-tenth the distance.

"It is not possible," says Macario.
"Of course, it's possible. Doesn't this river pass under that claptrap bridge?"
"Yes, señor, it is the same river, but the return must be surmounted in the same manner we arrived. To do otherwise is impossible."
"How do you know it is?"
"Well, if somebody does it, maybe it won't be so impossible for the next guy," I grin.
"I'd take his word for it," says Dot.
"By all means," insists Ramundo.
"Jalcomulco is Macario's home. The Río Pescados is a treacherous river even without the monsoon rains."
"I'll meet you guys at the bridge," I say, handing Ramundo my five-weight flyrod and fishing vest.
"I must ask you not to drown yourself while you are in my care," the guide insists politely. "It is very bad for business to lose gringos. There is many great rocks and raging water.

There is hydraulics, whirlpools and hissing waves. And shark," he adds.

"Sharks!"

"Well, not much shark, but there is the Bruja Blanca, the White Witch. This river is not for swimming. I know another place where beautiful women bathe without no clothes. I will take you there."

"I'll tell you what. When the rapids get dangerous, I'll swim out and walk around them."

"I don't theek so. Bruja Blanca will not pause kindly as for Moses fleeing the Egyptians. It is foolish to keel yourself far from home."

"I've seen worse than this," I counter. "Back in Georgia we've got the Chattooga."

"I too have seen worse. Between here and the bridge there is worse. Bruja Blanca, she is worse."

Guides are by nature overcautious. They think your hiring them evidences an inability to take care of yourself. I realize he loses face when a client takes off alone, but I'm doing him the favor of not having to call in the president of the republic's chopper to airlift me out. I'll keep my shoes on, I decide, my head up and my feet downstream. How bad can it be? I can always wade out and take the high road. I squat into the current and turn loose. "Adiós!" I yell. "Yippie-ki-yi-yeah!"

Our guide crosses himself sadly. "*Vaya con Dios*," he mumbles, shaking his head.

Into the first bend I'm having as much fun as a grown man can have. Wow! This is great! The raging river tugs at my wet clothes and tries to suck me down, but it's easy to pogo off the bottom with one leg, pointing the other downstream to deflect the rushing boulders. Man alive, this is more fun than the Tilt-A-Whirl! I'm really hauling ass now, better than the Log Flume at Six Flags. Bleached rocks, a scrub pine and a maguey blur past. Around the next dogleg, I'll pull over for a break. No sense getting in a hurry so far ahead of my compadres. I'll slow down and smell the Mexicali roses.

The river accelerates. I'm still skipping along at a formidable lick, sculling with my palms, the warm tropical sun on my face. My shoulders have started to stress from treading water, and my neck is stiffening from stretching it above the chop when I hear a tumultuous roar around the next turn and see the bank transforming into a vertical stone precipice. Hmmm. The noise must be magnified by the high cliffs around the bend where the river cuts through the gorge. I guess I'll pass through the cut before I work over to the bank for a rest.

As I approach the bend, the river beyond belches thunder. My cramped neck bristles wet hackles as the current snatches me around a dogleg, where I see what nothing in my previous life has prepared me for: the Bruja Blanca, where the forks of the Pescado converge, each into its swollen twin, forming a mighty conduit of brown water compressed into a narrow strait, the velocity geometrically increasing into raging, cascading violence with no end in sight—a tempestuous gut of exploding rapids walled on either side by high cliffs. Macario is right. There's no way to squirt in one piece through the violent bowels of Bruja Blanca, the White Witch.

Even before I can fully realize my predicament, I'm riding the crest of the horrible wave formed by the union of two mighty forks, hurling me pell-mell into the craggy jaws of the canyon. I'm caught in a surging dung-tinted avalanche of water.

"Oh shit!" I scream as the wave peaks and buckles, tumbling me down into a gauntlet of rocky hydraulics that snap my human meat like Macario's shirt in the bed of Paco's truck. I glance off rocks, spin, kick, struggle, fighting halfway to the dim surface before I'm body-slammed into another boulder then sucked into and spit out of hydraulic after hydraulic.

On and on and on and on, spinning, twisting, tumbling, helpless as a lone white sock in a washing machine, I'm finally too tired to struggle, swim or care. My life and wives flash before my muddy vision as my lungs squall silently for air. My heavy limbs tug me deeper as I lament my unfinished novel and reckon sufficient postage to mail my body home to Kimbrell-Stern Mortuary. I surrender to the destiny of mortal flesh and nudge eternity with one final kick of my toe as the outer dark swirls and pools into shimmering light and muddy water leaks into my lungs. I think of Fred, my pet frog whose home was a fishbowl on the back of the toilet. Inspired by a flush, Fred leapt high, landing popeyed in the swirling bowl, kicking pitifully before my childish eyes as the enamel throat gulped him into labyrinthine darkness, a White Witch. Come back, Fred! I cried. It's too deep! Come back!

A profound calm displaces my walleyed fright, and I become deeply grateful to the women in my life who chose to love me, forgiving the ones who turned me down flat or garnisheed my houses. I'm dead now, I decide. And it's not as bad as I thought. Not as bad as Omaha or Tupperware parties or Disney World in July. Not as bad as Darton's preregistration or Fall Faculty Workshop, where I'd be if I weren't at the bottom of Río de Pescados drowning.

Suddenly, I cork to the surface, vomited upward by some random gushing current, cast up by the Bruja Blanca as surely as Jonah was spat forth by the leviathan. Helplessly I wash between two sharp rocks that hold me cruciform beneath the armpits, moored and bobbing on the ruffled bosom of the White Witch.

I cough and sneeze, percolating beige foam from mouth and nose. Dry air burbles into saturated pulmonary bronchioles. Delivered from the churning belly of Bruja Blanca,

I rock in the cradle of the river. When I have floated and rested and even dozed, I wiggle free and drift downstream into quieter waters. I approach an iguana as green as emerald, hemmed with a spiked draconian seam from foolscap to tail. He flips out a venal tongue and watches with ancient eyes set into sockets wizened as elbows.

  I grasp an orange-size stone from the bank and covet the succulent white meat packed in a beanbag creature that does not cry when you kill it. My first thought after emerging from the jaws of death is to murder something living and eat it up, the true meaning of life: kill or die. Nothing's created or destroyed; we just pass around the cosmic food chain from one predator to another. After the girls and wives, the Tupperware parties, the faculty meetings, the root canals, taxes, dental floss and insolence of customs officials, the bottom line is just flotsam washing down rivers and galaxies, snatching a protein here, an electron there, a cheap thrill from a flickering bank.

*

My friends are relieved when I drift living beneath the bridge. I pass Mexican women pounding laundry on sun-blanched rocks, and they flash gilt smiles of relief. Macario has convinced them that Bruja Blanca has eaten me and that the village will be defamed. Now he smiles, swinging a dead armadillo by the tail. Anna, Dot and Ramundo sigh, delivered from spending the rest of the faculty development workshop recovering remains and making grim arrangements to transport funereal artifacts across the border.

  "Did the armadillo cry when you killed it?" I ask Macario.

  "*No tanto,*" he says. "Not too much."

The Wisdom of Solomon

Though boys throw stones at frogs in sport, the frogs do not die in sport, but in earnest.—Plutarch

*T*wo Indian kids in a dugout, one in a Yankees baseball cap, scull in place with hand-hewn paddles. From the shadow of Kestyll's beam, they watch me pretend sleep in the deck hammock. I snort a perfunctory time or two for credibility, hoping they'll leave, but the pretense nudges me into a serious siesta. When I wake up, they lurk in a longer shadow. Unlike American kids, Indians know how to wait. The secret is they aren't waiting. Everybody has to be somewhere; this is where they are—on the Caribbean coast of Panama at Laguna de Bluefields, named for the 17th-century Dutch pirate Abraham Blauvelt, who introduced Darwinian economics to the area a century and a half before Darwin.

My audience has grown, the CSY 44 a hub of Ngobe-Bugle dugouts pointing their noses—fishermen, grandfathers, pretty teenage mothers with infants, children caring for younger siblings. A brave new world has anchored in the lagoon, a UFO with flapping canvas, clanking halyards, rattling windlasses and aliens with guttural dialects and washed-out eyes. Indeed, no UFO could inspire more community interest. Starts and stops, arriving and leaving, mealtime, work, rest, repairs, refueling, abrupt changes in the continuity of living. Hurry up and wait.

Yachts fascinate Indians, whose pace never mends. It's not unusual to wake up in the morning to brown faces framed in portholes like family portraiture, watching alien gringos sleep. You can almost hear them thinking, Have they mated yet? Probably they will mate, and we will learn how gringos multiply, more each dry season. No, the grandfather of the dugout fleet will reply, I do not think they have mated yet. Even the gringos cannot couple continuously.

Intermittent spumes of bilge water issue from surrounding *cayucos*, blurred hands bailing with coconut halves faster than the registry of human eyesight, like cats scratching fleas. Perceived in the compass of entirety, the flotilla resembles a pod of blowing porpoises. Incidental to keeping the leaky cayucos afloat, the ejected bilge water rains down to imitate baitfish twinkling on the surface, attracting cero mackerel. Whatever else moves them, Indians are perpetually, effortlessly foraging food.

I groan, kicking my legs out to straddle the hammock, flat feet slapping the deck. Spectators mutter. The kids back off a stroke or two, eyes widening. The gringo, a time and a half larger than your average Bugle, is rising like an ugly sun. I yawn, addressing the kid in the ballcap.

"Want to climb up?"

The boys glance at each other then back to me, nodding and grinning. They tie their cayuco with horsehair twine to a shroud and scramble over the gunwale into the cockpit. They've never been aboard a yacht before, not even one grown long in the tooth like Kestyll. They sit quietly, eyes sawing, hands in laps, the older Eusilio pretending teenage nonchalance.

The younger boy, Donaldo, offers me a cowry the size of a pelican egg. "That's a good one," I tell him, turning the glazed mollusk over in my hands. He reaches into the pocket of patched and piebald cut-offs, offering another. "No, joven," I smile, "one's plenty. I'll hang it up here to keep you in mind." I force the serrated labia of the mollusk over a hemp strand of the empty potted plant net hanging from the Bimini top. The tropical sunshine fried the pot plant an Argentine hitchhiker hung there. Maybe somebody watered it with seawater.

"But there are many," Donaldo pleads, tilting his head, still proffering the shell, as though a treasure not shared is devalued. It's like when your homegrown tomatoes all ripen at the same time; you've got to spread them around or watch them rot on the vine. There are too many pretty unshared cowries. Then, too, the kid knows gringos covet what sensible Indians discard, tossing delicious conch meat to keep the shells, sometimes exchanging money, a commodity introduced perhaps by Blauvelt. Maybe Donaldo approached with the intention of selling his cowry, deciding to give it instead.

The power of cowries, of any gift, awaits the giving. Before Blauvelt and others introduced an enduring notion of piratical European economics, Indians couldn't hoard. After a day of lackadaisical foraging, having no refrigeration, they share. Greed and coveting opposes community gains. Yet Donaldo has a vested interest in the big boat now by virtue of the swaying cowry.

*

My nap has made me hungry. Entering the mouth of Bluefield Lagoon, I snagged an arm-length cero mackerel. All the Indians know I have it, a fact of life. "Want to eat some fish?" I ask the boys rhetorically.

"Clearly," says Eusilio. Donaldo nods, grinning. His cowry bought supper. I filet the cero, offering head, skin and backbone to a pregnant mother about 13 who nurses a newborn she must've delivered in the bottom of her cayuco during my siesta. I dust the fish in cornmeal and fry it up with pan perro, my neologism for hushpuppy. I've yet to see an indigenous Panamanian—Kuna, Embera, Ngobe-Bugle or Wounaan—who wouldn't kill for dog bread. It's an Indian thing. James Oglethorpe swapped out his grandmother's secret for shepherd's pie for a Yamacraw recipe at a fish fry up the Savannah River. The best way to break the ice with an Indian is serve him up a lump of fried dough.

My plans to weigh anchor early tomorrow fade with the setting sun and a pair of enormous doves flashing from a wall of jungle green across the bay. They fly like grouse, with elastic necks, whirling wings and elongated palmetto tail feathers, angling into a lonely ceiba tree on top of a Prudential-looking rock island a thousand feet offshore. I point my fork. "Lots of palomas around here?" Like the Bugles, I ruminate my next meal on mouthfuls of food.

"Demaciado," Eusilio mumbles, his cheeks puffed with dog bread, "too many."

"How, too many?" Whoever heard of too many doves?

"They eating all the rice."

"Why don't you shoot them?"

"My uncle has a slingshot to shoot them."

"I mean like with shotguns, escopetas."

"No, we don't have no guns here. Before, there was some .22s but the government has took them. Now you must get permission to have firearms or buy cartridges, which are too dear for anybody but soldados and ricos anyway. There no soldados or ricos here."

"No police?"

"*Tampoco*. What we need police for? There nothing much to steal but the rice the palomas eat. What the *policia* will do about that?" Eusilio tells me the farmers must erect effigies, presumably of Blauvelt, to frighten the doves from the rice. Bluefields is starting to sound like my kind of place.

"Maybe I can help you out with some of these palomas," I offer. I haven't had doves in onion gravy since I left home. These birds are the size of pigeons, almost too fat to fly. *oodoo*, the Bugle call them. To the equally onomatopoeic Kuna they are *nuu*. Maybe Eusilio's uncle can limit out with a slingshot. Of course, there's no limit on pests in the Ngobe-Bugle comarca, no game wardens to enforce one if there were. Wonder where I can score some grits?

"Why do the oodoo go to that tall rock, for grit?"

"To rest. They go there to rest."

"Rest from what?"

"From eating rice."

"Why don't they rest in the jungle?"

"Too many vipers in there."

"And monkeys," Donaldo adds. I picture troop of howlers and white-face capuchins snatching doves off the roost, holding them in hairy fists, biting the heads off, eating them like tamales wrapped in corn husks. Who owns this island where they rest? The kid shrugs. "Nobody. Everybody. Maybe Solomon. It is called the Rock of Solomon."

"Where is this Solomon to ask permission to shoot them?"

"I give you permissions. You don't need no permissions to kill mosquitos or oodoo here. The land belong to everybody. Me too."

As if conjured by machination, an old man with spectacles thick as Petri dishes sculls up with two grandchildren—Solomon. I invite him aboard for coffee, hot chocolate for the children. Solomon stirs in extra sugar, making simple syrup. "Will you kill the *tigres* too?" he asks politely. "The tigres are eating my chickens, sometimes my cow. I hope you will kill the tigres."

"I'm not much on killing tigers," I explain, "just critters to eat."

"You will eat the palomas?"

"Clearly."

"Not much meat on a paloma," the old man laments. "You must shoot the garzas. More meat on a garza." Surely the Guaymi dialect distinguishes egrets, herons, storks and ibis, but in Spanish the Indians lump wading birds together as garza.

"We don't eat garza where I come from."

"Where you come from?"
"Albany, Georgia."
Solomon nods like he's been there.
"You got garza in Albany, Georgia?"
"Plenty."
"You make big mistake not to eat them garza. There is much sweet meat in him."
"They're not fishy?"
"Sure, he fishy. You don't eat no fish in Albany, Georgia, neither?"
"Well..."
"There is much sweet meat on a tigre," the old man suggests. "They not so fishy as the garza."
"My tío say it's no easy thing to kill a tigre with a slingshot," Eusilio interjects.
"What's a tigre taste like?" I ask the old man.
Solomon stares off at nothing through thick glasses, politely considering a stupid question. "They taste a lot like chicken," he informs me, "if they been eating them."

*

I dinghy to Solomon's Rock the next afternoon with Eusilio and Donaldo, finding a slope I don't need pylons to climb. The boys scramble up the high bald rock like goats, waiting for me under the ceiba tree while I pole myself up with the Remington, clutching roots, slipping and sliding. I'm winded and sweat-soaked by the time I reach the top, marveling at forces of tropical nature that can drive roots of a ceiba tree through solid volcanic rock. Solomon and his grandchildren watch from his dugout 200 feet below. Other cayucos are attracted. I load the pump.
"How many shoots?" Eusilio wants to know.
"Six."
"Why you put in only three tiros?"
"It's too heavy with six," I lie. I don't want to get into a

discussion of magazine plugs and game laws that won't make a lick of sense to a teenage Indian. The Remington, my protection against latter day Blauvelts, isn't plugged. I just load three out of habit. That, and I've learned that after I miss something three times, I'm not likely to hit it with a gun too hot to handle.

A few palomas fly under me, swooping up on the way to the roost. My first shot catapults a blizzard of snowy egrets from a patch of mangroves below. Garza. The Indians watch them fly off with mouthwatering sadness.

Shooting down on the doves, I have to watch out for cayucos gathered to observe the gringo with the thundering *escopeta*. I've never fired down on birds before, so naturally I miss a few. Also, it's easy to misjudge the range and speed of birds twice the size of mourning doves. With their burnished copper necks and capes and red feet, they seem to just float around under me barely airborne, but my pattern on the bright bay below tells me they're hauling ass and I'm not leading them enough. I can't swing through without endangering dugouts loaded with Indians, which in combination with their hoots and laughter throws my marksmanship off even more. A few dugouts rush to my shot patterns in hopes the stippled surface imitates baitfish and will attract cero.

I finally bring down an oodoo, hitting it twice with high-brass eights. It tumbles into the bay, where Donaldo's job is to wet-retrieve it before a shark, barracuda or maybe a crocodile beats him to it. "Donaldo is quick," his brother assures me.

The companion of the floating bird circles and lights high in the ceiba tree.

"Shoot him," orders Eusilio.

"It's in a tree."

"*Claro*," he agrees. "Make him ours."

"It's not sporting."

"¿Como *sporting*? You killing the oodoo to eat him?"

"Well, yes, but it's not considered good sportsmanship to shoot birds from trees."

"They easier to kill from trees."

"Don't argue with me, Eusilio. Throw a rock. Scare him out of there."

Eusilio frowns, fingering the ground for a suitable missile. Selecting one, he stands erect, shoulder lowered, arm hanging to absorb the stone's heft. The supple veins of Eusilio's forearm suggest the untested potency of Michelangelo's adolescent David sizing up Goliath.

"I ain't sure I can kill him with a rock from here," Eusilio ventures. "My uncle ... "

I'm ready, one foot forward, clicking off the safety. "Shut up and chunk the damn rock, Eusilio."

The kid, afraid I'm fixing to shoot him, winds up. His bony knee cocks clean to his nose. Leaning backwards at an incredible angle, he extends a bare foot, sighting the cooing oodoo between splayed toes. Brown knuckles touch the ground behind him in perfect alignment with a trembling foot, and the kid lets fly.

I figured an Indian born to the wild would be able to chunk proficiently, but *son*! This kid can chunk! Cocked and coiled sinew, muscle, grizzle and bone snap into an explosive blur of violent release. The rock, farting through the air with incredible velocity, defies gravitational trajectory, hooking at the last moment a centimeter wide of the dove. A blast of green confetti and a loud *THWOCK* launches the astonished bird upward with no clear directional intention. For a moment it hovers, suspended in air long enough for me to miss it twice before its afterburner kicks in and the fat oodoo squalls off at Mach speeds into a crimson sunset.

In movies I've seen medieval catapults lay siege to moated castles. The outsized engine is cocked by an elaborate system of pulleys and gears, the heavy stone lifted and nested into its breach by two bullet-headed soldiers who aim the weapon then chop rawhide restraints with a broadaxe, releasing terrible missiles that penetrate castle walls. This celluloid scenario is the closest approximation I can manage for the fury of Eusilio's chunking style. The recoil of the rock's release actually lifts the Yankees baseball cap off Eusilio's head; its arrival severs the limb the bird perched on. My near misses send more green confetti whirling and fluttering in the light breezes off Solomon's Rock as the Indian flotilla boos and hisses.

"You should've shoot him from the tree," the kid pouts. "My uncle..."

A hateful squint stifles him as I clack a new shell into the chamber. We have both missed the same bird before an audience and are pissed about it.

Donaldo climbs the slope, dripping. He reports that another Indian got to my downed dove before he could. Shading my eyes, I look down into the wrinkled bay where a bucktooth brave in a dugout dangles the purloined bird provocatively, flashing white teeth.

"That's my dove!" I yell. "Tell that son of a bitch that's my dove!"

"He say it his."

"How his?"

"It fall from the sky near his cayuco. This his lucky day."

"Does he know I'm fixing to scald his lucky ass with a high-brass eight?"

Eusilio cups his hands, yelling something in Guaymi to the pesky Bugle, who grins wider, jiggling the bird like a dancing puppet. "He don't think you can hit him from up here. He sporting, too," interprets Eusilio.

By the time the doves stop coming in and the cayucos peel off to be elsewhere, Donaldo has retrieved three palomas, two of which—I confess it—were shot off high limbs of the ceiba tree, necessity having exceeded sportsmanship. It's not all that easy to knock a tough bird out of the top of a thick tree the height of a telephone pole. I got tired of entertaining a perimeter fringe of Indian spectators who don't understand the sportsmanship of harvesting small game with shotgun shells that each cost a day's wages in the local economy—who don't realize it's impolite to laugh at the profanity of near misses and the hubris of sportsmen who flush food from limbs to make it harder to kill and easier to cripple. Not even Donaldo can concentrate his full attention to retrieving doves that drop into steep jungle undergrowth among the vipers.

It's hard to shoot down on fast-flying birds without dusting off a dugout full of Indians, especially when some are rushing around to cast hand lines in the temporary stipple birdshot makes on still waters. Even if my marksmanship were impervious to ridicule, it's hard to score well with one eye on the target and the other scanning for an unpopulated field of fire.

Real sportsmen would understand the logic of my failure; they'd see why style demands risking lost and wounded quarry by flushing it into those wild kinetic gyrations dove are capable of. Wounded birds lost to jungle undergrowth support diverse ecological populations, such as hungry vipers. Real sportsman will understand all this together with my reluctance to leave a tribe of one-eyed Indians in Bluefields Lagoon. I shuck the plump palomas, puzzled but not surprised by how thickly feathered tropical birds are. I've dusted more than one into explosions of feathers, causing nothing more mortal than a burst of accelerated speed.

Cooking the purple meat, I discover another reason oodoo are difficult to bag: They are tough as motor mounts. I parboil them in wine and cream of mushroom soup until midnight, the aroma drifting over the bay to bait up more Bugles. When my indigenous guests rub their bellies and burp, I wind up with an overcooked ort gamier than a mourning dove and substantially chewier, more like crow, which Solomon says tastes like chicken if they've been stealing hen eggs.

Solomon says oodoos darken the sky when rice is planted in the river swamps. I promise to return with the rainy season when the Indians broadcast seed by hand over spongy jungle patches cleared by machetes. I'll protect the planting and share the doves.

Solomon is delighted. "Perhaps you will change your ways and kill the tigres, too. Perhaps you will shoot into the plump garzas roosting in the mangroves for you and learn the grace of accepting the gift of his life the oodoo offers when he sits for you in the trees." In the Wisdom of Solomon, where perpetual foraging is a way of life, a sporting Indian is a skinny Indian with no abundance to share with others.

Sportsmanship is superfluous when supper is stalked with a pocketful of volcanic rocks.

Donaldo and Solomon fall asleep. Eusilio sucks the last sip of marrow from a wing, and I ponder the bad turn civilization took millennia past when the pure art of chunk gave way to gadgetry. The bow and other contrivances that store and release independent energy came from mediocre hunters too lazy or inept to chunk their way into the best buckskins and roomiest caves, where wide-hipped debutantes gathered for partridge, tenderloin and reproductive snuggling. That first separation between arm and projectile broke the natural kinetic continuity between predator and prey. The club, spear, atlatl, jai alai racquet, Orvis 5-weight, Prince Pro and Louisville Slugger are all evolutions inspired by man's dissatisfaction with the length of his chunking arm together with his creative urge to extend it. The catapult, a deadly extension of the human arm, lacks joints and flexibility to give it the accuracy and grace of a well-oiled chunk.

    Slingshots and arrows produce outrageous and unfortunate opposition to the connection between pure Zen energy and motion—a break from the deadly eye of a hungry hunter to charmed quarry—from marksman to target. Gadgets that store and release energy gave rise to the corrupt line of crossbows, snares, firearms and nuclear warheads. With gadgetry, even the ineptest wiener in the gene pool could bag his self a possum or armadillo and fetch up a mediocre woman once in a while if she was hungry enough and he cooked up his kill in cream of mushroom soup and garnished it with hushpuppies. Thus began the decline and fall of excellence, the end of great hunters and heroes, the bureaucracy of grocery chains, fast foods, game laws: the decadence of man.

    Technology is a history of bad ideas. I realize that without skill's forfeiture to gadgetry I wouldn't be here. The mediocre Eve of my line lurked in the shadows of flowered walls, adorned in buzzard plumes. She wore possum fangs around a thick hairy ankle and a tit-chafing push-up bra fashioned from twin armadillo husks. I know I'm lucky to have survived the cut to witness a mutant reappearance of extinct prototypical chunk, the rudimentary vestiges of which infrequently flicker dim but prodigious shadows from the clay mound of professional baseball diamonds.

    "My uncle," Eusilio begins, lifting the wishbone and sighting cross-eyed down his nose, "has a slingshot..."

Dog Snapper

A fishing rod is a stick with a worm at one end and a fool at the other. —Samuel Johnson.

A Suzuki outboard flits over from one of the uninhabited islands of the Coco Banderas, setting upon us with the same tactical suddenness of the patch-eyed pirates who bushwhacked Spanish ships laden with Inca gold. But the dugout that grapples our beam is personed not by patch-eyed privateers but by three *omekits*, Kuna men who choose to live as women, selling molas, ornately embroidered and layered dress panels as finely crafted or better than those sewn by their rival gender. The crew buys molas and some trinkets, and the omekits, careful not to break a nail, crank the Suzuki and depart toward Nargana, waving warm, limp-wristed farewells. It feels good to be back in the *comarca*, where children are respected and people are free to choose who they are, including their gender.

Just four of us now—me, Cochise, Simon Coconut and Will—all with South Georgia roots more or less, enroute to return my vintage yacht, Kestyll, to her lagoon in the San Blas Archipelago of Panama's Caribbean coast. "Pigpen" Keenan, anxious to get back on his Epistemology Crusade—whatever that is—jumped ship in Cartagena and flew back to San Francisco. We're anchored for the night in the lee of a barrier reef and can be home among my Indian friends tomorrow afternoon if we sail as soon as the sun is high enough to illuminate the shoals and coral. Crashing surf against a wrecked freighter and a yacht provides an ominous reminder to navigate gingerly through these sparkling waters during daylight hours only, the charts being off just enough to transform a sailor's hull into a fine habitat for tropical fish.

  After a supper of fried venison brought frozen from Baker County and the backbone of a gold-plated mahi-mahi that took the fantail spoon and drowned, we relax in the cockpit, basking in the night air beneath Orion, Taurus and the Pleiades, burping heartily and passing a joint, generally awed by our view from the outer rim of the Milky Way Galaxy. Urban life has blinded us to the stars. Except for Cochise, electric lights have kept us chronically oblivious to the night sky. Without predawn hunting excursions outside the city glow, we'd never see the stars. Someday I'll learn enough to navigate by them.

  Even in the brightness of this gibbous moon, we see more stars at a glance than we've probably seen since childhood. What can be said for the general intelligence of a race of people essentially oblivious to the sky above their heads? Who are unaware of horizons except for a dim sun above a gauzy canopy of pestilent vapors, and roofs, car tops and office buildings? Of the upper half of our visible world, we are as ignorant as cows.

  Simon Coconut notices line steadily ticking from a freshwater baitcaster he rigged with a crappie hook, lashed across the Bimini top and forgot about. He frees it, picks it up and gazes curiously as the 12-pound monofilament stitches a slow silver seam across the still water. "I've got a bite."

  "Bullshit."

  The Coconut tightens the drag as far as sea-salt corrosion permits and sets the hook, backlashing the old Garcia with a flatulent sigh without notifying whatever is on the other end of the engagement. I don't know how this fossil fishing rig came aboard in the first place. It belongs in a boathouse dock at Lake Blackshear, something for the kids to tangle up.

The line continues to tick out effortlessly, white flakes chipping off reel cheeks.

"You've snagged the bottom," I advise the Coconut.

"Un huh, something's on there."

"The wind's swinging us around on the anchor rode." We sight on the dead sloop three-quarters eaten into the coral, moonlit foam swelling through open chest and fractured ribs. We're hanging true to lee. The reel's growling complaint is magnified on the drumhead of the Bimini. Then the dozing Garcia squalls like a four-dollar alarm clock, spewing white powder off the spool.

"Whoa! Hold her, Coconut! She's headed for the barn!"

Mysteriously, the chimera, or whatever the Coconut has snagged, halts a few turns from the end of the line, yawning, presumably, before strolling back toward the boat Simon reels in slack hysterically until the fish or whatever it is dives under the keel, doubling the rod and bending him headlong over the lifelines. "Hold that mother!" we shout.

"How?"

"He's trying to turn over the boat!"

"He's big, all right," I quip. Kestyll weighs 25 tons. A coincidental gust against the bare rigging heels us a couple of degrees. A maverick swell splats the side of the hull, adding a couple more.

"Did the fish do that?"

"Sure, everybody lean to the other side."

"I don't think it knows it's hooked!" Pausing directly beneath us, our "catch" lumbers aft.

"Aw right! Aw right! If we can fight him from the fantail, we got a chance!"

By his progress we see he means to orbit. We scatter and regroup, spreading ourselves along the gunwales, shouting and passing the rod fire-brigade fashion down the deck, around Bimini bars, shrouds, cables and stays as our prey magnetically tugs crew astern. "Don't let him wrap the prop! Keep him abeam."

"How?"

"Talk to him."

"Please, Mr. Finn, come now peaceably to the pan... "

"Don't horse him."

"Horse him? He's horsing me!"

"And quit pointing the rod at that fish!"

"Jesus!"

"Tighten the drag!"

"It's all the way tight!"

We take turns on the tackle, pumping, snatching, bitching. "Gimmie that rod, Will, you got no idea what you're doing."

"I do too; I've caught a fish before."

"When?"

"With my granddaddy, at his farm pond." American kids don't have fathers anymore, though some have grandparents.

"This ain't your granddaddy's pond," bleats a voice from the darkness, somebody cutting up, maybe me.

"And that thing may not even be a fish," somebody points out.

"It ain't the bottom."

"A manta ray!"

"A shark! *Bum, bum, bum, bum.* The hunters become the hunted, the fishers the fished!"

"Jawwwws!"

"Russian sub, is what it is!"

Rounding the fantail, the great fish heads forward to the starboard beam, tugging us along the starboard catwalk as we fumble the rod around and through rigging, relaying the screaming tackle hand to hand, a baton with a fish on one end and a ship of fools on the other. This thing can shrug off ten feet of line on a whim and a shudder.

At the bowsprit, the fish makes short, desultory runs each

time we try to rein him back, forcing the drag each time we try to raise him. We take turns coaxing it, whatever it is, under the anchor rode, back along the port beam, pumping and reeling, stumbling until our mildly inconvenienced visitor strips all the snaggle teeth off the brittle gears. The only way we can gain on the thing is tag-teaming it: one of us carefully lifting the vibrating rod so the fish doesn't feel it, dipping it quickly so another can take up the slack by hand, somebody else reeling the profit onto the spool.

The reel is fading fast. The stripped shards and fragments grind noisily beneath the crank like nutmeg in a grater. We've known since we hooked the fish that we had no hope of landing it. It's a game; keep it on as long as we can.

With flashlight beams we slash the depths, blue as ice, still unable to see the thing on the end of the line. The artificial light attracts a half dozen green needlefish and a five-foot bull-jowl shark of a species known as salty lawyer, a bottom feeder that doesn't hunt, cruising instead for gastronomic scraps derived from the mortal predicaments of others.

"We've got a shark, we've hooked a shark!"

"No, no, that's not him. He's deeper, deeper than the shark!"

The rod springs straight. Another fish rises on its own into the limelight, perhaps to discern the source of disorder. This fish, we think, is ours. We stare at our presumed adversary, gigantic, goofy and ferocious, a cluster of sharp fangs overflowing its lips like the grin on a bucktooth collie, a remarkable creature nearly a yard long of olive and gold with prismatic pinks. It's a dog snapper, *pargo pero*, plated with silver coins the size of half-dollars. It churns phosphorescence with pectoral fins the size of human hands—a rainbow in a tropical sunset.

We are attached very thinly to our quarry. Our pitiful blue hook is stitched into its upper lip above the bristling incisors, which is why he hasn't bitten off and gone on about his business of overturning omekits and swallowing giant squid. It lies incandescent beneath the stars and the moon-slung shadow of our yardarm, generating its own haunting light. Unless it incidentally dies of natural causes, we have little hope of landing such a fish without a gaff or a landing net.

The snapper takes a long look at his tormentors and sounds, trailing phosphorescence like a meteor and clots of monofilament like a kite tail. Simon and Will handle the line like it's hot, braking it with the heels of their hands against the rod, the guides of which ping off like the buttons of my old Army jacket. I go below for the Colt Woodsman. Cochise scrambles off the fantail into the inflatable, pulling himself along the gunwale to the origin of our original encounter, more or less where this fiasco began.

I chamber a hollow-point and hang over the lifelines. Will and Simon try coaxing the fish back to the surface. The spool spins freely now, completely disengaged from its handle. I expect the reel to die with the fish, crumble into a heap of rust or transfigure into a pillar of salt.

"You ought to take better care of your equipment," Cochise observes from the dinghy. Suddenly, of its own volition, the snapper rises in a glimmering halo of cold green light.

"Awesome!" gasps Will. "Shoot it! Shoot it!" He jabs my ribs with his finger as though to discharge the .22 pistol by remote control. "Shoot it! Shoot it!"

Each jab sets my jackknifed torso writhing on the lifelines.

"Stop it, Will!"

"Shoot it, shoot it!"

The barrel pulses like the needle of a heart monitor with each stab of Will's index finger.

"I can't shoot with him poking me! Simon, will you restrain him?"

"Who? Will or the fish? I'm doing all I can with the fish."

True enough, Simon holds the butt of the useless baitcaster pinched in his crotch. In his hands he holds a wad of tangled monofilament the size of a beach ball. If the fish makes another run, it will trim the Coconut's fingers like a weed whacker.

"Restrain whatever's jabbing me in the ribcage every time I line my sights."

"It's getting away!" Will bellows. "Don't let my fish get away!"

"Your fish! God's own fish!"

"Hush, Will! Simon, knock him out with the flashlight if he won't hold still."

"I've got my hands full," answers Simon.

I lean over the dancing ripples, sighting down the beam of the flashlight Simon has miraculously pinched in the nape between earlobe and shoulder.

"Watch the dinghy!" Cochise calls out from the darkness beneath us.

"Don't shoot my dad," bleats Simon. The flashlight rattles to the deck.

"Jesus!"

"Awesome!"

In the light of the moon, with the extinguished image lingering on my retina, I shoot the fish—*pap, pap*—group two just forward of the gills. Will picks up the flashlight, illuminating the last round of battle royal. The snapper cants, trembling, circling centrifugally on the end of a nylon leash and trailing a thin cloak of bright red through translucent green.

"Uh, good shooting," someone remarks of my dubious shot in the dark.

Cochise on his knees in the floor of the dinghy, paddles with his hands, stirring cold light as if washing them in stardust. He reaches—reverently it seems—into the pool of bioluminescence ignited by death tremors.

"Watch your fingers," I warn. "There's at least one shark down there, and that dog snapper has teeth like a buzz saw."

But the fish remains broached, calm now as if offering itself up. Cochise lifts it into the inflatable, where the circle of innocent blood spreads. We cheer and slap each other's shoulders and backs.

Simon receives the snapper from his father and places him on the deck, forcing open the operculum and trickling rum over crisp red gills, our manner of subduing a fish we want to spare the dishonor of clubbing, especially if we have dishonored it already by shooting it. But this fish doesn't need the rum. It has fought us long and well nearly to its death only to be ignobly dispatched by a handgun. It gulps a silent syllable or two, an abbreviated prayer.

"It doesn't feel quite right," I say as bright hues fade into pastels.

"We didn't have a gaff," offers Cochise. "Not even a club." The fish billy rolled off somewhere in The Windward Passage, and I've never owned a gaff. A dedicated marksman, I'd rather shoot my catch and feel like hell afterwards.

"Look at the size of that fish!" Will is hopping, flapping his arms. "Wow, wow, wow!"

"It's no worse than a gillnet or a long line," Simon consoles. We're all feeling, except for Will, on the downside of good, ashamed of our dumb luck.

"Just look at him!" Will says. "He's a lot bigger than the one me and granddaddy caught."

The snapper's goofy teeth are unearthly white in the anchor light. "You could've lipped him, Cochise," I strain for humor, "and grabbed that shark with the other hand." Cochise doesn't bother to respond, doesn't have to.

The snapper stains the deck like it will bleed forever, the stoned, bucktooth smile beyond folly, not so much defeated now as just plain dead, slaughtered by a gaggle of yelping and blasphemous yahoos.

Simon Coconut shucks away at the silver scales with the point of a machete, Kuna style, tossing glossy viscera into the dimpled water where pickers and stealers swarm and the salty lawyer returns for his percentage.

It's almost sinful to take a fine fish the way we have taken him; it's like killing a 12-point buck with a logging truck. Even Will senses the truth of this, but after you've pulled the trigger, the lot is cast. You've missed, killed or crippled a living creature—a fellow mortal—and this underlines the importance of doing everything as innocent of pure dumb luck as you can before clicking off the safety with a firm and responsible decision to subordinate a life to yours. Any subsequent redemption lies in reverence, not pride. To a man we'd gladly eat canned tuna for the rest of the trip to undo the murder. Though bringing this thing back to life even now seems eerily possible, we can't. Loath to dishonor it more, we can only prepare its flesh carefully and partake of it with good fellowship and honest wine.

"Leave the head on," I tell Simon. We'll take it to Ukupseni and share it with my Indian friends, a gift more presentable whole, though the Kuna believe that a fisherman must not eat the head or the fish will learn how he thinks and living fish will no longer be outwitted and caught. My friend Luz will cook the dog snapper, and we'll share with her family to celebrate a homecoming. Though Will doubts there's enough fish to go around, Luz will spread the snapper thin, garnished with breadfruit and fried banana. She'll make coconut rice and serve plenty of bread, the daily madu with burnished gold crust and foam white center—the best bread there is.

So, what's all this misty-eyed introspection over food that doesn't come frozen and wrapped in cellophane?

What's this shame that carnivores and fish-eaters kill

instead of ordering out or passing a summons to grimmer grocers? The slaughtered snapper will be fresher, more intimately enjoyed, more fully honored. Kestyll's crew will eat the head ceremoniously, and Caribbean fishes, learning our scatterbrain strategies, will arise berserk to the moon, scuttling themselves on reefs where freighters and sloops gnaw niches into coral and are themselves steadily digested. But the dog snapper still may declare itself in memory as a resplendent living thing sacrificed to less perfect critters, enriched and sustained a little while longer on their brief journey beneath the infinite and largely unnoticed sky.

Magdalena's Crocodile

Woo't weep? Woo't fight? Woo't fast? Woo't tear thyself?
Woo't drink up eisel? eat a crocodile, I'll do't ...
—Shakespeare

I'm basking in my hammock strung between the mast and forestay when her guide Gordo paddles her in his dugout to my yacht a mile from the village. I lower the ladder and they climb up to come aboard. Leaning over to help her up, I notice her designer khaki shirt is open at the top, a tiny gold cross nestled in cleavage.

I haven't seen see many non-Kuna single women since I sailed down here to get away from an ex-wifeís lawyers and restore my soul. Kuna women are taboo for *merg*—Americans—which I learned the hard way when I sailed off with a young widow to a nearby island. The chief, the sahila, banished me but let me come back after my friend Lucioís intervention, but Iím still on shaky ground with the villagers.

"Thees is Veektor," Gordo says by way of introduction. Gordo, the guide for the ecolodge, is also its chef. "He keels the crocodiles, and all the childrens knows him.

"The sahila, he say she goes tonight with thee to making pictures."

Because I shot one nuisance crocodile, I inadvertently became the tribeís nuisance crocodile killer, wearing the teeth of the first one around my neck as an honorary badge of office. Itís almost never that crocodiles gain the courage to venture into a village, so I figured I could rest on laurels indefinitely without ever having to fuck with a living crocodile again. Now another one shows up. Iíll have to at least try to kill it just to save face.

The tooth necklace made me a favorite with the village kids. I won their affection with Flintstone vitamins, Zodiac rides and candy. Sundays I set up a generator and DVD player on deck to feed them popcorn and play Disney movies. I was anxious to impress these wonderful people, the Kuna Indians of San Blas. They accept me as a kind of curiosity, a mergi mascot more foolish than brave. If I can get back in with the women through the children, I'll be in good with the tribe.

At the women's insistence, the Kuna chief, has ordered me to dispatch a second rogue that has lost its fear of the Kuna—next to pigmies the smallest people in the world. They said an enormous crocodile crawls ashore at night after the village generator shuts down, stalking dogs and chickens in the dark dirt alleys between the thatch huts. To the Kuna killing crocodiles is taboo as they may embody demons from the underworld, *poni,* whose hypnotic eyes can catch souls and spirit them back to nether regions. A mere glance can cause pregnant women to bear children with rough, scaly skin. The sahila ain't worried one bit about my soul since Americans don't have them. I'm pretty sure I got the honorary position because nobody else wants it and because I've got the only a gun capable of killing a crocodile, a .44 magnum revolver I keep locked in my cabin for protection. I haven't fired it since I shot the first nuisance crocodile. There's a spray of rust across the cylinder from the salt air and the brass bullets have tarnished green, but I'm pretty sure it still shoots.

"So, you're the famous crocodile killer," says Magdalena, her dark eyes sparkling irony.

"I reckon so."

"You're not from around here."

"Neither are you."

"Do we have to go at night?"

"If you go with me you do."

"Who else can take me?"

"Nobody."

She wipes a lock of crow-black hair out of her eyes. "I just don't understand why it has to be at night."

"It just does."

"It doesn't seem fair."

"It ain't supposed to be fair, Honey. It ain't no sport. Call it euthanasia. Night's the only time I can get close enough to shoot him with a pistol."

She looks at me, squint-eyed and critical. We sit in the cockpit. I serve them sweet tea. She tells me she works at the Spanish Embassy in Panama City, travels on weekends to remote locations to photograph exotic flora and fauna. The sahila has given her special permission to bring a camera to the village, where she is strictly forbidden to photograph Kuna men, women or children without their express permission since a photo can be used to cast spells. I'll be double damned if she takes a snapshot of me killing a crocodile and shows it off around the embassy. I'd be fined, maybe thrown in jail, if I ever leave Ukupsini, beyond the sahila's jurisdiction. I'm not planning to leave this Caribbean paradise, where I'm anchored between two small islands of coconut palms. I figure on staying forever if they don't they run me off again.

"Why is it your job to shoot it?"

"I'm the dumbass with the gun."

*

Magdalena sees this maverick crocodile business as another male excuse to murder something, holding that one well-fed crocodile is worth any number of emaciated Kuna dogs, even a male kid once in a while. She has learned everything there is to know about crocodiles but hasn't seen a wild one in the flesh.

"I want to go out with you," she says, "but I don't want

to be party to killing endangered species, which is, by the way, against the law." On the boat ten minutes, already she's captain.

"The sahila decides what's endangered. I do what all he says do, which is why I'm taking you out with me tonight. I don't want to shoot that crocodile any more than you do. The first one like to killed my ass. For the record, this expedition was instigated by the women, not me. Hell's fire, I'm a goddamn environmentalist."

*

Dressed traditionally in colorful molas, arm and ankle beads and gold nose rings, the women had gone to the sahila demanding that he rid them of this current nuisance crocodile. In this matriarchal society, what the women want gets done. When the women accept me, the men will come along.

Anyway, that's how I got assigned the duty of cruising around the village after dark in my dinghy, flashing my spotlight on the garbage littered shore to keep the women off the sahila's back and the sahila off mine.

I'd already made Magdalena's environmental argument to the chief. The last thing I ever wanted to do was tangle with another crocodile. The first one dislocated both my thumbs by spinning when I lifted it heroically by the neck, showing off, thinking it was dead.

*

"Crocodiles are endangered," I reminded the sahila when he assigned me, from his official hammock in the congreso or community meeting house to exterminate another bold reptile that came ashore prowling for chickens and dogs. Crocodiles are attracted to garbage tossed into the tidewater around the island, freshwater crocodiles that move in from mangroves and jungle after the village generator cuts off and the village is dark and quiet. The women fear the encroaching reptile will sooner or later snatch a kid wandering around at night under a full moon, as Kuna children will. Especially when they're wired up on sugar.

The sahila in his hammock wore the traditional dress of Kuna men, a ball cap, T-shirt and flip-flops. He kickstarted his hammock with a small brown foot on the dirt floor. When it ran down, he dismounted to speak with the authority of office.

"Yes, endangered," he said thoughtfully, raising his arms like rabbit ears to receive a clearer vision, "to children, to dogs, to sleeping men and to women big with child. The poni is endangered to thee too, mergi," he continued. "Thou must kill him carefully so he don't catch thee with his eyes."

The shaman has declared this crocodile a *poli* with fireball eyes, snorting smoke. According to Chino, the Panamanian policeman, he makes a regular show at the police outpost where the footbridge connects the village to the schoolyard and airstrip on the mainland. Chino claims to have seen him many times. He pot-shoots the little crocodiles with a disreputable revolver, bitching that the reptiles interfere with the perpetual domino game outside the outpost where he sleeps. Players slap their dominos emphatically, which attracts the crocodiles chummed up with table scraps and outhouse waste. Whoever sits with his back to the shore can't concentrate for fear of getting snatched. An apprehensive glance over the shoulder occasions the other players to peek at his dominos, so he says. I don't depend too much on what Chino says.

"Why don't you shoot his ass?" I ask Chino, whose soul, because he's a Panamanian policeman, is as expendable as mine. The chief has his own police force, armed with intricately carved wooden staffs. They have no guns to kill nuisance crocodiles with.

"We do," he insists, brandishing the antiquated .22 revolver with a duct-taped grip, "but he don't die. This one much bigger than the little one you kill."

"That little one was over nine feet long."

"This one much bigger than that."

I doubt Chino has ever shot at a crocodile in range. He can't shoot a pistol worth squat, and he's not inclined to let his target get close enough to bushwhack with a Saturday night special.

"This a very big cocodrilo we speaking here. And too we National Police must account for our cartridges. He must be keel before he eat Raul." Chino points the careless firearm at a swag-belly hammock close to the shore, from which issues mighty snoring interrupted by snorts and whistles. Raul's apnea and the creaking hammock perform one of the many village rhapsodies that lure in crocodiles. Chino will wake up Raul if a crocodile gets too close to the pool of hissing light from the gas lantern where the dominos are played. It doesn't occur to the players to stop slapping the dominos any more than it occurs to Raul to stop snoring or to Kuna women to stop tossing garbage into the tidewater.

Chino holsters his revolver front and center between his thighs. He gazes covetously at my .44 revolver, long as his forearm.

"I'll be out tonight," I tell him. No boats are allowed in the sound after dark, a tactical measure against drug trafficking, or something.

Chino is thinly tolerated by the Kuna, who rebelled against Panama in 1925 when Panamanian police and Catholic priests tried to exterminate them, stripping them of their identity, outlawing their religion to absorb them into Panamanian culture to take their land, taking the gold rings out of the womenís noses. They won their independence when the U.S. supported their rebellion with a gunboat offshore. Long before that, they sided with English pirates against the Spanish. Many still bear English names. The Kuna remain the worldís largest organized tribe of Indians

*

"There was a six-footer last night under the foot bridge," I tell Magdalena. "I'll show you that one. If we happen upon the poni, I'll take you back to the eco-lodge and find me a more willing apprentice."

"The police?"

"Nope. Lucio."

Ordinarily my first mate and sidekick, Lucio, goes out with me on these sorties. A converted Christian, he doesn't worry about poni now that he has the Devil to contend with, but three would overload the inflatable. I'd been trying to crawfish back out of this mission until one night leaving Lucio's hut after a supper of *Tule masi*—fish and plantain stew?— flushed a tremendous crocodile out from under his dock, the dock where I tie up my dingy and where kids swim and play. I knew I'd feel like hell if the poni hurt one of them on my watch while I was aboard the sailboat in my hammock shirking my only tribal duty and drinking beer. It's rumored that this crocodile or one like it swallowed three chickens and a dog on a nearby island. That's what they say.

*

We cross the bay toward the dark village, careful of needlefish leaping toward our flashlights. The outboard propeller churns pyrotechnic pinwheels of blue-green bioluminescence. Halfway across, I cut the outboard motor to drift in the moonlight and listen to the jungle and smell its funky perfume in the offshore breeze. An alpha howler monkey roars like an asthmatic lion while the rest of the troop chitter just inside the dark wall of jungle spangled by fireflies.

"How's this for a romantic interlude?" I try. "Just listen to them monkeys."

"Let's hurry up," she says, "I need to get back early to wash my hair. Big day tomorrow."

Tourists aren't allowed to go around the comarca unattended. Tomorrow her guide Gordo will show her the cemetery, where the dead are buried in hammocks beneath simplified huts. He'll take her up the mountain to the waterfall with winding pool under it and the defunct herbal garden that the curanderos stopped tending when mergi botanists ran out of grant money.

*

I crank the Evinrude. It stutters, coughs, and backfires before it starts—water in the fuel line most likely. We cross the bay dragging a trail of cold blue light. With the village generator off, the moon silvers a flawless bay and the thatch roofs of the negas or huts along the shore. Votive candles and nuchus—wooden household gods—are set in the windows and doorways of the dark thatch huts to prevent evil spirits from entering. Or demons disguised as crocodiles.

As we reach the sound between the island and the mainland, I scan the shore with my headlamp, insects buzzing to our light, swarm our faces. Under the footbridge on the schoolyard side shines the red neon eye of a crocodile.

"There one is," I whisper. "Let's try to get in close enough to snap a photo before I rush you back to the ecolodge so you can wash your hair. I'll pick up Lucio and go ahead on making our rounds." I was sure the offending crocodile, if it was still around, haunted the north side of the island near Lucio's dock, where I first saw it.

When I first came to Ukupseni, parents ferried their children dressed in blue and white uniforms back and forth in dugout canoes to school. Now there's is a walking bridge between the school on the mainland and the village. The police outpost is on the village side near the footbridge. I'm taking Magdalena to the opposite side of the island from where I saw the crocodile in question up under Lucio's dock. I don't want to engage the poni with her in the dinghy instead of Lucio.

"It's not the big one?" she whispers.

"Uh, uh. this oneí' a pup. He'll look ferocious enough in a photo with nothing of scale in the background. The bull of the woods ain't around or it would've run this little one off."

We putt toward the blazing red eye doubled by its reflection, bright as a taillight though there are no cars in Kuna Yala, no roads, only trails maintained by the Kuna through the jungle and up into the mountains.

The crocodile lies in shallow water submerged except for the head. As we approach, I suddenly realize what we'd thought was the whole reptile is only his head. It's the poni I've been hunting. "Yikes! Whoa!" I slam the Evinrude into reverse, killing the engine, the momentum gliding us helplessly toward to a warty head the size of a mule's.

"Hold the light in his eyes, Magdalena." I whisper, drawing my pistol. "Keep him blinded." I scramble to the bow where Magdalena sits frozen, shining her flashlight into the crocodile's bright eye. The motor off, there's no reverse to slow us down, nothing to keep us from plowing smack into a warty head slap full of overlapping teeth. Closer we drift until, leaning out over the bow, Iím directly above the monster's long black head. I hug Magdalena's shoulders to keep my balance and steady my aim as we drift helplessly toward the hypnotic red eye. I cock the hammer. The crocodile regards the click without interest, Chino having dissipated any fear of firearms.

"Don't shoot!" cries Magdalena. "It's a baby!" But she holds her flashlight steady, mesmerized, perhaps, by the fiery windows of crocodilian over-soul.

"Hush, Magdalena! Cover your ears." Aiming at the invisible spot behind the skull where the spiked neck starts, I pull the trigger.

A blinding flash. *Ka-boom!* The apocalyptic report of the .44 magnum reshuffles village tranquility, reverberating down the dark alleys between huts. Sleeping Indians jackknife in their hammocks. Domino games abruptly halt between final click-clacks. Kuna spectators appear magically along the handrails of the footbridge. Children wandering around in the moonlight come to see their popcorn knight embroiled in action.

In the muzzle flash I see a bullet hole dead center behind skull, but the drifting dinghy has cornered the reptile against the bank, forcing it to charge under us to get away, diving under the dingy. Boney ridges scrub the hull as the mortally wounded crocodile scoots under us in a streak of turquoise light, beaching itself on a shell mound at the shore of the schoolyard. Well, hot damn! Nothing to it. The poni lies dead. Mission accomplished and mission ended. Not near as bad as I expected, not near the trouble of the first one. A piece of cake. From now on I can stay in my hammock on deck evenings, swaying in the cool breezes tumbling down from the mountains, drinking beer, restoring my soul.

Ears ringing, sucking breath, I beach the dingy on the shell mound where the crocodile lies prone and still. I step over the rubber gunnels into the shallow water, marching up the mound on shaky knees to see for the first time how really big this sucker is. Man, he looks like a hot water tank with a tail, fully capable of snatching Raul out of his hammock and gobbling up Chino and his dinky pistol too. Careful not to get too close, I pace him off, 12 feet. I'm not sure the Evinrude's reverse can drag the heavy carcass off the shell mound. It is longer than the dinghy, where Magdalena sits statuesque, a slain monster spotlighted in the wide beam of her flashlight, the whole village looking on. A gallant quest fulfilled. A maiden saved. A dragon slain. The village will honor me now. At least the children will. The men will envy, the women satisfied.

"You done good," I tell the silent Magdalena, who still shines the beached monster, her empty eyes fixed on the dead crocodile. I'll just tie a rope on him and drag him off the shells, across the sound into the village.

Having no cordage but the rope spliced to the bow ring, I drag the loose end to where the reptile lies, making a noose to slip over its tapered bill and around its thick neck. No way I'm going touch that crocodile or get anywhere near its head or tail. Injured crocodiles, I learned killing the first one, are more dangerous than the ones you leave alone. A bullet to the head can disconnect whatever restraint the goober-size brain is capable of, unleashing the mindless violence that Mother Earth and Father Sky bestowed on it a hundred million years ago when crocodilian forebearers wallowed in muck with dinosaurs. A prehistoric monument to evolutionary durability, the reptiles have more brains in their tails than their heads. Like mergis who tie their dinghies to brain-dead crocodiles.

I've already started strutting back to the inflatable when I hear murmuring voices from the bridge. I turn back around to see the monster coming alive pushing up on powerful shoulders, resurrecting, scatting with arched back and lifted tail, quick as a lizard back toward the water, clawed toes scratching shells, splashing in beside the dinghy.

"Whoa! Hot damn! Shit!"

The slack in the bow line snaps taut as the beast splashes into the sound, snatching the dingy around, tugging the silent Magdalena out to sea.

"Jesus! Magdalena, hang on, Honey! Hang on!"

I dash after the dingy, getting one leg up over the rubber gunnels, hopping on the other foot to catch up and jump in. Yonder we go, the crocodile towing us around like a rubber duckie. The great tail splashes whitewater as the crocodile dives to the bottom, where it starts spinning in a manner typical to dying crocodilians, churning up galaxies of sparkling mud, bobbing us bow and stern with intermittent pulses of postmortem fury, winding itself up the bow line like a yo-yo, lashing itself fast to the rubber gunnels, close enough to smell, the creature's fury transferred to the dingy, where Magdalena and I hang on to D-rings and each other like wet monkeys on a bucking bull. Thick hide squalling against rubber as the rough beast squirms, Magdalena's flashlight slashing its beam every which way as the dingy lurches and bucks with every slap of tail and every beat and tremor of the ancient reptile's persistent heart.

"Help!!ȋ" The terrified knight in shining armor cries. Do heroes never yell for help? The one quick word that transforms tragedy to comedy, heroes to clowns.

"Help!!" the delighted children cry. "Help, help!" The children's parents laugh.

Only Lucio tries to join the skirmish, climbing down the bridge abutments near the water, too far away to help without swimming. God knows what he plans on doing when he gets out here where we're lashed like Ahab to a dying beast. I've lost my headlamp and fumbled my pistol into the bilge with Magdalena's camera.

"Shine the light, Magdalena! Shine the light!"

Indians chant from the footbridge, presumably for us, the women's colorful dresses muted in moonlight. They don't much seem to care who wins as long as it's a close game. "Shine the light," they mimic, cheering us on, laughing. "Shine the light, Magdalena! Shine the light!" My Indian friends enjoying the show, laughing at me in my time of peril. Humiliated in the eyes of the people I'd hoped to impress.

"Thou hast angered him!" laughs Chino from the bridge, waving his revolver.

"No, Chino, no!" the glowing crocodile towing us into deeper water under the bridge.

"He don't look too dead, mergi," offers Chino, leaning over the railing, duct-taped pistol in one hand, his flat Asian face illuminated by a quick slash of Magdalena's flashlight. "Dust thou want me to shoot him again? Kill him some more?"

"No, no, Chino! Shit no! Don't shoot!" Chino's revolver, lacking the ballistic authority to subdue a crocodile, is fully capable of punching a hole in me, the dinghy or Magdalena, the bravest woman I've ever seen.

"Remove thyself a little bit. I kill him for thee, mergi!" cries Chino.

"No, Chino, no! Somebody get his pistol! *Toma su* goddamn *pistola*!" I scream. The women surround him, taking away his .22 revolver.

Tangled in umbilical coils of bowline, the crocodile raises his sinister head above the water. With quivering sights, I aim at the bullet hole I'd made before and shoot, the blowback spattering Magdalena and me with cold blood. The crocodile settles back into the water, sinking tail first. Muscles will twitch and jerk the whole time as Gordo, the ecolodge guide who doubles as its chef, skins him, the poni taking a long time to die before returning to the Underworld to incarnate demons and rise again. The meat will be served to mergi eco-tourists since the Kuna, who savor Iguanas, won't eat crocodiles or snakes in keeping with the taboo.

Chino struts bowlegged, fretting and shouting orders, his empty holster wagging between his legs as Gordo, surrounded by Indians, eviscerates the crocodile by the hissing light of gas lanterns. A hairless ocelot, maybe a pet, plops from the sewage of his belly. No dogs. No kids. No chickens fall out.

Magdalena in the dinghy is still as stone, her black hair

dripping sequins of seawater, her khaki shirt, open at the top, spattered with crocodile blood, her olive complexion blanched white in moonlight, a cameo face illuminated eerily from below.

*

Trailing a turquoise wake, we cross the bay in silence back to the ecolodge. I'm supercharged with adventure and won't be able to sleep. I figure Magdalena won't be able to either. Now we have adventure in common to talk out, making a story that leaves out Kuna laughter and my humiliating call for help. After being in the fray herself, how can she judge me coward. Maybe she'll want to decompress back on the yacht with a hot shower and a rum or two. Maybe a joint. Review our mutual adventure. Talk late into the night. Who knows what might transpire? I put forth the proposition.

"I'm sick," she moans, staring into a full moon's reflection on the sparkling water. "When I close my eyes, all I see are his." There's a tiny speck of dried blood on her forehead. I reach to wipe it off. She jerks back like a rattlesnake fixing to strike. "You promised me," she says.

Back at the beach of the eco-lodge, Magdalena steps out of the dingy headed for her hut without another word, leaving me to wonder what ails this ghost of the chatty girl I took out to photograph nocturnal fauna. Reckon the poni caught her soul, *or does she just want to wash her hair and go to sleep,* dreaming of crocodiles?

Bad Thinking

There's nothing either good or bad but thinking makes it so. —Hamlet

*E*very dozen steps we flush stingrays, which rise from the silty bottom and fly off like gray moths the size of dinner plates. Agustin, my guide, has told me to wear my chews and shuffle my feet, but the waterlogged Docksiders are abbreviating my breath, wearing me down. I'm soaked to the crotch in tepid water and from crotch to cowlick in sweat. Soon there's the faint pulse of oncoming angina, softer footsteps getting heavier. The stent my cardiologist installed before I sailed to Mexico was working fine until the girl jumped ship in Isla Mujeres, leaving me arguing only with the two Boykin spaniels.

We hit a reef off Bahia de la Ascención which is what I get for arguing with dogs: They say the girl flew hoping to find a real life.

I get barefoot and tie my shoelaces together. A stingray barb has to be less lethal than a heart attack unless, exhausted from dragging my feet, I stumble headfirst on one and take a hit between the eyes. Agustin stalks our quarry like a cross-country skier, hardly glancing down. His Mayan ancestors used stingray barbs to pierce tongue and penis for sacrificial bloodletting while consorts knelt to catch the sacrificial drippings in a bowl. You come from a line of folks like that, and you don't worry so much about your feet. I've had plenty of time to read up on Agustin's ancestry while I wait for a blacksmith to hammer out a prop that looks like the lid of a C-ration can hacked open with a bayonet. I mostly blame the dogs.

My guide turns to see what's holding me up, wagging a

brown finger as I hang the chews around my neck and spray a cold mist of nitroglycerin under my tongue.
"You aren't wearing yours," I remind him.
"Sì, Veektor, but I have deed thees before."
Agustin seems a little arrogant for a guide, maybe because nobody's paying him. His boss, Sirena, a sixties flower child named for a mermaid fetish, made him take me bonefishing to improve my attitude and to give him something to do during the off-season doldrums. Sirena has survived four shipwrecks and was herself abandoned by a husband right here in Punta Allen, where she made the best of things by renting palapas and providing fishing guides. She knows what it's like to take a hit in a foreign country, figures a macabi on a fly rod will cheer up anybody. According to the dogs, my attitude needed work long before the girl went AWOL and we climbed the reef. The upside of this trek is spending an afternoon away from judgmental dogs.
Impatient with my pace, Agustin smiles faintly. He must think the pink nitro spray is to sweeten my breath. Maybe he's insulting me so I'll make him take me back. Or maybe I'm being paranoid. It's true, this is my first time out for bonefish, for macabi.
From experience I know jilted lovers and novice fishermen can be touchy. To be fair, my guide's under no particular obligation to fawn. He's used to sportsmen thrilled to death to fork out big bucks for the chance to shuffle around in mangrove flats up to their nuts in stingrays. No fool, Agustin knows my cracked and occluded heart ain't 100 percent involved in this exercise. I appreciate the gesture, but I've never been much of a saltwater man in the first place. When I run out of canned tuna, I drag a church key with a hook wired to it behind Kestyll: meat fishing. By the time I notice something white skidding around in my wake, it's drowned and inflated. Big ones still kicking I shoot with a Colt Woodsman. If they flop after that, I pour rum in

their gills. The girl fought fish on a nice saltwater outfit she trolled off the stern rail. I'd head up so she could play them. I admit, it was sort of fun to watch her. She'd get so excited she couldn't keep her little feet from dancing. I haven't fooled with her tackle since she left: too much trouble to mess with alone.

*

Agustin slows his stalk and I moonwalk behind him, my knees bumping his hip pockets every time he pauses to scan the glare. A flushed ray hooks around to hide in our smoke. It grazes the top of my naked foot, and I climb Agustin.

"Ess too hot!" he says of the water, squirming out from under me. "V·manos a los manglares." He gestures toward a mangrove patch with his 9-weight. "Over there maybe I show to you some caimanes."

"Do what?" Caiman is a polite misnomer for crocodile in these parts, which translates into a heap more than a souped-up gator with an attitude. The first one I messed with down in Panama broke my thumb after I'd emptied a .44 magnum into it. I don't want to mess with any caiman with a 6-weight Orvis, though I'm no coward. I've even considered suicide as a respite from my latest rejection, maybe leaving a note on my webpage so the world won't view my leaving as just another absentminded blunder. I've fantasized hurling myself off a rocky cliff in Guatemala, where I was headed before engaging the reef. Maybe I'll just sit tight right here in Punta Allen until the next hurricane comes along, but even in my darkest hours of despondency, being torn apart to putrefy piecemeal in a crocodile den yaws far alee of my romantic musings of demise. I'm not afraid of death, just crocodiles, though I suspect Agustin is trying to spook me back to the skiff so he can go home to eat beans.

"Let's go back to the skiff," I suggest. "I've seen caimanes, plenty of them."

*

Agustin poles us around in the skiff. He wants to be able to tell Sirena he gave this venture his best shot.

"*Busca las plumas,*" he advises.

"Feathers? Bonefish have feathers?" There's the plumed serpent of Mayan mythology K'uk'ulkan. Maybe there's a plumed fish, too. Or maybe my guide is taking another jab at the new kid on the block, but I already know what bonefish look like. I've seen plenty of them in fancy magazines like *Gray's Sporting Journal,* some dude in a ventilated pastel shirt bent over one he's fixing to release, grinning like he just sired and delivered the damn thing. To me, bonefish look a lot like bugle mouth bass, which is what we call redhorse suckers in Southwest Georgia. A sucker on a cane pole can give a very decent account of itself, too, though they're mostly taken with gillnets during a spawning run up a creek. Served with grits and hushpuppies and a slab of fatback on the side, there's nothing tastier than a bugle mouth bass, a gourmet fare that inspires a wagging white finger from my cardiologist, but if you ever get invited to Julian Morgan's wild game supper outside Coleman, Georgia, you better scalp your symphony tickets and get on over there. Julian serves everything from rattlesnake to chitterlings, but good ol' boys in the know school around the washpot of sizzling bugles. Old Julian's a good writer, too, and he can yelp spring gobblers into rakish acts of perverse abandon.

Maybe Julian knows if a sucker will take a doughball imitation pitched in with a 3-weight. I'm sure that stalking macabi, a fish you can't even eat, has never entered his mind. So, I digress, a symptom of homesickness I'm entitled to under the circumstances. I'd go home to Mamma, but she's dead.

"The tail, they raise the tail so you will know they are hungry!" Agustin appeals to a Virgin in the perfect Yucatan sky: Maria, Guadalupe, or one from the Maya pantheon recruited into Catholicism by Spanish conquistadors. Mexicans have more virgins than we do. Agustin wears an icon of Guadalupe on the front of his ballcap. Maybe he's torquing his eyeballs up to her while I'm wondering if my meat fishing bothered the girl. Maybe she thought my ideas of closure lack finesse, but to me, boozy euthanasia or a quick pap to the back of the skull is more humane and less messy than gaff and billy club.

*

"She was too young for you, anyway," Bailey, the younger dog said just before we tagged the reef, which is what comes of listening to dogs.

The fickle SOBs view life from a strictly carnivorous point of view, and the girl fed them. It hasn't dawned on them that I'm the one feeding them now, so they do a lot of bitching without contributing much to the overall program, especially Bailey, who's still got a lot of puppy left in him but won't admit it. The young fool knows absolutely nothing about courtship. He tries to hump everything that moves when we go ashore, even cats. I don't know why I dignify his remarks with reply.

"The hell she was!" I shouted, taking my eye off the fathometer to nail him with the captain look, where the buck stops. Translated into English, the captain look says: We're out of sight of land. Which way would you go if you had to swim for it? Bailey snorted, resting his head on oversized paws. Old Rufus, the aged eunuch asleep in the sunshine, hardly stirred when the 25-ton yacht beneath him shook like a wet elephant and squalled to a grinding halt. He just yawned, broke wind, and settled back in while I ran around wondering what to do. Bailey ran around on deck barking at the whitecaps breaking over coral. I need two dogs on a sailboat like I need a case of the clap.

*

"*Tíralo, tíralo!*" Agustin whispers, pointing to the clump of tailing bonefish. I squint into the tropical glare, but the wet shoes around my neck have fogged my glasses. Oh yeah, there they are. The only movement looks like eelgrass waving in current. The fish are standing on their heads, maybe a couple dozen of them in deeper, cooler water, waist deep on me, more critical for Agustin, another reason besides tepid water, stingrays, and crocodiles to be in the skiff.

I'm not casting worth beans with the 6-weight and a hot wind to my back. I actually own an 8-weight I've used once or twice to troll for barracudas, but my guide rejected it on account of its fly line being crazed like Chinese porcelain with a memory like baling wire.

"Do what?"

"Throw heet!" he hisses.

With no cliental obligation to give me first cast, he hauls a couple of false ones 90 degrees from his target, then fires with perfect accuracy to the tailing macabi. His form isn't textbook, more like he's getting after a coachwhip with a tobacco pole, but man is he accurate. His fly shoots like a bullet and lights perfectly at the perimeter of the winding wad of fish. He strips in without a bump, mumbling trilingual curses under his breath.

"*Tíralo, tíralo!*" he repeats, remembering that Sirena told him to make sure the gringo catches a macabi. I'm gawking from the bow, fly line curled around my ankles. Somehow, I manage to get a loop airborne. The wind catches it, and the fly, something small enough for bluegills, makes a couple of bolo flips, alighting in a coil of leader yards wide and short of the tailing school. Again, Agustin appeals to an airborne Virgin, maybe to all of them. Stripping in for another try, I feel a bump—I'm almost sure—though maybe I've snagged a blade of eelgrass. But no, Agustin is watching my line.

"*Pica*," he whispers. "It pecks." More bird talk. Ancient Mayans made no sharp delineations between species. Snakes had feathers and men had claws and wings. Mountains have pissed-off spirits that make them shake and fart fire. Ten meters from the tailing school a truant macabi has picked up my fly.

"I've got one," I announce prosaically. Agustin has told me to point my rod tip down in the direction of the retrieve, has stressed that I set the hook with a firm snatch on the line. Accustomed to crappies, however, I raise the rod gently. I've caught a million speckled perch and know what I'm doing.

The macabi feels something funny and takes off like a sneeze, slack line lashing wildly, scalding my fingers, snapping against the cork butt and whipping out drag.

EEEEEEEEEE EEEEEE goes the little Battenkill. *REEEEEEEEE EEEEE*. I try to slow it down with my hand, but the blurred handle spins like a masonry saw. It strikes the nail of my index finger, spattering blood thinned by anti-coagulants. Now, this hurts. Well, of course it must hurt some, the dogs will say. No, I'll tell them, this Really Hurts!

"*Déjalo, déjalo!*" screams Agustino. "Geave heem eet!" The run spurts into the backing. I'm holding the 6-weight in one hand, the mauled finger of the other clamped between wet knees. Ow, Ouch, Ooow eee!

The fish stops somewhere out yonder on the horizon. I examine a black nail and plug the stricken digit, salty with seawater and blood, into my mouth. It throbs like it's been hit by the power stroke from a claw hammer. I pull it out, fan the air, and put it back in. A barracuda must've hit the bonefish after I hooked it.

"Damn!" I tell Agustin, "That 'cuda must've been eight feet long."

"Reel heem!" shouts Agustin.

"Oh, he's gone," I assure my guide. "He cut me off and kept on trucking. That sucker is in San Pedro, Belize, by now." Or in Florida with the girl, if that's where she is.

"Reel heem!" Agustin has stopped whispering. I wind with my thumb and pinkie.

Sure enough, something is still on my line. The barracuda must've chomped off the bonefish at the gills and left the head. The line goes slack again, though I still haven't retrieved all the backing. The floating fly line canes around, heading our way as if some jagged ort of the barracuda's leftover lunch means to attack the skiff.

I reel as fast as I can with two fingers, like a Colonial Dame holding a teacup.

Then I turn the whole outfit upside down, swapping hands and reeling backwards, recovering all the backing and about half the line before this thing Agustin still insists is a macabi makes a second run even more violent than the first. The first run must've woken it up, energizing its potential. I press down on the rim of the reel to brake it, burning the palm of my good hand (the one without black nails). From the poling platform, Agustin, his drop-jawed chin touching crucifix, leans toward me, holding his 9-weight like a suitcase, while I whoop, bare feet slapping the deck, dancing in a solo joy the girl will never see. The third run melts the drag clean out of the smoking Battenkill, silencing the inverted reel, slinging hoops of line into a bird nest the size of a soccer ball.

I've never played a fish on the reel before, and I'm still not convinced a fish not much longer than my foot can raise all this hell. Even lunker sow bass don't run into the backing. They sound or head for a deadfall, but they don't run, not like the silver-plated son of a bitch I'm connected to. My stented heart thumps painlessly in its bone birdcage; the forgotten nitro spray canister has rolled off into some cranny of bilge. I'm as happy and alive as I've ever been. Mako or mudcat, I don't care. My stagnant lungs are full of fresh air. Infected by my excitement, Agustin is also transformed. He pumps his fist at the Virgins. "*Eso!*" he shouts. "*Eso!*"

The macabi, tiring finally to manageability, glides alongside the skiff. Agustin moves to release it, but I have to have a picture of this fish, which bears absolutely no resemblance whatever to a bugle-mouth bass. I fumble for my camera, as the tamed bonefish swims circles. Time after time I force it toward a photograph. Each time it spooks from the white moon of my face. Escape attempts weaken finally to impotent spasms. Hell, if I can't eat the thing maybe I should get it stuffed, but where would I hang it? There's no taxidermist this side of Cancun to mount it.

It cants, beaten beyond will, sinking into the disturbed silt. Crimson webs trail from laboring gills. The macabi has swallowed the fly. Hey, wait! I don't want to kill it. I can measure it with my foot for the taxidermist while it's still in the water. We're not talking bugle mouth bass here— something to be cooked and eaten. I've just killed the wild, wild thing that unwound my despondency into the backing. Brief joy sours into a ponderous catharsis of sacrificed innocence. I've reached into nature for a wild, wild thing, and my clumsy touch, like a thumbprint on a butterfly, has destroyed it. I've played it too hard and too long, killing it just when I realize a desperate personal need to set it free. Dead, a bonefish, I suddenly know, is nothing! Lost to any definition of essence and not worth remembering. Inversely, by killing it, I've made impossible any kind of spiritual union with its energy, depriving it even of whatever skittish savvy could've survived in its primordial recollection of our encounter. I've disappeared myself, leaving not the dimmest recollection to testify this brief union.

After I've hurled myself off the precipice in Guatemala, no living testament beyond a scarred reef that I ever passed this way will survive me. I wish the macabi, like the girl, had broken off before I took too much. I panic, seized by the nauseating loss of equilibrium of the vain youth who steps up to the mirror to shave a five o'clock shadow and discovers a sagging mug dour with grisly stubble. I suddenly know I should've attended fewer funeral viewings of dead friends and released more fish, not dragged them behind me leaching their bright colors. I wish I'd cut more leaders and ended more contests with coups, not coups de grace from a Colt Woodsman and a shot of cheap rum—wish, at least, that the girl had witnessed less of it. This time I can't even blame the dogs, who, thank God, aren't around for censure. While I'm beating myself up, I could've denocked more arrows, clicked more penultimate safeties back on. Sport that kills needlessly isn't sporting. Even bullfights make more sense than killing a bonefish, and bullfighting's not even a sport. What's in a man that makes him seek out the holy things to destroy? I should've let more contests end before the end—especially with the crocodile. I should've let that one end before the beginning. I should've just tipped my hat and gone ahead on with a happy thumb and no further need for mano a mano engagement. I could've photographed more covey rises...I could've...Whoa.

In my telepathic vision, both dogs raise their heads from cool holes they've dug in Sirena's flowers. That's excessive, they bark. You're going way too far with this thing, past your own nature and beyond the bearable limits of your friends of canine persuasion.

Agustin, uplifted by my elation, seems puzzled by its quick descent. He's stuck with the same glum gringo he started with, but now there's an identifiable cause, a tangible sadness. He lifts the mortal fish gently, bends his flat Mayan face close enough to kiss it goodbye, biting off the line with strong white teeth. He lowers the macabi, saws it gently through the water until the bleeding staunches to a wispy crimson thread. It limps off leaning to one side like a drunk headed home from an Irish funeral. "*No lo pasa nada*," my friendly guide assures me. "It will be all right."

And suddenly everything is all right again. Just like that. The sun sets over the bahía and the sky darkens further by a purple-black cloud larded with lightning that hovers over the jungle. Chaak, the Mayan rain god, comes. Skimming the still water, the skiff leaves a faint phosphorescent trail—cold light that brightens with darkness. I've never understood why phosphorescent plankton lights up, how asexual creatures survived the evolutionary theater of fang and claw by drawing, when perturbed, luminous attention to themselves. According to Sirena, the cold light evidences tiny sea creatures charging up a universe energized by love. Typically, I've tried to catch the green light in a pickle jar in order to own and agitate it when I wanted light, but microscopic dinoflagellates wouldn't bow to my heavy hand. I found myself shaking a beaker of dull seawater.

Though dogs doubt, I promise to teach myself the lesson of not pushing too hard, of not hanging on too tight too long, of not hacking away at veils of mystery shrouding magic. My contagious excitement and my empathy for a dying fish have warmed Agustin, melting the distance between us. I've made a new friend in a land where I thought I'd lost my last. He'll come out tomorrow without being sent. He'll invite me to try out for *palometas* or maybe sábalo.

From Serina's flowerbed the dogs greet me, wagging happy tongues and sawed-off tails. Sirena offers icy glasses of *agua de Jamaica* under the ceiba tree, where we absorb coolness from desultory breezes. "How was it?" she asks. "You get your mind off her for a little while?" My head's still spins, the little Battenkill's drag singing me back to crystalline flats.

"Who?" I muse.

Juice and Joy

What is all this juice and joy?
A strain of the earth's sweet being in the beginning
In Eden garden...Innocent mind and Mayday in girl and boy... —Gerard Manly Hopkin

"*Is* it a swamp hare or a cottontail?"
"Don't know, Vernon."
The rabbit swims from the shoreline, brush and blackberry fringing the slough. A dozen yards out, it turns toward the boat. "You don't reckon it means to attack?" I ask my 80-year-old fishing guide, recalling President Jimmy Carter's 1979 assault by an aggressive bunny he had to repulse with a boat paddle, but this rabbit swerves at the moment of truth, fixing us in a complacent stare of one obsidian eye, swimming by us on the mirrored surface of Lake Hamilton.

"He's throwing them dogs," Vernon concludes. "That's what he's at. Washing his scent." Earlier we saw a few Walker hounds sniffing through the mayapples without supervision. Vern says they swim over to islands to hunt on their own. We'd rousted a yearling whitetail from its hidden bed of bramble and blackberry at the water's edge. It ambled up a hill where dogwood petals floated through late March woods charged with the grand gold of nature's first green. The little deer, like the rabbit we watch now and the hounds it lackadaisically eluded, seemed involved in some perfunctory Edenic venery utterly lacking in urgency.

I've never seen a rabbit in water, though of course I know they, like all natural creatures, can swim. The passing bunny manages at least as well as a yappy dog, quiet as a cat, ears back, nub tail raised coquettishly to keep dry. At first, we mistook it for an otter, dragging a subtle V through the spatter painted pine pollen on the skin of the slough.

I doubt the rabbit could drown its scent to more committed hounds. By fall the entire company—hare, hart, and hounds—will quicken the chase, but in this early Arkansas spring the woods are peacefully involved in quiescent new beginnings.

Originally drawn to the Ouachita (wash-she-ta) Mountains for the area's natural beauty—its refreshing absence of billboards, its scenic rivers and grand lakes, including the 49,000-acre Lake Ouachita—I needed a break from gourmet meals and gallery receptions. Staci, my resplendent and sympathetic tour coordinator, scheduled a fishing guide who took sick, calling Vernon Neighbors to rescue me from a red-carpet tour of a spring water bottling company.

Gratefully, I sink into the bucket seat of Vern's bass boat, sponging sunshine and rigging the multi-piece fly rod I packed into my luggage. Vernon knows what it is, but since his first commission in 1947 he's never had one aboard.

"You set that thing aside, I can put you on some fish," he counsels. "I got plenty of tackle."

Rigged spinning rods and baitcasters line the bow beside the trolling motor. Vern plunders the white plastic bag of last-minute tackle I picked up at Wal-Mart along with my three-day license. The only item he'll sanction is a crappy jig I'd thought to sling, if all else fails, into the stippled pewter shades of baitfish I've seen from the sixth-floor balcony of the Clarion, where I'm garrisoned for a press trip of travel writers. The tour has been tightly organized, rich and demanding. Hot Springs, Arkansas is a Mecca of civilized leisure, an arts community with resorts, gourmet restaurants, film and music festivals, health spas, golf courses, a hippodrome, and a wealth of pleasantly attractive places I've been trying to circumnavigate so I can go fishing.

Hernando de Soto, after stumbling upon the Mississippi River, was in 1541 the first European to visit "the Valley of Vapors," where warring Indian tribes buried tomahawks and puffed calumets for sufficient truce to steep in the healthful waters.

Generating from rain percolating 8,000 feet into the earth, the heated water seeps through cracks and faults leaching minerals from Earth's bones to resurface at the base of Hot Springs Mountain 4,000 years later in thermal springs pulsing a million gallons of hot artesian water every day.

In 1832, Andrew Jackson, notorious enemy to Indians, made Hot Springs the first Federal Reservation, and during Prohibition, Al Capone, as infamous as Jackson and de Soto for homicide, engaged gangland rivals in mutual cease-fires for peaceable soaks. Lucky Luciano was arrested here, ending his frequent pilgrimages to treat venereal diseases. Wyatt Earp and Bat Masterson gambled where Jack Dempsey, John L. Sullivan, Jim Corbett, and Joe Lewis relaxed. Frank and Jesse James robbed a train just outside of town. The Army-Navy Hospital at the south end of Bathhouse Row administered water therapy to wounded WWII soldiers and sailors. Hot Springs justly enjoys a reputation as a temporary retreat of violent factions, a solace for the wounded, infirm, and exhausted in a country's busy history of endemic strife and perennial war.

*

"Boat's old like me," Vernon apologizes, "but she'll get us yonder and back. Sixty- two is all she'll do."

"What's the rush?" For the last five years, I had cruised the Caribbean, reducing sail when my cutter approached 10 knots. The fastest boat I've ever owned was a Thompson Lapstrake with a Johnson Golden Javelin 35. During the middle decade of the 20th century, I tormented fishermen at 32 mph when I was 15 and Vernon was 35. Now I despise fast boats, with their screaming engines and jaunty rooster tails.

187

Vern punches the throttle. The boat squats, bow pointing first to heaven then planing off, lifting haunches to scat across the glassy lake, flushing wild ducks and then passing them. I reach for a seatbelt where there isn't one. Tears stream over flapping jowls into tormented ears. Maniacal eyes behind Vern's thick spectacles squint into the headwind, white hair trailing like an egret crest.

"Damn, Vernon, how fast we going?"

"Sixty-two."

Like most guides, Vernon assumes clients want to catch the most fish as fast as possible. In his arithmetic, we left the hotel dock late and were already in the red, and I spend the first hour trying to calm him down. We buzz from one hope to another like late bees before a cold snap, until we see fish pushing up shad in a bottleneck between wider sections of Lake Hamilton. Vernon cuts the engine. We glide into range.

I tie on the crappy jig and heave a high overhand like a first serve at Wimbledon.

The lure's trajectory hesitates at the neutral peak between momentum and gravity, tailing fly line into the shadow of shoaling fish. Vernon boats a largemouth and a Kentucky bass before I can strip in and sling again. My next cast, a double-hauled Herculean haymaker, nails the jig head smartly into the back of my skull with a report like a .22 short—*PAP*.

"Jesus!" I wheeze. "Ow! God damn!" I drop to my knees on the carpet. Vern, inspired by blasphemy and genuflection, tells me about his church, Mt. Olive Nondenominational, where he's the oldest deacon.

"I got to go with something lighter," I interrupt, rubbing the knot on my scalp. I try a white popper and provoke a strike or two before the feeding fish sink too deep. Vern puts a hybrid and another largemouth in the box.

"Let's just find a pretty place and fish the shore for prespawn bluegills and bigmouth bass," I suggest. "Just take it easy, enjoy the springtime."

"This whole lake's pretty," Vernon says, as indeed it is; a civilized, comfortable beauty inhabited by wealthy human beings. Eager to please, he turns his ballcap around, and we squall off again like a scalded cat past monumental boathouses and funereal lawns chalked by feral geese a long way from Canada. I stomp my own hat beneath both feet, bracing against velocities that water my vision and suck slobber from my mouth.

We yaw around a sharp turn into a quiet cove of deadheads and overhangs. Vernon kills the Evinrude, and we slide in close to the wooded island where we'll find dogs, deer, and a rabbit dallying in prelapsarian harmony, where Vern and I will settle into the comfortable friendship of two senior citizens fishing together on a perfect spring day in the foothills of the Ouachita Mountains.

A late March storm has dumped rainwater on central Arkansas, charging the hesitant hills with the verdant juice and joy of spring. It's unusual and a little haunting to fish with somebody two decades older than I am, a first since my father died. I listen to an abbreviated story of Vern's life in rural Arkansas, predictably fraught with poverty, hardship, booze, and disappointment. He grew up during tough times on the Ouachita River. He lost a child, buried the second wife he'd married after catching the first in adultery, and adopted children who went to jail. To land a job as a machinist, he inflated his four years of schooling to 10 and became a production supervisor of more educated men, who eventually exercised their own brand of white-collar mendacity to filch his pension, but Vernon doesn't linger on Fortune's outrageous slings and arrows, and I won't either. Now he's happily married to his son's mother-in-law, a complicated connection even by Arkansas standards. He courted his wife of 18 years on weekends from Texas after he started drawing Social Security, driving nearly a thousand miles round trip to take her to church. One evening a foreign voice spoke through his mouth.

"We ought to get married," he shocked himself by saying.

"Aw right then," she replied.

Driving home, he panicked over the notion of rushing into a third matrimony to a woman he'd known for barely 40 years. He quickly proposed a lengthy engagement, then came to trust the alien voice that had issued through his own mouth, reckoning the match made by the Lord's steady hand, and this—except for an undaunted willingness to hurl our brittle bones at fiendish velocities—constitutes my only glimpse into the nature of his faith. His ready conversation is seasoned with frequent mention of church activities without a hint of theology, no speculations or conclusions outlining the tenets of his faith, no system of rewards and punishment or prospects of immortality. It's as though the specifics of Vern's faith go without saying. He invites me to Wednesday church supper, a temptation eclipsed by a scheduled visit to Bathhouse Row, where Indians and gangsters before being driven to Oklahoma or arrested by the Feds, set aside fatal agendas to partake of thermal waters.

Amid placid coos of mated mourning doves, I indulge the whimsy of paradisiacal waters brooded by Mother Earth, her juice rising like Eden's fountain of four rivers, placating natural adversity in a garden of respite from war, feud, and venery.

Vernon has promised Staci he'd have me back at the hotel dock by 11:30 for lunch at Quapaw Bath House. At 11:25 we are at least five miles away. I'm flipping a mayfly in March to lethargic sunfish, knowing absolutely I should fish a Woolly Bugger, watching the dry fly float with thistledown on provocative wrinkles, anticipating the sip of bedding fishes where a rabbit rinses its scent to elude perfunctory hounds, and lazy yearlings amble up banks beneath snowy dogwood blossoms and rashes of redbud. I keep quiet about the time. If I can blame a missed tour on Vernon, maybe I can hook back up with him for the afternoon, haul over to the Ouachita River of Vern's invested youth, chunk flies to walleyes and smallmouth bass in whitewater riffles, or just drift on the bosom of a scenic river with a new world crawling by.

Vern releases our fish from the live well into the cove, holding back a bass. "I got a neighbor eats them," he reasons. The big Evinrude erupts. We turn our caps around and catapult as if launched by a slingshot to the dock, where the stately Staci awaits with itinerary and van. The wind has picked up, a chop rattling beneath the hydroplaning hull. "Four minutes!" Vern declares as we approach the Clarion. He kills the engine. The backwash pushes us in.

"What luck, you two?" Staci, in sundress and sandals, hails us with a smile warm as spring sunshine. Self-consciously raking my nails across my disheveled skull, I finger wisdom's latest lump on a thin scalp. As Vern crawls forward to tie us off, I venture one final oxymoronic and impotent gesture of hope: "We wore a hole in the water pulling them out," I testify. "Climb in and hang on; we'll take you where they're thick as fire ants and lions lie with lambs."

"Some other time," she declines brightly. Staci has a delightful capacity of feigning temptation, when in fact she'd rather go in for a root canal than scoot off with two old farts in a vintage boat at velocities that would righteously wreck her hair. "Promises to keep," she reminds me. "We've just time to scrub you up for lunch."

I crab along the dock on bandy legs, taking down the rod. A quick 30 years ago I'd have followed this gorgeous girl gleefully to a chamber reception or on a pale horse through concentric chambers of Hell, but today I yearn only to stay on a clean lake in Arkansas with an energetic guide old enough to be my dead father, swapping gourmet fare for the thermos of coffee and cookies Vern carries to tame his diabetes. I want to drone among early flowers with fumbling bees, to recall bright waters and dream of eternal springtime forever budding and fish waters that sink to the depths of Mother Earth to purify and return. For a precious moment, I want to leave pretty girls on land, anticipating reunions on distant shores with my father, casting milksop and honeycomb into lakes of swimming rabbits, where indolent hounds trail placid deer. I want to lay down pen and books and study with Vernon the ways of fishes, releasing our catch into wobbling reflections of renewable green.

Ideals

...and the waters were divided. —Exodus 14:21

$\mathcal{S}$couting the aisles of Kmart between blue-light specials, I sniffed out a clearance on trout flies and offered $200 for the whole enchilada. The manager sent back the pretty salesclerk with permission to sell them for a nickel apiece.

"Tell him take or leave the two hundred, honey," I said, holding firm. "I don't want you working late counting all those flies."

It's a common infirmity of old farts to buy up useless stuff in bulk because it's there and cheap enough that we think we can afford it. The girl, puzzled that anyone would pay money for artificial pests, made another roundtrip through the swinging doors.

"Aw right, then," she said, loading my shopping cart with armloads of clear plastic cubes labeled by size and pattern, each promising in regal font that it was HAND TIED IN CHINA. It was enough flies to last the rest of my life if I fish them, which I probably won't, as I can't see well enough to tie most of them on.

"They got a sweet deal on a five-gallon bucket of paper clips at Sam's Club," whispered a fellow codger as I stooped for a fallen cube, and rose to a dizzy swarm of floaters, or maybe Chinese flies.

I told Dr. Hotz about it, blaming my new blood pressure pills. "I see spots when I lace my boots, and they dampen my libido, I think."

The specks, he said, are *Muscae volitantes* (literally "flitting flies")—spots, not clots, drifting around in the vitreous humor of old eyes.

"Forget about it and go catch some trout," he said. "'And

stay on the pills or blow a vascular gasket."

Hotz and I used to fish together until his office manager quit letting him take off, which is what happens when you marry your office manager. Now we're basically just trying to outlive each other. I'm older, so his prescriptions assume a canary-in-the-coal- mine ambiguity, but I'll go fishing, and if he's worth a damn as a doctor, I'll outlive him and inherit his stuff

"You got a prostate like an Idaho potato," he added. "Be glad you can still piss standing up."

*

Back at the Airstream, I discovered my father's only son held firm to twice the nickel offer for the flies. "Buy high, sell low," Daddy advised from the hereafter. "Make it up on volume." Surplus breeds generosity, I rationalized. If I stumble on a pattern that will raise a fish, I'll bestow samples upon my fellows of the stream. I need new friends, my old ones being mostly dead.

Online investigation into my floaters additionally identified *Musca* (fly) as the southern constellation that used to be called *Apis* (bee); that *Musca Nova* is a binary object consisting of a star and a black hole. Following the trail of unsolicited information, I somehow discovered my flies were tied by a female adolescent called Min Yon, confined to a rude table in underground Beijing, where she flings her childish soul against tedium, tying imitations of things she has never seen. Her caddices and mayflies are prosaic and uninspired. Her drys, wets, and nymphs lack soul, as distantly removed from the originals as my plastic Jesus, manufactured two doors down the hutong, is from the Transfiguration. I've no more hope these flies will tempt a trout than my dashboard Savior will shunt a collision with a logging truck.

Min Yon has seen mosquito larvae in pools of basement

water and insect husks in dusty webs. Through the tiny window of her cell she has seen locusts and grasshoppers. She knows crickets in cages, and skippers in food. Chinese fish, if any are left, must eat terrestrials. Because hers are good enough, and cheap, too: a nickel apiece if I hadn't bargained up. Because I paid too much, I'm obliged to use them. And there's one pearl worth the whole tribe: a black ant larger than life but not by much, like Greek heroes and duck decoys.

Curiously, there's only one individual in this cube. Into it, from her shadows, Min Yon has woven adolescent dreams into this singular creation, the perfect alchemy of innocence and longing distilled by art into the ideal pissant.

There were, of course, the usual difficulties of internet translations from dialectal Mandarin to Hanzi to English, triggering vernacular ambiguities in international matchmaking services and erectile dysfunction pop-up ads. Still, a background in college teaching has honed skills of intuitive scholarship, except in business, and this enabled me, with patience, to discern the hawks from the handsaws.

*

Following Hotz's orders, I gather bare essentials, including a new motorcycle and Min Yon's flies, and tug my Airstream to Blue Ridge, Georgia, where a warming globe and a lingering drought caused the Department of Natural Resources to dump most of the state's trout hatchery into the Toccoa River at the tailwater beneath Blue Ridge Dam, where even in this drought it's cold enough for arctic char.

The stocking point is popular among both fly rod aficionados and corn-slinging locals with Zebcos, both castes discernible by attitude and attire. Weekend visitors sport the latest catalog garb, heads crowned with Havelock caps that shade pallid necks and Western-style fedoras, as though they'd arrived on camels and horses instead of shining

Land Rovers and Escalades, parked alongside rusting Datsuns and new Harleys in the TVA parking lot.

  You'd think thereíd be territorial fistfights, but the climate here is symbiotic, because fly fishermen never keep a fish and locals never toss one back, hauling home stringers of stocked trout like banana stalks. Until the visitors start bringing stringers, they'll be tolerated as a source of amusement and revenue, and the townies won't run their dapper asses back to Atlanta and Birmingham.

  By their general exodus, commuters alert locals when the gates of the hydroelectric dam will be opened, at irregular intervals without warning lights, bells, whistles, or sirens but posted via a recording on the TVA's 800 number. Locals monitor weekend transients, who with cell phones pinched ear to jaw, monitor the TVA, and, never wet below the knees, withdraw to high ground in plenty of time for locals to take their places for a few quick casts before hoisting their stringers and climbing the berm, timing their exodus just before a wall of whitewater crashes through turbines that would douche them like Egyptians right down to Mineral Springs or Horseshoe Bend or even Copperhill, Tennessee, where the river changes its name to Ocoee. I have the TVA's number in my vest, but I don't own a phone. I just mind the locals.

*

  Arriving in late afternoon, I elbow, unwelcome, into the skirmish line, anomalous to both factions in my high-end yet threadbare gear inherited from a heart surgeon felled by thrombosis. Wearing my dead friend's stuff is next to having him along. I almost feel his hand on the butt of his old Sage, my floaters a warning we might be fishing the same turf soon.

  As the hydroelectric-release shift changes, I sling my ant upon the waters, hooking a native brookie that glitters among the pale stocker rainbows as a pearl lagged into a marble ring of snot agates. A wild brook trout, made by a master jeweler of gold and rubies set in turquoise rings covering firm flesh stained wild-azalea pink right down to the tiny spools of his ribs. A native born into this stream, or at least a holdover with enough time in grade to know an ant was something to eat.

I'd like to say I released this trout and came to know her inner beauty through meditation, but I can't: It inhaled the ant with such wild hunger, I couldn't retrieve it without mortal consequences to one or the other or both, and I'm loath to lose a fly that catches fish. I confess it was in preparation for the pan that I delved her singular beauty, examining twin lobes of pomegranate roe, intruding a thin digestive tract peppered with pissants. But who could shun communion of that consecrated flesh, the host of that wildest spirit, her future doomed to either cannibal browns or peanut oil?

After supper, I sort my flies for Sunday fishing, singling out the special ant and sundry related terrestrials, when suddenly a living hornet dives upon my ant, winds up to maximum RPMs, and lifts off vertically into a poplar. So far this ant has duped a brookie, and now a bee. It would fool a bird, likely, or perched on a scoop of potato salad, me.

Astonished, I resist my hand's urge to swat. I ponder how so little can become so much, how everything is all, woven into the fabric of creation, the seminal energy of the Big Bang, but beyond ethereal. Like my ant, crossing the threshold of perfect illusion to become naturally selected by predator as prey, depriving me of my first mystical connection with the Far East since I was over there in the 1960s and up to no good.

Through musca I scan the dark lace of leaves and evening sky for my ant, hoping the bee will sense fraud and drop it before heading for the hive. Perhaps Min Yon has imparted some mysterious martial element that turns an opponent's bulk against it.

Perhaps the bee, after a quixotic joist of stinger and hook, will soon tumble in mortal missionary tandem with the ant through layers of light-fingered gravity. I vector drift, looking upward through constellations of hypertensive sparks, and suddenly my ant floats down as easily as an actual ant might fall. I tie it on as a dropper dangling from a yellow hopper a stocky might mistake for corn.

All this reminds me how precious my ant is. I'll never find its equal. Min Yon could perish in an earthquake or a cultural revolution or lose her art to puberty or even transfer to the Plastic Jesus Mill two dungeons down. I burn to save her from the Asian Rumpelstiltskin and his prenuptial agreements. Through Matchmakers International, I imagine mail-ordering her for my bride and waiting for her majority. She's maybe eight; I'm 66. When she turns 21, I'll be 80, old for honeymoons, but her magic dubbing will be mine. Spare the goose and win the golden eggs, my father may have said. With proper lighting, her genius could aspire to even better ants. If nothing else, her little fingers, nimble as chopsticks, can tie a tippet.

*

My belly boat provides a forward edge to compensate my casting. I haul it deflated on my motorcycle to the parking lot where I exhale into it sufficient air to displace 240 pounds, along the way flushing up a swarm of floaters. As I descend the high bank into a world spinning on its axis, my float tube gets away, blooping down granite boulders, gathering momentum, T-boning a commuter with a cell phone, punching him headfirst into his honey hole. I thank him for stopping my tube, don swim fins, and fudge in past the skirmish line, vintage waders trickling refrigerant at the crotch.

A few begin catching fish. Then everybody is. A little girl Min Yon's age is tearing them up on her Donald Duck combo and a white Rooster Tail. Rocket Joe, a retired scientist who fishes daily, says he's caught and released 75 since daybreak. You can barely see the bottom for the trout—rainbows and browns, running like mullet. The lawyer who bulldogged my tube and shares my place hooks one too big for a landing net. It peeks through the melting surface like a grouper winched popeyed from the deep, sounding back into our hole.

"You need a gaff," I say.

He clears a space to fight. "Gangway!"

His trophy breaks the tippet. Dejected and wretched, he swivels toe to heel and sloshes up the bank, late again for wine and cheese in Buckhead.

I tilt forward, lashing line and mending down. A strike! Another native flashing gold! Resplendent in my landing net, burnished by fast water into the symphony and song of trout.

I spin my tube to show off my treasure and find myself alone. How much better can it get? A blanket of mist descends, dimming the sun, as on the first morn in Eden. Then, as though the upstream corners of the blanket were grasped and shaken, the static fog becomes a roiling sea of gauze with troughs of silk and peaks of gossamer. I've died and gone to heaven, I decide, a squirming brookie in my hand, a river to myself.

In old black-and-white buccaneer movies, stormy seas couple with fog, illustrating mighty contentions of wind and wave. This is just such a scene, though everywhere but Hollywood it's known that mist and squall don't flock together. But here in the throes of thermal differential, icy air collides and braids into a muggy lull. I feel myself becoming symbolically transcendent, mediating molecules of meat and sky and river—a flightless water bird afloat in water deeper than my legs. A sitting duck.

I barely see the hoary hair of the river hag combed to curls by turbine teeth. I faintly hear the hum, the hiss, the rumble. I faintly feel the upstream suck into the reunion of parted waters rushing the river valley in a crescendo of white noise.

Transfixed, I bob and squint beyond the roiling mist into a wall of roiling water. Angry, spitting, hissing, feline water. A cauliflower ball of boiling water. A mushroom cloud of water. Waterfalls of water falling. Cold as frozen razor blades.

I run in place. Flailing arms and sculling feet.

Help.

Lifted upon the blade of a tsunami, I surf the curl until it tacos me, somersaulting cartwheels, floaters into bubbles, river into shards of fallen sky—now a centaur, now Bruegel's Icarus, nose turned keel, webbed feet kicking sky. Waders ballooning water cold enough to stop a reptile's heart, I spit and gasp, inhaling mist and spray. My tube, slack with shrunken air, is swept through the channel's curve and into the skeletal arms of a bone white sycamore.

A frantic squirrel, I claw the branch that bends me to the sinking bank, snatching at eroded roots. I crawl through brambles on knees padded thicker than some thorns, through a nebula of systolic fireflies, dragging my dead friend's Sage by the tip.

Above the threat of rising flood, I turn to watch the flotsam of my flies, my magic ant, my twitching net, dissolving into a vortex of spangled fog, into adjacent dimensions where ideal forms exist in perfect worlds of fishes. Where nothing ever lives or dies but as potential.

Fish Tale

Many men go fishing all of their lives without knowing that it is not fish they are after. —Henry David Thoreau

"Whoa! That's a real by-god Native American person down there by that waterfall."

She pulls over. "What makes you think so?" Forever skeptical, this 40-something-kid forgets I cruised the Caribbean for five years, my first mate a Kuna Indian.

"Trust me."

Crabbing down the bank, I hail, "How do I get to Shaver's Fork?"

He points his pipe upstream, a New Age gadget, glass and chrome, no calumet. Fetid wisps of smoke drift into the falls, folding into mist.

Who else but a Cherokee, squatting on a rock, dreadlocks sprouting from an indigo headband like a crow stuffed in a coffee can.

"Say, is that *asema* you're smoking there, chief?" Wherever I find Native Americans, I ask around for *Nicotiana rustica*, old tobacco eight times stronger than a Lucky Strike, grown in lightning strikes, stowed underground in deerskin, hair-side out, used these days for ceremonies, and to commemorate the poison they laid on Sir Walter Raleigh a while back as an act of long-range vengeance.

There's a corncob pipe in the glovebox, a hillbilly gag acquired from a welcome center after we'd spent a night in a place raped by mining—truncated mountains, jagged craters, bloodshot clay spray-painted with grass seed and abandoned to four-wheelers and gaunt elk roaming chain-link perimeters dreaming of forage and euthanasia.

"Ugh," he weeps, wiping his nose, offering.

"I'm good for now," I say. "How about I score a pinch for later?"

The girl up there honking. Afternoon oozing west.

*

Three months from now we'll watch these woods fill up with snow, the stems of autumn leaves snapping beneath the weight of diamond dust, spilling whole galaxies into the tawny beams of morning sun. But now I sit on a warm rock dripping shadows. I knot a bead-head dropper on the Dave's Hopper that duped a fingerling, light the corncob stuffed with rustica, and through a cloud of pungent smoke I watch my fly box—damn—wink through a riffle, bob around the bend.

I hop off my rock, loping downstream and giving chase, sloshing crotch and jamming toes, spooking trout from here to Maryland, until it dawns on me it's a rhododendron bloom I'm after and all my pricey flies have gone the way of the fishes.

Where File Creek meets Shaver's Fork, the bird-track map makes sense.

Railroad tracks, for stocking trout by the boxcar. I snag a pale brookie just upstream from a Fish for Fun sign nailed on a juniper.

"Aw," says the girl tugging on hip boots, "a baby!"

A woman's heart for infant creatures, scorpion or shrew. Without her censure, this fish would sizzle in a skillet—my first catch in West Virginia, July having stewed all but mudcats to lethargy.

A sheepish grin puts supper back. Writing or fishing, I'm haunted—this editor, who wasn't even born when I returned from some Asian mischief. Yet still, she mothers me, ever since flying to Belize to get me out of jail, my yacht stripped raw by pirates, abandoned like a shoe on a dead reef in the Bay of Honduras.

She says I'm not a sailor, should return unwanted to the classroom, out of harm's way. But no: I'm more than that. I'm all I've ever met. I've drunk up *chicha*, eaten crocodiles, and have a heap of noble work still left undone.

She'd have me finish novels, bury life in print and sum it up, but old men know the final quarter is the time to grab the ball and run, not huddle up. Her love would undo what I've done. Yet I must also love this muse and warden, whose nurture underrates a winter lion in his time to roar, not yodel on in swan songs sung too long.

I give her all, is why I ramble on.

And on," she sighs, wading up as I start down, alone together.

*

Yikes, bare shins twisting braids of white-haired water witches. It's cold enough for arctic smelt in here, this lonely, lovely river, stained sepia by summer rain, these wind shadows burnished bronze by summer breezes. I pause with heavy breath. The leaden air I suck transmutes, and everything turns amber, amber, amber—windswept clouds spun Rumpelstiltskin gold in fencing strobes of sun.

Here's déjà vu: Bit by a rattlesnake one fall, I watched an autumn breeze transfigure Georgia pines and all the world to shades of El Dorado, a gilded world with vibrant undercoats of tarnished antique gold. Look, look! I marveled to the pal who sped me to a surgeon.

Hang on! He said.

Now, free of angst, I watch again a leaden world transmute—a mountain stream, wood, tree, and rock imbued with aureate magic. Shivering, I sit on a warmer rock, anoxia of the chase fanning this lonely river valley with a golden breeze that sizzles aspen, bone-white sycamore, and ash to miraculous transfiguration. Broke loose by dizzy-headed coughing—how did they get Sir Walter to smoke this stuff?—another rhododendron plops in the drink. Well bless my soul, I've stumbled on a perfect place to fish: a little waterfall, plunge pool of molten iron webbed into a net of flaxen gold, as if this moment stalks me orbiting against the clock into a ducking vortex with the bead-head on the hopper, spinning in and out of time and self.

But wait! A flash of white eclipses half the pool and swallows up the whirligig of tandem flies, tumbling, a towel in the port light of a washing machine, flagging out of sight into the *chiaroscuro* of slashing light and sepia shadow.

Throbbing heavily, this thing turns inside out, a flower folding in upon itself. Dead weight and living pulse too strong to be a fish. But what? Some lobe-fin throwback from a mucky age? Landlocked salmon? Water witch? Uktena? Water cougar? Siren or Lorelei?

A 3-weight rod won't pry this kraken up, but like the new-growth green of orchard switches, neither will it break from lashing childish legs in howling circles.

Thump, thump it goes. Sparring, shadow boxing, throbbing around down there, getting bearings, making plans.

I know I'll never land this monster's mother; I just want to see her, know how big she is—what the hell she is.

She shoulders from her cave to take a walk, feel out the opposition. Then quick as youth she jerks my line downstream—*joo—joo—joooup*—my yo-yo of a reel spewing line out to the backing. Then pausing for a somersault in amber air, she shatters all the world's unraveling tapestry, splitting even me in two. One half, a younger me, gives chase downstream, kicking lace behind him like a coot. My other half, a gargoyle squatting on his mossy rock beholding the blither spirit in gilded nimbus and a better hat, who waltzes stones across a sighing river—rod high, immune to gravity—in a poetry of motion that puts to shabby shame Brad Pitt on the Gallatin near Missoula.

So goes this interplay of youth and jaded doppelganger until a sudden clack of knees on stone recalls them both—the stuff of dreams and meat and uncut rustica, converged into a single epiphany of howling agony.

Then pausing for a farewell somersault into the amber air, the fish-monster flies—sweet Lord and Holy Mackerel—shattering topaz into shards, trailing pearls and prisms. What is this thing that flashes arcs of Iris, and where's my editor? Who'll witness this and who'll believe?

Who hasn't felt the slump of soul when floating line falls slack? I've waited all my life for such a fish—a life of fingerlings, small minds, and tedious law; of pirates, apathetic students, harried wives; and now my proof and prize has disappeared as though it never was. I want to die, to sleep, to tumble fin and elbow down a continental slope, sink into the death-wish fishing shadows brings: to die, to sleep into the icy, golden world of fishes, a better place to go, it seems, than Third World prisons.

But whoa again! The fish starts back upstream, towing 90 feet of line, a Grendel's mother scourged by a buggy whip and headed home. Back under me, the bloody knees that never crooked in prayer. A reeling frenzy gaining line, a lunatic who'd save a diving kite.

Returning to her cave, she churns the passing pools to smoke. I've never known a better fish—not photographed, not mounted on a Buick dealer's showroom wall or laced in parsley on a silver platter.

Locked in timelessness, she moons the tighter orbit, sluggish as a flathead cat, heavy as a flooded wader. If I don't land her soon, she'll kill herself and maybe me, my nitro in a glovebox where a corncob used to be. I swear I'll never fish again without a net.

Oh God, the single need to touch where first I only sought to see—to spark the gap of our divergent worlds, the Sistine fingertip that charges latent clay with mortal hubris.

205

Please, fish, come in and let me let us go—I swear to God I'll break us aloose from each other.

I drop the rod and dog-crawl after her to shallow water, and the rod transforms into a serpent hopping on its tail in puffs of silt, the haughty tip striking like a pissed-off rattlesnake. I lift her in my arms and fall back on my ass. Great God! She's in my lap and longer than my leg! This gulping maw could swallow up my arm.

Embraced, we roll. Face to face, blurred nose to nose. Crowned teeth gnawing on a uni knot. Sipping where she sips. Lips touching lips. How can I know her eyes don't close with mine?

Cherokee immortals living under rocks can snatch a human soul beneath a stream. The slough returns to masquerade to wives and friends and dies.

This fish and I are bound and tethered by tangled line and moiling webs of blood from leaking knees snatched at by minnows. My hands support her throat, saw her through quicker water. I feel a colder pulse, more frantic even than my own, a knot of tachycardia, a twisted vein in palsy ribbed around by numb arthritic fingers. A kinship of fellow mortals inspired by ragged lungs in hyperventilation.

She kicks away and sinks into a stagnant pool a fathom beneath a mirrored gargoyle's sagging face, a wobbling rainbow canted on the mica-spangled sand and polished pebbles. She's suffocating, stressed past recharging breath.

A nimrod Beowulf plunges down to swim her up before I know it. A frail old fart in foggy spectacles on a dripping nose emerges through the mosaic of fractured sky, dog paddling with one paw, the other hooped over a giant fish like wino lovers crabbing home.

I'd never shame this rainbow to a record book. It never crossed my mind—I swear to God, except a time or two—and I'm loath to mount her visage rocking glassy-eyed on an Airstream wall beside *memento mori* of turkey beards.

I'd sooner snag my lip while gnawing off the dropper and have her drag me to her treasure cave to hang with cloudy carapace and mortal coils. But now a duel of clumsy cunning has broken her, doomed her to carrion for swarming crawfish.

Away with that! By God, if she must die, I'll build a fire right here with soggy matches, cook and eat her gravely as a cannibal an only child, host made by danse macabre on two ends of an orchard switch and eaten. Where should our rainbows fade but down the gullets of a kindred kind, committed to the timeless fang and claw of definitive predation?

I fumble up a passing stone to bludgeon her. So, what's a couple hundred yards and who's to know? And man's law, anyway. Alone, the girl upstream, in all these million acres of shrinking wilderness.

An amber bubble wobbles up and winks?Iíll know! The fish mouth yawns. And you will, too, you lawless son of a bitch. But go ahead, Iím tired and grown too old almost to catch enough to eat.

To kill a talking fish?more blasphemous than murder. Then we are swept into hissing run, tumbling over rocks that crawl upstream above the buried voices, when suddenly a sluggish tail kicks free into a twisting, effervescent chute: a miraculous resurrection.

*

Back at the truck, the girl red-marks some poor jerk's manuscript, not mine. I stumble up confounded with the goofy grin I started with at birth, the world I've tumbled through restored to innocence of milt and honey.

"Good God, what happened?"

"A fish," I whisper, shivering. "Don't speak, just feel this slime on me. Oh, don't you see the very air is fretted even now with golden fire?" Thin arms span monstrous fishes, amber skies.

She wipes her hands. Her skeptic squint. "You've got your shooting glasses on," she notes, this Apollonius, her sharp eyes melting every shade of fantasy. "You lost the Polaroids a week ago in Tennessee."

And true enough, the glasses off, the splendor dims a shade—but not altogether.

"She slimed me boot to belly. Just feel of it all in through here."

"She?"

"Female."

*

Back at the Airstream she measures me as for a coffin. Her seamstress tape snakes ankles polished bare by seven decades of socks. It crawls beneath her fingers around a knobby knee made proud from kissing stone. It slithers past atrophied thighs loosely bound in Jockey briefs. It stops as if to coil upon a fleshy mound around the rifled crater of a belly button.

How thin these flaccid limbs have grown so soon through age and jail house dieting; dull alabaster, tattooed with marbled veins of lapis lazuli, cross-hatched now with ruby scratches like a child's switched in howling orbit.

Uncapping pen, she enters measurements into the flyleaf of an ex-wife's Bible, the kind of thing a woman leaves behind with fondue forks to make more suitcase room for silver.

"You didn't stretch her out a little bit?" the cynic says.

"For who? This keeps a living fish from growing!"

"For whom!" she edits. "My, my, is this a little much?"

Behold a fated love affair! This girl who touched my slime and still lacks faith, the relic of a wet belt coiled yonder, minutely spangled in Lilliputian sequins, with one much larger diadem of cloudy mica.

"You had slime," she says, "all over you."

"I never claimed she was as long as me."

"As I," she clucks. "No, not even you can write that in a Holy Bible."

So unembellished here by burnished leaves, October snow, or offshore breezes lies the bottom line, raw statistics noted in a holy text absent of names of born and dying kin:

Rainbow 31.5 inches. 7/26/09, 5:30 pm, Shavers Fork off File Creek Rd. 3 wt line w/6 x tippet, #8 Dave's Hopper, bead-head Woolly Bugger dropper.

*

The fish I grappled for my soul and lost to water spirits, released back to the web of living things by the better man we all become by dying.

Great fish will spawn or go by process through the bowels of poets, kings, and beggars. Our lives sans soul embossed on Grecian urns or buried deep in odes.

Without some testament, our rainbows fade into the common light of day or flit away on threadbare spinner wings.

It's better not to mouth these things too much, but writing's what I do and thus am bound to scrutiny of infidels and editors.

Our souls, thank God, are lent, not lost, to water spirits hostage underneath the river stones where they belong. Our mortal portions stagger home to walk with sweethearts, wives, and friends, but when we feel the loss most keen, we take a Bible out and read a testament beneath a maiden name who never set a stylish foot into a travel trailer.

By wrestling angels, devils, editors, and fish, we learn what snatches souls and how to get them back. So, where's that matchbook map, my 3-weight wand, Uktena scale and corncob calumet? There may still be residue of windbroke hope for grace to conjure pristine rivers, golden dreams.

The Devil's Game

Though wast not born for death, immortal Bird! No hungry generations tread thee down;
The voice I hear this passing night was heard In ancient days by emperor and clown. —John Keats

*B*efore Orion fades into a frosty Dixie dawn, we step from a stolen rowboat into the owls. We've spent the night at my house on the Flint, swept ourselves downstream with Tillie's broom to a spring-fed backwater, where wood ducks feed and roost year-round. Johann has my daddy's solid pump. I tote a nickel-barrel trap gun from a cousin once removed, twice if you count his one-way trip to England in 1942, the year I became heir and incarnation of his grieving parents' legacy.

Tillie will raise hell about the broom when she comes in to get my younger sister off to school. "The debil in them boys," she'll tell my high-strung mother. "They both slap full debilment."

With first light the woodies whistle in, plopping like footballs into webs of silver.

The drake ordained to forever haunt me appears, chuckling to his hens by way of introduction. He swims in range of where I squat sucking breath to quiet my drumming heart. At 15, I know it's a deadly sin to shoot a wood duck on the water, but I'm scared if I jump him, he'll scat back into the outer dark. I can't tolerate the thought of Johann bagging a duck before I do.

Tillie's devil tells me, "Shoot!" The muzzle licks lightning into partial dark, stippling the floating silhouette, thunder launching Johann wide-eyed from his stump.

*

Mother Nature underwent a hormonal spasm creating the wood duck, a creature of splendid excess that the dull mind disremembers, like a bluebird's blue, from one sighting to the next. Each feather sings a microcosmic miracle that patterns all creation: buff, chestnut, gold, iridescent green slashed in chevrons of transfigurative white. I've heard it bragged that eastern fly fishermen can swap out wood duck feathers for Western wives.

My murdered prize floats head down in feather shavings and trembling quicksilver. From an acrid mist of cordite and sulfur, I rake it to me with a broken limb, Johann bleating blasphemy from across the pond. More ready than adept, he hunts because there's nothing else to do but go to school. His dad, a chemist, escaped the Third Reich for Philadelphia, where he married the eleventh child of an Irish railroad executive, who escaped the 1937 West Virginia flood. To Hans she bore Johanna, a timid scholar with a perfect grade point average, and Johann, of whom we roughly speak. Hans brought them south to a white house in a pecan orchard right next door to Merck, where he brewed up toxins to discharge into the Flint River four river miles downstream from my house. Away from his crucible, Hans bowled, a suspect avocation in an agrarian South where fathers fished and hunted. I don't remember Hans at home except a time or two, his elbows propped on a tablecloth of Irish lace from Mrs. Bleicher's doomed trousseau. Alone, he grunted down his supper, rushing with his balls and bowling shirt uptown to Midtown Alleys.

Mrs. Bleicher, the most alienated papist in the Jim Crow Bible Belt, was the loving presence in our lives, her living room a sanctuary for broke-wing birds, stray cats, and poisoned dogs she took into the house she never left except for Mass.

War babies sired by war babies, we'd have whiskers before television or conditioned air, the final generation crawling between heaven and earth in the grim penumbra of the National Conscription Act, the mandatory manhood that eclipsed us from our mothers before we got old enough to vote or drink a glass of beer.

In the urgency to live out childhood before unsown wild seeds got fed into the national grist, we enjoyed an easy truancy enabled by permissive mothers who feared surviving us, whose maternal instincts told them "police actions" were as dangerous to sons as world wars were to husbands, fathers, and cousins.

The mothers gave us boys wider tether than their daughters. Even Johann's mother grimly acquiesced to the provincial assumption that marksmanship trumped algebra as the more immediate survival skill, and Southern boys entered basic training knowing how to shoot.

For us these were the best of times, for we had woods and fields to frolic in. By and large we were pampered, irresponsible adolescents whose fathers hoped we would mature in the army, if we survived it.

*

Johann, alerted that I've duped him to the hind teat of the action, scrambles upon a foot log adjacent to the fiddlesticks beaver dam I crossed in moonlight. Midway across, he's covered up with ducks I've flushed. Shouldering the old man's scattergun, he splashes backwards into the misty pond without a shot as I return swinging the garish banner of my duck. He flounders up an icy bank, furious, armed, and soaked through bulky clothing to the marrow. At first there's nothing mortal in the lay beyond my school chum's murderous rivalry. The pond's springs exit limestone bedrock at a constant Fahrenheit of 68 degrees, more than twice the temperature of our ambient air, so there's absolutely no threat of hypothermia until his garments freeze, hoarfrost forming on his cap. We know we'll never sweep the boat upstream in time to save his life or get to school on time, so we set out through catclaw and palmetto, following a discharge pipe to Johann's mother's snug menagerie of convalescing critters.

Johann lurches woodenly along in frozen clothes, legs splinted stiff, swinging arms encased in sleeves of ice, each footstep crackling shards between his socks and bowling shoes, while I galumph along bearing shotguns and a swinging duck. I goad him, aping his singular ambulation. "It's alive!" I taunt to the cobbled heap of scavenged parts self-exiled to the Arctic Circle, but he's too miserable to throw a punch or run me down for murdering.

At home, his mother ushers her iceberg offspring into a tepid shower. Cloyed with hot chocolate, we hitch to school a little late, the duck ensconced into the game pouch of my canvas jacket. I'm scared to leave it in Mrs. Bleicher's Frigidaire lest she pluck and cook it before I'm done coveting—an improbable notion for a woman who'd never go near that duck unless to nurse it back to life.

At school, the devil makes me yank it out and wag its neck at squealing girls. We are what we are, blunt-fanged carnivores who breed and feed and sleep and wallow in a mire of ignoble imperfection.

But there's solace at Johann's house, when Hans is out of it. We'd barge into Mrs. Bleicher's sanctuary, where she sat in her wingback chair, serene as a bodhisattva faintly smiling, a Beethoven concerto winding out of the Victrola, a bandaged critter in her generous lap. It ain't no telling what we'd be without her loving presence in our lives, for she was quick to nurture critters great and small, including me and Johann.

We'd spend our first year of college in Mexico. Rivals for our high school sweetheart—my first wife. We'd climb the ice-glazed slopes of sulfur fuming Popocatepetl. Spikes, ice axes, winding buzzards far below, but soon the '60s slung us into different orbits. Johann, a weekend warrior, would end up bivouacked in San Francisco's Haight-Ashbury, where he and the other flower children dreamed better alternatives to perpetual war. I would watch long V's of ducks flare and wobble over Fort Knox rifle ranges, conveying my lonely spirit over burnished autumn hills to Georgia, then from isolated observation posts in Korea's DMZ, where Asian flocks fled the harsh Manchurian winter to warmer latitudes. Maybe Viet Nam.

I might as well own up to one other drake, shot down on the cold, cold morning of my first wedding day, back when cypress ponds still froze. Two woodies whistled high and fast—ear, ear, ear—above the trees into a solid gristmill pond. I heard the trap gun blast before I knew I'd fired, in a Hail Mary farewell to bachelorhood. Incredibly, the duck folded into a meteoric arc that smacked a silver web into the ice, skidding for a football field to rest on a thin smear of heart blood between Glory and opaque reflection.

This time, the devil didn't make me do a thing. He shot that duck himself with the trap gun I acquired with the removal of a second cousin.

*

A half century after his baptism in the beaver pond, I locate Johann, an alternative-school principal in coastal North Carolina, asking him if he remembers hunting ducks with me. "When the skunk sprayed me and the teachers sent me home?" he wants to know.

"No, no. When you fell in the beaver pond and damn near froze to death."

"Oh, then."

"Come home, we'll hunt some more. I'll keep you dry and let you kill a duck."

"We're too old to steal another boat," he says.
"I've got a boat, a little outboard on it."
There's a pause of slipping cogs. "Hey, lookit: come up here to North Carolina.
We'll make Justin take us out."
Well, I'll be damned: venery stifled in the Bleicher line erupted into Johann's oldest son, a guide for salmon in Alaskan summers, for winter ducks on the Outer Banks.
I'm not even sure wood ducks live on the coast of North Carolina. My provincial heart's geography says summer ducks live and nest in trees year-round exclusively downriver from my childhood home. A duck to Johann, who's never even shot at one, is a duck, but there's a roundness to the plan: two old farts nudging a seventh decade, winding closer to the falconer, undertaking a bygone enterprise botched 50 years ago. This will be a time for summing up, for finding ourselves in what we used to be, seeing ourselves somewhat as others see us. I sure as hell ain't up for scaling any Mexican volcanoes.
"Uh, well, aw right then."
Killing ducks had never been much more than it was for Johann or Ben, the third musketeer, whose challenged eyesight would save him from the draft. Unlike bullfights and police actions, duck hunting didn't absolutely require blood sacrifice. Wood ducks taste good, sure, and Tillie cooked them up more succulent than anything that flies. Still, we invited Ben, whose parents had known he'd be deferred and disallowed his cutting school for venery. He said Hell no, he wouldn't go, although he'd grace us with a bit of solid information.
"Do you bastards even know why the V is longer on one side?"
"No, why?"
"More ducks on that side!" He hangs up the phone.

In all these years, except a time or two—one funeral, and a boozy school reunion—we haven't seen each other or known wives and children. Launching our skiff, a younger Johann peers from Justin's easy smile. A stocky outdoorsman in his 30's, some twice the age of Johann when his Jockeys froze, he has suited up his dad in thermal coveralls, a Russian cosmonaut's leather cap, and gigantic boots that could've printed man's first step in lunar dust at a time when his dad and I were attending graduate school and learning to be teachers, because we didnít know another blessed thing.

Slipping on the frosty bilge, we fall down on our asses, pawing around like polar bears, wind-broke and wheezing by the time Justin drags our collars onto a seat.

Bouncing across the sound through frigid spray reminds me why I quit hunting ducks along with soldiering in the 1960s.

Justin's blind is built on a spot held exclusively for duck blinds since hungry generations of carpetbagger industrialists flooded the flyway after the Civil War. In a flotsam of decoys, we huddle around a propane heater. A great orange of a sun rises out of the Atlantic, coloring the shallows of Currituck Sound on a bluebird day—the kind of dawn that jacks quail hunters out of bed and rolls a ducker over back to sleep. It's cold as Korea, a bitter wind pushing out the low we should've hunted, inspiring migrations of ducks, geese, and swans flying high as clouds, if there'd been any, hitching the wave of high pressure on down to South America.

This bothers Justin, but not us, especially not his father, who's never killed a duck. We're toasting hot chocolate to Mrs. Bleicher when the brace of pintails drops in like timid guests arriving late.

I cleanly miss the half-ass shot I take, but Justin drops the mated pair with three apologetic shots that bark like bells in high cold air. Johann blinks. Predictably, on purpose, he has left my father's pump, unused for half a century, in Justin's truck.

Pampered by dove fields and indoor living, my neurotic Boykin spaniel wakes up yapping. He springs into the icy sound to find his tennis ball, tangling in decoys. Justin steps down into the hidden skiff to rescue him and retrieve the ducks—beautiful ducks, wonderful ducks—but not woodies.

*

I go back to Georgia without the closure of the shame acquired a half century ago by blasting a wood duck on the water. I launch a boat I paid good money for and scoot downriver. I load the old man's pump with high-brass shells, stepping back in time into the swamp. Though Merck has closed, the crusty pipe's still there. The pond is lower now but the dam's still there, too, managed by living, gnawing beavers. Algae-tinted water trickles through the daub and wattle where crystal ribbons once gushed.

Johann's foot log, thinned to a heartwood core, still bridges stiller water. I sit on Johann's stump, made softer now by spongy moss. I know the drake will come, the same or its perfected progeny. This time I'll take him properly in flight and wind up this shame before I die—this deal is that important!

Before sundown they splash in as if ordained, the fated drake swimming eagerly from the flock, the pumping iridescent neck dragging silver where I squat, as unafraid of me as if I've already died. So near he comes, I think I see my youthful cameo in an obsidian eye set inside a ruby ring. This alpha and omega duck, a first transmogrified into the last, I mean to skin out with a scalpel, flay the colored hide into a cloak of many colors, tufted topknot to the claws on golden webs, a cloak more precious than a borrowed wife or homespun flies bestowed on living friends.

I'll scorch the oxblood heart in steaming gravy, stuff the breast with orange and slather it with marmalade to slowly bake until the wine-dark meat falls from alabaster bones. I'll make its wildness mine in unctuous mastication, feel my pores ignite to sips of moonshine.

"All this," says the devil at my elbow, whose kingdom comes when all green twigs are dry and every precious living thing that can turn a buck is sold. "All this to justify one damned duck you busted on the water fifty years ago. You'll wing it or miss it if you let it fly. Who's to know?"

I'm not surprised to find him here again. He snaked his way into this fading paradise through a crusty discharge pipe, just like before.

"I've shot ducks on the wing," I brag. "The morning of my wedding day, I stood on ice and..."

"You think I wasn't there?" he snorts. "I put you on those ducks and fired the gun. You'd never make that devil of a shot alone. Look at you now, a shadow of the lousy shot you were and ten times slower. You'd better blast again before it flies."

This time, by God, I shun temptation. I've lived a whole life to get this right. No way I'll miss a duck I've been shooting for 50 years. I'll kill it on the wing or dare damnation.

My blood is up. I'll jump this duck and take him as he levels off, before he turns on his afterburner. "This duck is history," I hiss.

"Well, pride's my business, too," the devil says. "I'll bet immortal youth against your soul, you'll never even get your safety off in time to nail this duck. But win or lose," he adds, "I'll grant one bonus revelation."

"You're on," I whisper, springing from my stump. The

crack of stubborn knees erupts the flock, kaleidoscopic shrapnel twisting up like bats fired from a cannon. "Get behind me, devil! Clear the firing line!"

The drake, betrayed by brotherhood, splashes off the water, trailing pearls. As the squealing anthem of his fellows fades, we rise together (standing up so quick I get a little dizzy). The low sun sets my rising drake on fire. He tumbles higher, slinging embers, sparks, and prisms.

I hoist the gun, appendage of predation, from port to shoulder, suck penultimate breath. I have forever. Still he doesn't level off, but rises higher. I push the safety—damn! Push hard—trigger finger blanching to the knuckle—son of a bitch! I quit the safety, tug the trigger till it crumbles. The duck, ascending higher, trails a wake of sparks and ashes through cauliflower clouds until I lose it with my soul in the setting sun, where what decays is seared into becoming, fading into the tender, cold, eternal night.

"Well, I'll be damned" I say. The devil's in the details and the vanity of preening wives. "Well then, what's the wisdom that my soul was bartered for?"

Fiendish laughter ebbs to baleful grinning. "Just this," he gloats. "The soul's a happy accident, quickly lost as falling off a log. You should've oiled your daddy's gun."

A Fine Kettle of Fish

How cheerfully he seems to grin, How neatly spreads his claws,
And welcomes little fishes in,
With gently smiling jaws! —Lewis Carroll

Joe Lawson, a crabber who took me under his wing and introduced me to St. Marks society, showed me where to go—a backwater slough of the Wakulla River, where the bream are bedding in water too shallow and too clear to fish in full daylight. I paddle my kayak through the mist upstream to my waypoint, the first of Joe's crab pots, marked by his green Styrofoam buoy. The slough opens into a lagoon, where the full moon brings spring tides and bedding bluegills. There's no dry land at the eastern edge of the beds. The shore is swampy with pickerelweed, water hyacinth, and hydrilla.

Beyond that is a tropical backdrop of cypress, tupelo, water oak, and one palm tree. I arrive by kayak in darkness, just before the full moon sets to a rising sun. A low lying mist tickles my nose.

The source of the Wakulla River is Wakulla Springs, the largest and deepest spring in the United States. Through glass-bottom boats, tourists can see mastodon bones at the mouth of the cave, 190 feet from the surface. Tarzan movies starring Johnny Weissmuller were filmed here, Hollywood's idea of Africa, where monstrous alligators standing in for crocodiles bask in the sunshine. A horror film, *The Return of the Creature from the Black Lagoon*, was shot here as well. The wide-bellied cypress trees with Gothic roots and long beards of Spanish moss lend themselves to an eerie setting in the moonlit fog. The Wakulla is nine miles long. It joins the St. Marks at Fort St. Marcos, and together they flow into the Gulf of Mexico.

I scan the thin mist with my flashlight. Red alligator eyes glowing like automobile taillights are scattered across the lagoon, more than a dozen pairs. I paddle quietly through them, each submerging tail first as I pass. Judged by the distance between eyes and nose (an inch between eye and nose equals one foot of gator), most of the reptiles are less than five feet, but there are some eight-footers and one or two larger than that. Gators can get big in this tidal river. Joe has a skull in his living room more than 12 inches from knobby eye to button nose. He measured the monster at just over 13 feet. I nurse a grudge against Wakulla alligators, since one caught and ate my beloved Boykin spaniel, Geechee. Joe showed me where the dog tracks and gator tracks commingled at the low-tide mark near the ramp at Shell Island, where I'd set up my Airstream for the summer quarter, clearing out cobwebs gathered from teaching freshmen how to write. I suspect the big gator that hangs around the fish cleaning station. You've got to blame something else when you know a misfortune is your own damn fault.

The bream that inhabit these crystal waters are the sweetest you've ever tasted. I've bought a sturdy chain stringer at Shell Island Fish Camp. I plan to fill it with bluegills and return to camp with the rising sun. There I'll fillet them, dip them in corn meal, fry them up crisp, and serve them with cheese grits and hushpuppies to the staff of the fish camp, my Florida friends. I told them dinner is at high noon. Anybody can fry fish, but crafting a good hushpuppy is an art form I take pride in. Anchored in a lagoon near a Kuna Indian village in the San Blas of Panama, I fed my Kuna visitors hushpuppies the size of cow pies. Pan perro, they called it, "dog bread." Whole families came out to my sailboat on Sundays in dugout canoes with bright sails. I set up a generator and a TV monitor and we watched Disney movies and ate dog bread and popcorn. If you ever want to make friends with Indians, feed them fried bread. At the time I didn't realize the irony that my mere presence among the Kuna threatened the purity of the life I so ardently admired.

In the dark, I smell the bream beds—funky, fishy, and fecund. I ease my kayak as close as I dare, blindly casting a popping fly in the area where yesterday Joe showed me the sandy piebald circles at the edge of floating hydrilla solid enough to support wading birds. The fly lands, broadcasting tiny rings of moonlight. A big bluegill slurps it up—*thup*. I set the hook to the smack. The bluegill fights hard enough to pull the kayak, running in circles and figure eights. Plenty of action on a 3-weight rod, especially when the fish manages to tangle itself in hydrilla. This first fish is too wide to grasp with one hand. Holding my flashlight in my crotch and the fish against my chest, I remove the hook. It's a bull-headed male with a deep-russet breast. I undo the first clasp of the stringer, add the fish. Worried that the bluegill has tugged me too close to the beds, I backpaddle a few strokes and cast again. Another bream smacks my popping bug. I'm casting to smell, setting my hook by sound. Nearly every cast is met with a sip or a splat. A streak of pink and smut on the horizon heralds the promise of a new day.

*

Joe is one of the remaining few native Florida Crackers, an endangered species facing extinction in the Florida Panhandle, and one of the very few people I know who might survive a power grid apocalypse. He hunts, traps, fishes, and crabs for a living. A stocky outdoorsman in his 50s, he has close-cropped hair and a beard the color of wheat stubble, thick forearms and solid round shoulders of a crabber, a ruddy complexion burnished by salt and sun together with a jovial disposition and a disarming grin around broken teeth. He and his ex-wife's half-sister occupy a double-wide mobile home next door to the house he abandoned to his ex-wife and their redheaded spawn. Dogs, cats, and kids meander freely in and out of both houses. The dogs and more bizarre pets are collectively owned, as are the kids—children of both women, his and others of his wives' previous unions, common law and nuptial. The redheaded children are clearly Joe's.

The yard is strewn with stoved-in boats, outboard motor parts, and rusty boat trailers together with towering stacks of crab pots. The myriad of heavy-headed dogs are inbred into a curious uniformity, unlike any canines I've ever seen. Mixtures of Lab and country bulldog with long black tongues of chow. All but the puppies are scar faced with tattered ears from catching hogs and fighting each other.

The cats warrant notice as well. Some are house cats, some feral, some flat-ass wild. They range in colors of orange, gray, black, white, striped, and spotted. There's a caged gray squirrel on the screened-in porch and a wild sow with piglets in a muddy sty off the kitchen. I spent one winter night on Joe's sofa for an early start to hunt wood ducks. I woke up before dawn to a pet pig licking my face.

When he was a young man, Joe married a Seminole "princess." He caught her in bed with his best friend, shooting the friend and chasing his wife out into the street. "I tried to shoot her, too," he confided, "but the tears blurred my sights." The best friend and the friendship survived, if not the marriage. "I don't blame him," says Joe. "He couldn't stay off her no better than I could."

Once a year, the generous Joe barbecues a whole wild hog, inviting the children's various and sundry fathers and stepmothers, a gala outdoor event that proceeds a heap more amicably than one might imagine. The men sit around the fire drinking beer and eating stone crab claws while the women provide covered dishes of greens and grits. They collectively mind children and serve the food.

Besides the gator skull in his living room, Joe's doublewide is decorated comprehensively with artifacts collected over a lifetime of "rooting," as he calls his local excursions. Here are handblown bottles with tiny bubbles in the glass, lead musket balls, clay pots, and framed flint points, one of them a Clovis found with mastodon teeth, 12,000 years old. Joe's avocation has garnered him an impressive knowledge of regional history, as Fort San Marcos, at the juncture of the Wakulla and St. Marks Rivers, has been occupied by Spanish, Native American, English, American, and Confederate alike. Union soldiers tried to take Tallahassee by a nocturnal approach up the St. Marks, Joe told me. They were ambushed and routed at Natural Bridge, where the St. Marks River goes underground for a quarter mile, by old men and teenaged cadets, scattering the Yanks throughout the mosquito-, alligator-, and snake-infested swamp. Tallahassee remained the only Confederate capital uncaptured by Yankees.

The battle of Natural Bridge was the last Confederate victory of the War Between the States.

*

The moon sinks into the western horizon, splashing silver lace through the treetops. The emerging sun in the east does the same in bright, gold filigree. By the time it clears the trees, my stringer sports a bluegill on every clasp. I start back to the fish camp, trailing my catch, which rises to the surface with each paddle stroke, sinking back down as I glide. The stringer of fish catches scratchy tendrils of hydrilla that I remove every now and then. With bright colors hyped up by the early-spring spawn, these saucer-sized beauties are fashioned by the Grand Jeweler Herself—ruby red breasts on the males, antique gold on the females, silver sequins that fade to pewter in the open air. I'm happy as a man can get with his clothes on. Every once in a while, I lift my catch out of the water just to admire them and to hear them rattle the chain, a bouquet of lovely flowers. Soon I'm back to Joe's crab pot, the green buoy smothered by strands of hydrilla swaying on its tether at the ledge where the channel drops off.

Suddenly the clear water boils sediment and tendrils of moss, fizzing like ginger ale. There's a sharp metallic rattle as the kayak is lifted, plunging backwards. A quick drubbing of triangular scutes runs the length of the keel—*buripp*—as if it were raked lengthwise by a crosscut saw, a vibration that rattles me tooth and bone. The stern is snatched under. Water rushes into the cockpit. I grab the gunnels, losing my paddle.

"Hey!" I scream. "Whoa!" The swamped kayak wallows backwards, the raised bow wagging. The wide head of a bull alligator parts the water behind me like a hideous idea, a genuine creature from the Black Lagoon. There's a quick jerk and a loud ping as the clasp securing the stringer to the stern ring snaps open. I'm eye to amber eye with a creature that crawled through primordial slime with the dinosaurs. It rattles my lovely stringer of fish in his toothy smile, sinking slowly back through the surface. Gone is my double-blade paddle. Gone is my bright bouquet of fish.

Now what? I'm sitting in a swamped kayak that wants to capsize, impotently splashing water out of the cockpit with the palm of my hand, leaning to one side as far as I dare. I'm drenched all the way up to my armpits. I'm shaking all over, but not from the cold. My stricken heart thuds wildly in my chest. All my neurotic aversions and petty fears have dissolved into one orgasmic moment of stark and unmitigated terror. The cobwebs swept from my soul. My paddle floats in the water 10 yards away.

Now the morning sun is well above the horizon. The

moon is down. The vision of the creature has left me shaky yet curiously elated, glad to be alive. Long strings of black cormorants fly across a blue-gray sky from their roost upstream. A cruciform anhinga perches on a channel marker drying her wings. Migrating upstream, silver mullet take their oblique plunges into the air, plopping tail first into the channel. Gaudy gallinules and spade-toed coots walk on the thick mats of hydrilla, an invasive species imported as aquarium greenery that threatens to clog every lake and river in Florida. A great blue heron spears a minnow and lifts its head to gulp it down. My blood still sizzles with pure adrenaline. I have no bright ideas of what to do next beyond sitting in a swamped kayak contemplating how quick a man's good luck can sour.

Before long I hear the distant burble of an outboard motor, amplified by fog. Soon I can see the outline of a Carolina Skiff, a stocky boatman standing midship steering with an extended tiller. Joe, bless his rugged heart, blooms through the low mist. The top of his head catches a ray of early sunshine like a golden crown. He pulls up alongside, grinning that broke-tooth smile of his.

"Boy, am I glad to see you!" I squeak.

"Morning," he says, "this looks like a mess only a college professor could get himself into. I thought I'd taught you better than to hang a stringer of fish into the Wakulla River."

He helps me up into his skiff. We lift the kayak, empty out the water. We recover my paddle, he pulls his crab pot, dumps a couple of blue crabs into a dry washtub, where they scratch around, facing off. I'm still shivering. He thinks I'm cold. He hands me a yellow oilskin with a fishy smell and helps me back into my kayak.

"Join me for lunch at the fish camp?" I stutter.

"Sure, what we having?"

"Pan perro and cheese grits. Maybe a blue crab or two."

Pork

After (Circe) had given them (Ulysses' sailors) food and wine mixed with a pinch of something, she waved her wand and changed them into swine. —The Odyssey, Book Ten

The hoar haired pariah in Liberty overalls and black rubber boots steps out of the swamp, his most remarkable feature a wide pug nose like a double barrel .410 between beady, red-rimmed eyes. Any closer I could see the old manís brains, though my gut says back off.

"Hey boy!" He addresses Michael, our youngest hunter. "What you doing out here with these reprobates of a Sunday morning?"

"Running hogs, same as you."

"Where's she at, then?"

"Where's who at?"

"That pretty gal you left in bed to engage in this here unholy enterprise."

"Asleep at home," Michael says, ìsafe from the likes of you."

"What you reckon safe about a bed?" he grunts.

Deer season gone, swine wranglers have the turf, serious business—no guns, no bows, nor noblemen on horseback swishing lances. More than medieval sport, this venery derives from pioneer husbandry when livestock was fenced out to forage common wilderness, not in, when spring round-ups mixed rustling with rodeo, family feuds with homicide. Clans captured, castrated, and earmarked every feral hog they caught with unique or customized notches. Older stock developed ears reduced to tatters or missing altogether. The wildest fled into deeper wilderness, reverting to type, culminating gloriously in the infamous pineywoods rooter, as hunchbacked as an alley cat with trombone snouts and ears that bloom like jungle flowers.

As suddenly as he appeared, the porcine old man, almost an apparition, wags his head and sloshes back through the deadfall bog, galoshes sucking tracks that fill with black swamp water.

"Who's that?"

"He ain't us. Likely out another caste," says one.

"You can't put a dog down, he don't show," another says.

"His boys in here somewhere, claiming ever hog we bay to ground."

"That the one called Shoat?"

"Sheriff Barrows," Michael adds.

"Hell."

Calhoun County boils with hogs, hounds and hoggers. Action on the paw and cloven hoof, no sport for sissies. Compact pickups cancerous with rust and dog boxes and swishing antennae. Few of us even know each other, bound by a mutually perverse attraction to swine. I'm out for pork and they are willing where there's pork galore, meat never wrapped in cellophane. If I can't shoot, catch or run over it, I've vowed, I'll forage with the vegans.

Like Irish Saints and English poets, wild hogs, *Sus scrofa* of Old World ancestry, are more honored dead than living. Five hundred years ago Hernando Desoto came through here from Florida driving hogs to provision a swinish army rooting for gold and setting mastiffs on Indians, who thought copper was what the bastard was looking for since they had no gold. His 300 pigs contaminated the new world with plagues as genocidal as the pestilent hearts his pockmarked soldiers stewed in breastplates. With no natural predators they couldnít handle, escaped swine flourished to the proportionate demise of Indians. Between Desoto and Lasalle, an estimated 96 percent of the highly civilized Caddo and Coosa Indians perished, deteriorating a highly sophisticated culture into the 'Stone Age savages" English settlers defamed when showing up to steal the land.

Imported for sport, Russians and Eurasian boars leaked genes into a hodgepodge heritage, culminating into the infamously glorious pineywood rooter with stain fanged snouts on slender hams and bristled backs as highly arched as graveyard cats mustachioed with tush and whetter that clack like synchronizing castanets when brought to bay, that can gut your dog and peel your britches to the bone before you holler soowee.

*

Bubba's a gold-hair youth with a classical profile and a taciturn disposition for a hog man, lean, strong and fleet of foot. His shirt has torn open, face and chest burnished red as a Georgia brickbat, not scratched up much as you'd expect. The dog leash across his shoulder that could hold a rhino. Lengths of parachute cord dangling from the hip pocket of canvas britches. Bubba's quick to grin, slow on conversation, like he needs every bit of air he can suck to run a bayed hog to ground. A latter-day Adam, the noble savage the Creator had in mind from the prelapsarian get-go, innocent of all industrial evil. Bubba with a dubbed in voice could be on daytime T.V.

"Say son, don't I know you?"

"I'm Bubba. You taught me English, fall of '89."

Typical among my students who held the notion, not without foundation, that good old boys and girls fare better with a homeboy freshman English teacher inclined to view dialectal interference as respectably Elizabethan to be preserved not decimated.

"What you doing these days for subsistence, Bubba?"

"I farm some, run hogs on Sundays."

"Any money to it?"

"Naw, just pork."

"And sport?"

He looks at me like I've inquired if he likes, girls, cold beer and Georgia football.

"Well yeah."

He cups an ear to a distant hound giving tongue, takes off toward the strike. "He can outrun a deer," Guy Oglethorpe says, blue-eyed, swag bellied good old boy without an ounce of fat. "Robert yonder can outrun him." Bubba's mentor and the honcho of this enterprise, salt and pepper headed Robert, is older than the other hunters, younger than me. A hardcore hog man up from Defuniak Springs, he's married to a schoolteacher I'd love to meet.

We watch Robert light out behind a 120-pound gilt that broke loose from the other dogs. He tackles and bulldogs her, pins her squalling with his knees, binds hocks with parachute cord. He clean jerks her over a shoulder, totes her back across soft winter rye like some Biblical shepherd, dumping her into the bed of a rusty pickup squatting on tired springs. To classical minds he might be a tusk-scarred Ulysses, who beguiled a lovelorn Circe to release his sailors she charmed to swine.

To quiet the mournful hounds, he bashes the metal dog box with a bat of stove wood—sad-eyed, scar-faced hound and bulldog crosses with souped up noses, balls of brass—dogs blood fated to run and bay the thing that kills them quickest. The hounds broil inside like maggots, shutting up, but the unblinking catch dogs gnaw their tethers, keeping up a high-pitched whining through larynxes compressed to make room for bear-trap jaws. Bad-ass canines squeaking like Chihuahuas that should roar like lions—*aw please aw*—begging to rip some living thing asunder—dogs who'd scat Desoto's mastiffs from a pit.

Oglethorpe holds Strawberry. The roan pit bull in a Kevlar vest squats on the ground, quiet and deadly as a sphinx on bench-leg haunches. His awful head from waist-high vantage, surveys the goings on with yellow rattlesnake eyes. Strawberry could catch a Hummer you don't mind the tires tore off.

The hounds are set down in a wallow of new-turned divots and hoof-pocked mud.

Stoic, fearless dogs who'll stand on a tailgate without a whimper to have their guts stuffed back and sewn up with dental floss or cat gut fishing line. They slink and sniff through haw and buttonwood, striking, giving tongue, *Baroop! Baroop! AW, Aw, Aw*—as rust gnawed pickups with oversized tires and swishing antennas scat around firebreaks to get in close enough to put a catch dog down. At first the two-way radios and telemetry keep track of chaos, but before the sun's up good, batteries die and the morning fills with the cacophony of pure chase.

On the first cast, I bottom out my truck in a soupy wallow, hopping into the high cab of a new GMC 4X4 stretch cab with a real estate broker named Martin, infamous—I learn too late—for driving like a bootlegger. This truck, slathered over front and back with hunters, replaces one he spun out, turning turtle, scooping through an open window a cab full of mud. Disinterred and shaken back to life, he blinked, rushed out and paid a higher sticker price than any house I've ever owned, leaving his wife the muddy one to make a yard art gladiola planter from.

In the brawl of bay and catch, excited human voices pitch higher than the dogs, hormonal cries of manly women at a clearance sale. In close there's no discernible sound, just the hellish cacophony of hogs, dogs and hunters.

Runk, runk!

Catch holt that sawn bench!

Ahrooo! Ahrooo!

Neophytes like me hang back when catch dogs are turned out, the chase far safer than the catch.

Yike! Reeee!

231

But now we're chasing a sounder of some half dozen multicolored porkers scurrying like lemmings through a wide field of sprigging winter rye.

"Look yonder!" hitchhiking hog-hunters holler, drumming the roof.

Aroo!

"Head 'em!"

Martin stomps the gas, spinning rooster tails of soup. We catapult across the rye, dumping hoggers into the bed among the jounce and squeal of hobbled hogs. We close the distance. A piebald shoat bouncing beneath my window.

The fishtail sliding me backwards against a sawed-off shotgun and Martin, tattoo of elbows upside my head, muzzle stabbing baby back ribs. Ow! Aw! Framed in the mud-spattered side mirror, Bubba catapulted off the tailgate, brogans spinning airily, lurching, making purchase in the soggy rye.

We pull away, hot after a spotted gilt to cut her off before she gets to the planted pines. The maniacal Martin actually gaining on her.

"Shoot her!"

"Hell's fire! Is this thing loaded?"

Bounding, we lurch beside the bouncing pig, Martin's boots stabbing at the gas.

She's underneath my window, but we're synchronized in opposition. Even if I could work the shotgun from between us, I'd shoot straighter from a pogo stick.

He swerves again to clip her with the front bumper, misses. Yaaaaah, no, no!

She scoots beneath our undercarriage, squirts into planted pines. Our truck spins out, blades of red clay berm to the door handle. I'm trapped by automatic door locks as clawing hunters are slung like water off a dog.

Grinning like a serial killer, Martin spins divots getting back to speed. Hobbled captives squeal and flop in altering gravity, bouncing the rear springs as we fishtail towards the woods. Pulling up alongside Bubba closing in on the hog.

"Hop on!" Martin yells as we skid by.

"Not on that truck!" Bubba's afterburners ignite, his rag of orange shirt trailing flames. In hot pursuit he dashes through the brake, gaining on the bouncing gilt as Martin puts the hammer down again to race across an irrigation dam. One captive hog's decisive flop could send us skidding off into the lake.

*

By early afternoon we've loosed captives into holding pens. Back in the muddy swamp, hounds strike again. We pile into the trucks, rushing down firebreaks to head the quarry off. At a junction by the banks of a wet weather pond, we pile out, cupping our ears to the rising cacophony. Anticipating the cast of hounds and driven swine.

Standing in this clearing, I have the leisure to imagine Bubba in his golden tresses now as Adonis fated to be slain by a boar, dismembered by his dogs and mourned equally by Love and Spring. A puckish Michael seems the spawn of Mars and Venus. Robert, a wily Ulysses with tush scars revealing his disguise. His shaggy sailors charmed by lovelorn Circe into swine. Such is the power of a woman's spiteful and redemptive love.

Like the beasts that draw them to the bogs, these hunters vary in a wide continuum of domesticity that fluctuates with age and habitat from mild as maids to hog-ass-wild. Hog wire or matrimony can divert them from a feral state to something manageable that can be trained to fetch a paycheck or truffles until a broken fence or marriage vow turns them out to retrogress to a purer type back in the wild.

Such is the flaw of woman's love to wilderness. As honey-headed Adonis might could testify, Venus and Venery are deadly kin and kind. Cracked corn and womení' love can dampen, but not quench, the swinish beast within—the latent rage in seething slums or thorny solitude.

They say one hunter's strands of DNA laid in a line could span the cosmos all the way to Heaven. They do not say what cul-de-sacs and crossroads we'll bumble on. Since Adam's Fall there's only two directions. From innocence that's dumb as dirt to greedy, sinister social institutions. Thermodynamic destiny of disorder unwinds us back to noble savagery.

*

As hodgepodge hunters grin around and text their wives, on tippy-toes we others stare into the tangled wall of briars sunlight nurtures as the swelling mayhem crashes through the brambles—a sooty Russian sow leading a stampede of hounds, shoats, gilts, and piglets striped like chipmunks eclipsing us into a rosy cloud of dust. Scattering like laundry, we scale everything ascendable—truck hoods, low limbs, saplings, each other. Michael hurtles a tailgate, passing himself and his amputated boot heel on the way back out when a piggy gentle as a lamb goes postal, snapping like a crocodile.

Stranded, I bounce in place, waving hands and feet, spastic jumping jacks inspired by sheer terror. The red tide parts miraculously, reforms behind me, scattering every which way again by a single gunshot.

Ruddy necks turtle into coveralls. As if sniffing out the source of flatulence, noses screw up tight. These guys don't like firearms, this business perilous enough without them.

"Who shot?" indignant voices hiss. A sheepish guy with the smoking muzzle shuffles over to the 90-pound shoat shot from his running board.

"Guess we better go ahead on and get the guts out this little hog," he tells his shoes.

Meanwhile, a dozen hogs have hit the pond every bit as

wild as those possessed by demons that jumped pell-mell into the lake at Galilee, which hogs will do, and drowned, which most hogs donít. All but the sow trail dogs through water to the other side. The shadow of a sow encumbered by a pack of dogs.

  Squeaking like a pump handle, Strawberry hits the water like a cannonball, dragging Guy into the muddy fray. Slinging hounds aside, he fights his way into the stormy cell of yin-yang violence, throttling Strawberry, holding him underwater to break him off the sow. The cherub Michael splashes in, ducking dogs and sow to break up the boiling cluster. Hellish noises rise in bubbles the size of circus balloons, exploding in deafening decibels erupting into air. Strawberry would rather drown than turn loose, but Guy drags him whimpering to the bank, handing off his leash to me together with a sawed-off Louisville Slugger.

  "Hold him!" he orders, splashing back to bind the bobbing sow. "Crack him 'cross the nose, he don't mind."

  What nose? Strawberry's face is flat as a fist full of nails. Mind? The only thing on Strawberry's mind is getting back aboard that sow. He starts that eerie squeaking, chewing briars and drooling blood, idling like a chain saw.

  I muster up the brass to bust him hard across the skull. He cocks his head, regarding me as somebody who's come out here to repossess his Buick. He snatches my bat and snarls. I back off smiling with my teeth, and the inescapable irony dawns on me: If you can hold Strawberry, you don't need a dog. If you could hold Strawberry, you could stall his Buick.

  A sidelong glance from Guy stands the bulldog down. The sow subdued, bound at the hocks and dragged to shore by a choker noosed behind a fanged snarl of upper mandible. After a right smart round of blasphemy and fumbling, muddy hunters heave her into the bed of Martin's GMC.

  "Here's your all's hog, professor," Guy Oglethorpe grins.

And she's a beauty too—high backed, bristled like a broom, a snoot like Joshua's trumpet sounding off. Unlike other hogtied captives—quiet as doves till somebody blunders close enough to lose a leg—this sow flops continuously like a gaffed marlin, rocking the truck on bitching springs, squalling discord, panting like a bagpipe. My barbeque! Oh man!

By late afternoon we've sequestered about a dozen hogs to pens and cages, killing only two—one shot from the running board at the firebreak stampede. Another Bubba killed with his pocketknife too deep in cottonmouths for extraction. He and Robert have disappeared to God knows where, maybe together. Last seen, Robert was loping on a pulled Achilles tendon after Sassy, his favorite blue tick hound. Before joining the search, Guy speculates the three by now have crossed the Chattahoochee into Alabama. Martin leaves his GMC at a firebreak crossroads with the apprentices to hunt the hunters with a tougher caste of men and recharged telemetry.

*

So, our novice straggle is left to hang behind, thinly knowing one another.

Suddenly, red dust rolls in behind a pick-up truck of unsurpassable dilapidation that rattles up and sighs. A one-eyed catch dog, crosshatched comprehensively with many honorable scars, is tethered with twisted barbed wire to a well-gnawed dog box squirming with mongrels newly acquired from the pound.

A clan of pre-human evolutionary throwbacks are strewn in and on the bed and hood and fenders as if they've fallen from an empty sky.

An elbow of a cured Boston butt angles from the driver's window, maybe holding the door shut. A skull tattoo the size of a magnolia blossom on the smoky patina of a bicep labeled Mother. The meaty head above it torques its mouth in painfully untutored elocution.

"Y'ens done any good?"

The Barrow Boys bail out and off a battered pick-up yawning back to higher haunches. Thick jowls, short necks, bowlegs, meaty upper lips and uniformly snouted, they're clearly sired by Shoat, the former and defunct sheriff who materializes and vanishes into miasmal bogs, with no genetic hint of maternity. Their domes are arrayed by mohawks, mullets, scalp locks and ponytails above multiple occipital rolls—fed out old boys and one of questionable female gender, tattooed comprehensively.

Without Bubba, Guy, Robert or the formidable Strawberry among us we look like Audubon birders facing off a Viking lynch mob. Goons and ogres, this porcine *posse comitatus*, rough clones of Sheriff Barrows in spit and image, holding us at bay in a circle of double-barrel snouts. Most us, by contrast, have daytime jobs and at least one necktie in the closet. These boys donít have a closet. Of hog hunters, theyíre the genuine article—ages staggered in accord with seasons. If old Shoat ruts another year, he'll sire an actual hog. A dim-eyed notice passes over us to the white GMC. They mill and cluster over to the tailgate peering over to inspect my sow.

"'At air's duh sheriff hog," the mohawk says.

"How's he marked her then?" I demand.

"Up under the tail they's a hole. 'At air sow belongs to the sheriff or used to did."

"Who's she belong to now?"

"They still his; it's just he ain't sheriff no more."

"Where's this past tense sheriff at?"

"Watching, I expect."

"That old man who got on Michael about his girlfriend?" I ask one of ours.

"Sheriff "Shoat" Barrows his own self," he whispers.

"Well, that's my sow in the back of that GMC," I assert with professorial authority, expecting backup. "She's got two holes up under her tail."

My silent delegation minds the sky and muddy boots as Barrows size us up with flinty eyes held narrowly apart by cloven tracks in sandy loam. Venue is useless here. No deed or lease can cleave this feral tribe's connection to the roaming swine. They grin together baring yellow pegs.

The one of questionable gender, a twin or triplet sister with a matted ponytail above occipital wrinkles, nose hole studded with a golden jewel, reaches lewdly in to pinch a dug. She could've punched the plunger of a Bouncing Betty.

In an explosive collision of meat and metal, the sow removes the tailgate, hits the hard red road, cleft hooves spinning. Careening through a barbed-wire fence, she scats through planted pines and barbed blackberries.

"She's done broke loose!"

"No shit!"

"Yonner go that bitch!"

"Head 'er!"

Yawlping hoggers charge the gap in wire she back lashed into concertina curls. A lusty chase, contesting primal forces. Bristling stand-offs. Snorts and charges. Flying tackles missed, reach exceeding grasp, fumbles, pileups, blasphemy. Action reversing as she pivots, charging the line of scrimmage, flinging rednecks.

But my blood is up with the threat of purloined pork. Unstable fear distilled to action volatile beyond the wisdom of my years, I spring into a flanking action to head her. I'm caught up in the chase, imbued with mob courage, beefy linemen closing on a pell-mell porker. Shouts, runks, blasphemy, clacking tush and whetter. Halts, hops, hasty retreats, and aborted advances. Monosyllabic utterances, porcine and humanoid. Primordial.

I'm charged by the elemental physicality of these goings on, immune to frailty, wisdom, station, regressed to type. I'm amongst it, egged to action, drawing courage from a moiling mob, an Edward Hyde among the Barrow boys.

By God, I'll head her off. She can't jump the road if I'm in it. Before me glides an apish shadow, abreast of the desultory fray, keeping the flank of boiling violence, an amorphous, black hole in all expanding night that fuels itself perpetually by sucking light and slinging Barrows every which way, but I'm abreast, a scarecrow fleeing corn. A dentist drill set free, the slack-string puppet of a palsied puppeteer. Mindless euphoria in a thoughtless brain. I've never dreamt of apprehending her. I chase only to hold my challenged claim, but, Jesus, here she comes. She angles off the fray to charge across the road I'm running down.

Suweee, Suweeee.
Runk! Ree!
"Hut damn!"
"Head 'er!"
Uh, oh, here she comes.

Immune to jumping jacks, she breaks back through the fence, slinging Slinkies. She vaults the ditch into the road. Which way to go! She zigs, I feign, she zags and runs slap over me. Into the silky purse-shaped shadow that descends, I reach and find and grasp salvation from the slashing scythes of grim reaping, unholy mower beheading me for hubris like Adonis, torn asunder by his dogs.

"You see that old sumbitch throw that hog?" I vaguely hear. "He's Bubba's teacher, used to be."

"It's her throwed him. He caught her ears when she run him over."

I'm buried utterly in sow, flat nosed, hot cheeks, and lips smothered. I'm all but crushed before a ton of beefy Barrow boys pile on, burying my wide mouth scream into a row of silky dugs, a womb of darker self and night.

My hearing, dulled by the military ordinance and a life of shotguns, returns surreally amplified. The heaving sow protests recapture—*Yeeeeeeeeeeeeeee!*—a locomotive locking wheels on a rusty track. My muffled, wind-broke cry beneath the squirming mound of pork and proto-human meat kneading me back into fecund firmament. My own voice bellows back to me from the place called Yonder, far, far, away and everywhere.

"Get off, get off you cretin, lard-ass, inbred sons of bitches!"

"He talk 'et way in the schoolhouse?" a voice past yonder says.

"Mona allowed he done so on occasion."

Above, far, far away, another voice, familiar and strange—a rasping voice I can't quite place but know I've heard before somewhere, someplace, some yonder.

"Git holt her hocks and pull her off."

The mound dissolves, a wad of blood worms writhing loose.

Mona Barrows. I'd clean forgotten her. Hardheaded little roan, face like a skull whittled from a cantaloupe, nose holes like a .410 side by side. Mona sailed through my bonehead English class into the nursing program oh-so-many-years ago. From a front row desk, she rattled me with silence, lifting her chin to words profound, inane, profane. I could not know her thoughts but thought I saw her brains.

"Load up the schoolmarm's hog and hep him up." Shoat Barrows says, "I 'spect he thinks he earned him a pound of pork.

Gravity slacks as Barrow boys drag off a hog kicking like a jackhammer.

"What's pretty little Mona up to now?" I wheeze, propped on a bloody elbow.

Shoat Barrows spits. "Pretty little Mona married out from here up north, twenty goddamn years ago, my onliest girl

to done me that-a-way, thanks to high-hat likes of you."
Indignation rising, he slaps his cap against a bandy leg
as if to goad a pale steed into the Apocalyptic sunset. His
bloodshot dome inflamed by peachy wisps of nappy hair, a
sunken halo or a crown of thorns.

One foot lies slue on a dog leg cramped into single genuflection, a blown-out knee that will hang me on a crutch for a half a year and could've saved me from the draft a half century ago. Shoat's wrath has scared the pain away. From my lower vantage, I can see into his heart, yet find no murder lurking there. We like to think the tribal kings benevolent.

"Me?" I peep.

"Grandbrats I never laid a eyeball to, tore by fancy notions off from blood of who they are and where they belong to be, so git this goddamn sow I give you out my woods. And take your high fallootin' ass out with her."

Epilogue

At sundown thirteen living swine are assigned to pens and cages—one transferred from Martin's GMC to my old Ford still dripping mud from reclamation. It's dusk-dark setting out for home to kill and butcher. My sow and I have had a long day. I'm scared she'll dehydrate and seize up before I can cook her up and pull her pork. I beg a coffee mug of water from the Hindu at the Flash Foods store, dot like a third bloodshot eye or pistol shot between long lashes. Stealthily I cross the tailgate, standing just off plumb by bracing on the cab. She seems asleep or dead already. I trickle water into a hydrophobic snarl. Her neck blurs out about a yard to amputate the hand that waters her, the Go Dawgs! mug launching into spiraling galaxy of pearls, shattering at the stylish feet of a lady gassing up a Beemer. Flatfoot on the asphalt we mutely gaze into each other's eyes, focused out about a thousand yards. My injured knee buckles, dumps my ass on ceramic shards of shrapnel.

We need a respite, my sow and me. It's way too late to butcher, and I'm not real sure how to begin. I know I've got to kill her first. I'm too squeamish to slit a throat in the dark even if I dared proximity. Shooting a hobbled hog in the bed of a truck seems an unsporting end to the drama of acquisition, not to mention the jurisprudential risk of discharging in the city limits a firearm of ample bore to dispatch a 350-pound sow of uncanny stamina. And after that, what then?

In the driveway of my girlfriend's apartment, I toss an Army blanket across a sow that clearly holds a grudge. I limp inside for beer and sympathy, rising the next morning in the dark before her neighbors do and find, uh oh, a tangle of nylon cord, a curl of feces, a tailgate hanging from a hinge. Loss and liability on the hoof, mauling her wild way through lawns and city parks and topiary hedges, flowerpots, and garden plots, repairing to the wilderness in a swath of devastation to rival retreating Russians or a Yankee general marching to the sea. I load up my tailgate, slinking out of town before the zygotic eye of dawning day.

Hooterville

Oh, blame it on midnight.
Ooh, shame on the moon. —Bob Seger

*M*ooney, Taze, and me are sitting in the den of Mooney's farmhouse-lodge, extrapolating solunar tables and wild hogs. Mooney's watching the Outdoor Channel, on mute night and day when anybody's here, maybe when nobody ain't. Trophy deer heads watching from walls, glass eyes flickering endless tragic flaws from a deer's perspective, punctuated by innumerable silent commercials hawking gadgetry made mostly in China. I take an armchair by the hearth, but it's too hot for a fire. All the furniture is upholstered in camouflage. There's no woman's touch at Hooterville. Even the bedspreads are Mossy Oak.

I'm pretty much keeping my mouth shut. At sundown I missed a white feral sow the size of a bear with Mooney's rifle, shot her right through the heart and she scatted off through the planted pines like a borrowed Lincoln on a honeymoon straightaway, piglets bouncing along behind her like cans tied to the bumper. Tracking her through labyrinths of catclaws and honeysuckle into the swamp, I found not the least blood spoor, and I lost my glasses. Again.

I tell Taze I view the active feeding periods as great tides of lunacy moving across the world—sea, swamp, desert, and shopping mall.

Mooney checks the tables. "There's a major at 1:45 a.m.," he says. "Not according to my calculations," I say. "I make it later."

For common ground, Taze and I agree all living things—everything from sunflowers to groundhogs, including plants and plankton—respond to the light and shadow of hours, days, seasons.

"When'd y'all starting hunting woodchucks?" Mooney wants to know. To Mooney wild hogs are a nuisance, not game.

"It's all about shadows," Taze pontificates. "The reason things get active when the sun or moon's at the zenith or at right angles. It's the length of shadows that makes things jumpy, tadpoles to tiger sharks."

Mooney thinks he knows a thing or two about a hog. "Mix you up some corn and water," he says. "Let it set awhile, then spread the mash where you want to find the high range of a hog. You don't bait none up, you can cook it off and get sloshed."

Taze and Mooney concur that fermented mash will flat draw feral pork. Ask any bootlegger if it don't. "Or put it in a timer on shell corn in a feeder and make up your own feeding pattern."

"Can you bait up hogs in deer season?"

"Sure you can, but I ain't sure it's legal."

In his wisdom or his cups, a ruminating Mooney says, "There's two kinds of places: those that have hogs and those that will."

*

De Soto brought the gene pool to South Georgia driving swineherds through here in the 16th century, a movable feast for soldiers with swinish appetites for pork and a lust for gold. The hogs probably brought more epidemic pestilence than the pockmarked Iberians, the combination essentially depopulating the new Eden of its native residents. The Spaniards finally left. The hogs thrived, staying on and mixing with new feral immigrants just to raise hell and havoc, running like backhoes through Mooney's food plots and peanut fields.

Mooney's pretty wife, Pam, an RN and a former student of mine, resists our camaraderie due to my professorially absent mind having degenerated into geriatric dementia, in her opinion. She absolutely forbade her sartorial spouse to set foot on the yacht I subsequently sank in the Caribbean. The year after that I got us stranded in a rare squall on the Flint River. Pam thinks we're both too old to hunt alone, so we meet at Hooterville, eat junk food, and take off in different directions, which I guess will work if something happens to me. If Mooney falls out, I won't have no earthly idea where either one of us is.

At the tail end of deer seasons he lets me shoot a couple of does for the freezer off Pam's private shooting house when she's working. Once after field dressing and hanging the meat, we had to return for the rifle I'd left leaning against a tree. Another time, my left arm in a cast, he set me up close enough to kill two with a revolver.

Mooney has tracked deer my arrows cleanly missed. I've snagged his scalp with popping bugs. Mutual tolerance testifies friendship.

"Antlers are nature's way off cooling down a buck during the warm months," Taze offers. "After the racks harden, the bucks fight with them and such, the cooler head prevailing, but all that's secondary to diet and shadows."

"What about the does?" I wonder. "How do they cool off?"

"They don't get as hot," says Taze.

"Well, your hogs are cooling down in the creek," Mooney says, "but you can't get back there right now without sinking to your nuts."

How about the runoff?"

From there the subject of deaf bird dogs is broached, how to work them with hand signals. The problem is getting their attention. Taze says shock collars go off accidentally and send bad messages to deaf dogs holding a point. I've got a young Boykin I shoot in the ass with a BB gun to get his attention, but he won't hold a point anyway, though sometimes I can stop him from eating the birds.

"You ever dust him off with a shotgun when it ain't practical to yank out your Daisy?"

"Ever which one's handiest," I lie. The only time I ever plink Bailey is to call him off the riverbank when Sharp, the resident gator, goes after him. I'm scared a shock collar in the water will fry the dog.

"Don't that make 'em gun shy?" Mooney says.

"Naw, it's the noise makes them gun shy. Noise don't bother a deaf dog."

Mooney's got him a couple of new dogs that hear a heap better than Mooney does, an English cocker and a fancy poodle cross that looks like something he won in a weight-guessing game at the fair, his lovable golden retriever, Beth, having died.

"Why don't you get you another dog?" Taze asks me. Mooney looks at Taze like he's just sprinkled cinnamon on his grits. My own jaw sags. Me and Mooney, deaf from a lifetime of shotguns, have a sentimental weakness for old dogs. We chew food for them after they lose their teeth, bury them tearfully beneath stone markers years after anybody else would have had them put down. Taze might as well suggest we upgrade family genetics by swapping out our homely kids or senile parents. At one time or another all our close friends and family have disappointed us, but none of our dogs have, although we've both had some sorry-ass dogs.

Dr. Andrew Mooney, Mooney's daddy the orthodontist, had a standard poodle he used to fetch doves until Mooney's mama broke that up due to sandspurs in the chenille. Dr. Mooney was Albany's only orthodontist when I was coming along, as they say. My sister and I were both bucktoothed as beavers, but putting braces on boys just wasn't done, and that set well enough with me. Dr. Mooney laid a smile on Sister to rival a '58 Buick, if she'd shown it, which she didn't, as I recall, for her entire adolescence.

The morning of her wedding she yanked the last wire out in the bathroom mirror with a pair of needle-nose pliers. Getting married in braces wasn't done either.

Mama Bud, our grandmother who lived in Macon, Georgia, gave me an official Boy Scout bugle on the day Sister's braces were installed, although I wasn't musical, the idea being the bugle would eventually shove my overbite into an acceptable plumb. It worked, too. What's left of my original incisors aren't canted out much worse than Sister's.

*

Full up with proverbs and bourbon, Mooney gets up to go to bed.

"The early bird gets the worm," he yawns. "But the second rat gets the cheese."

At 1:45 in the a.m., a mousetrap trips in the kitchen.

I'm awake, feeling around for the glasses I lost trailing a white hog through labyrinthine tunnels of cat's claws and honeysuckle. I slink along the walls, feeling for a light switch, tripping another trap with a naked toe.

I used to have an alarm clock like Mooney's digital, an electronically driven Rolodex of Arabic numerals that groans, squeaks, and slapjacks separate tin cards in every maddening increment of 60 seconds. One restless night some years ago I got enough of one just like it. I reached across a sleeping wife and shot it with the bedside .38. I don't know what it did for her insomnia, but it broke us from sleeping in the same room, eventually the same house. I was working more and hunting less in those days, and a lot more irritable because of it.

I dance on one foot, bitching. Since I'm up I might as well have a stick of deer jerky and a glass of buttermilk. Still too early to hunt, but the mousetrap and Mooney's groaning clock have murdered sleep. I watch mute expeditions of venery on TV with the glass-eyed wallflowers, munching camp food a dietician wouldn't step in. I plan to go out about an hour before dawn, walking in the moonlit fog to the rim of the runoff. When I hear or smell hogs, I'll stalk in close and wait for shooting light.

The world is blue in the moonlit mist, incandescent. If there's any movement of air, the fog doesn't show it. I feel like I'm swimming underwater in a stagnant pond, guessing the direction of my scent. You'd think with a snoot packed with mud a hog couldn't smell, but they damn sure can. You can't sneak up on a downwind sounder.

I stalk around like a ghost my own self in a lunar landscape, getting lost. I'll squat right down and listen up, assuming a half lotus in palmettos. I hear no hogs nor smell any. At sunrise I stand up in wet, still air, easing around blindly until I stumble up on a ladder stand against a red oak. I climb it to wait for the fog to lift.

Almost before I settle in, a gaunt buck with more rack than body mass slinks sheepishly under me. He's nearly invisible in the gray air, tuck-tailed and stinking from carousal. The rut has dulled his matted fur and, as they say, drawed him down considerable, caving in his haunches and puffing out his neck. His massive rack doesn't seem to have cooled him off enough. He's been making the rounds before last call, and he's wore slap out. We share an empathetic moment. The buck doesn't give a damn if I shoot him or not, but Mooney does. He'll fine me $500 for a buck that doesn't make the Boone and Crockett. He'll make me cape and mount it if it scores, which I can ill afford. Plus, the Airstream travel trailer I've been living in doesn't cry out for glass-eyed deer heads wobbling on concave walls. I don't bother to put the scope on him or count blurred tines softened by my aging eyesight in the mist.

When the fog lifts enough for me to find my way back to the truck, I return to Hooterville. The house dogs and hunters have gone, Mooney in town playing golf. Taze left last night, on the cusp of some hypothetical shadow. The cheese in the sprung trap has been eaten by the second mouse.

I sink into a camouflage armchair and disappear, the TV still broadcasting silent outdoor expeditions. In a sequence run backwards, an arrow reverses from the heart of a whitetail buck in slow motion back to the archer's nock. The deer getting up front first like a cow, walking backwards.

Quail, Dogs & Grandmothers

You will find something more in woods than in books. Trees and stones will teach you that which you can never learn from masters. —Saint Bernard of Clairvaux

It helps to know that grandmothers are still in charge in the Deep South, that hunting bobwhite quail is still a rite of passage, that future sons-in-law and trade associates still have their virtues weighed by dogs and guns before sober investments of cash or daughters. Our folk have been a matriarchal lot ever since Clovis nomads squatted down to grub a root. Muskogee princesses, absentee Spanish queens, frail belles, spoiled brats, and dusky mistresses—all conspired for power while males ranged out to drag home protein.

In Southern climes, egocentric Mother Nature bestows a seamless transformation on her daughters, who say their childish prayers and wake up as women and running things. Her sons, however, must re-smelt imperfections in cauldrons of puberty, swollen glands propelling meat into hormonal battles and idiotic wars. Girls simply have mothers and then become them, creating an omnipresent matrilineal network of grandmothers without whose temperament we Southern males would've exterminated ourselves 400 years ago.

Though generally disinclined to train the dogs or hunt the quail, these true rulers of the South rule roosting territories. Outliving mates, they hold title to hunting lands and impose etiquette. A careless hunter in some other venue may gain some "hubris of empire," even to a Vice Presidency of the Union, but down here in Georgia, an ill-bred thug who fires his gun with greedy disregard for dogs or fellows can't hope to reproduce himself. Without the blessing of grandmothers, these men must wander north or starve.

*

Patrick's grandmother, Barbara, whose daddy was our grocer, impressed me indelibly in the 1950s by laying rubber in the family Cadillac. Now, her grandson has moved down here from Iowa to live with her and the boy's father, her son, and she spends her days monitoring a police scanner. Chagrined that Patrick plays Mortal Kombat—a diversion she feels deemphasizes firearms safety—she told me to take the boy hunting, which was what was done with 14-year-old boys when she was, as they say, a girl. In keeping with time-honored caveats, I wasn't to let him get chilled, hungry, or shot. Plus, he couldn't miss any school.

"*School*? Damn, Barbara, I'm a college professor!" I say. "Or was before I quit."

"I know," she trumped, "and I'm his grandmother."

The law allows Patrick a choice of parents, and that's it. He can't drive, vote, work, or drink whiskey. He can't stay out past curfew, and unless courtship has drastically changed since I was, as they say, a boy, his female contemporaries won't pay him much mind until he gets his photo on a wanted poster or a driver's license.

Down here among the gnats and Spanish moss, hunting behind dogs of finer pedigree than their owners' remains, largely due to grandmothers, the most gentlemanly and least sanguinary form of venery and the best fun adolescents can legally engage in fully clothed, but for mortal consequences from a bungle, hunting ranks right up there with bullfights and juggled hand grenades. The etiquette of safe gun handling underlies Southern traditions against causing the death of somebody who don't need killing, and endorphin laced teens must be regimented like bred pointers to throttle instincts primordial. Patrick's grandmother wants him to learn to manage his mettle before 21st-century media technology transforms him into a psychopath with a mail-order AK-47.

When Jimbo, Patrick's father, brings him by, I'm astonished to see a normal teenager, tall and handsome with broad shoulders and basic manners. We take him out to Triple Creek Plantation to meet the Plumber, a pal of mine for almost 60 years. We find him at the trap range sitting on a plastic bucket on a grassy knoll between a new lodge and a sparkling lake, teaching grandkids home from college to shoot trap without encroaching on each other's slice of firing line.

Poleaxed by déjà vu I first mistook his granddaughter Augusta, cocked on one hip, a broken shotgun balanced backwards across a shoulder, for her mother, Beverly. It takes a long moment to get back to where and when I am. I'd taught these youngsters' parents and coached (if loosely put) Augusta's future dad in Spanish, but Gary "Plumber" Flanigan and Corinne Beverly go back even further, being the first of our high school class to get married without having to.

In those early days, Plumber and I weren't much company for wives, snoring in our boot socks by the hearth while the ladies scraped plates and fed the dishwasher, but Corinne stayed the course. She made their home and brokered real estate. She kept the books and raised pretty daughters, with bright brown eyes and crow-black hair from Plumber's line. Our camps were tents and campfires. Before turning in, Plumber would kick up a galaxy of sparks to Cassiopeia and Orion.

"I moan have a place someday," he'd say, "and the whole damn world can go to hell."

"Sure," we'd yawn. "Sure, you will."

*

"He's never shot a quail," I say by way of introducing Patrick.

"Them neither," Plumber says. He gestures with the trap remote to Brett and Blake, Lila's twins, and Beverly's Augusta, who wears the Flanigan hair down past her shoulders as her mother did, the shimmer of a grackle's iridescence, a trace of Plumber's cowlick at the forehead.

"Put him yonder with them," he says.

*

Plumber's grandfather, a hard-drinking redheaded locomotive engineer, settled in Albany, Georgia, the midpoint of his run. His flamboyant unpredictability at the junction earned him the nickname On-Again Off-Again Here-Again Gone-Again Flanigan.

Plumber's father, an affable plumbing contractor who rocked like a penguin when he walked, was called Old Man by the crew, including Plumber. Old Man brought blackened pots of turnip greens to camps, taking his teeth out to eat. Kids were drawn to him like he was made of candy. Unlike Gone-Again, Old Man lived for hard work, and Plumber grew up doing a lot more of it than the rest of us. For one whole summer his legs were nicked and scarred by splintered flint that a maul sparked from river rock he broke for walls.

Cursed and blessed with continuity, I taught college English in my hometown for 30 of the 60 years I've known the Flanigans. I taught both daughters. Pace, a future son-in-law, I tried to coach in Spanish. Teaching Pace—too wired to sit—was worse than herding cats. I marched him through the pinewoods drilling verbs only because his saintly uncle, Bill Pace, had signed me out of school to take me quail hunting when nobody, especially not girls, would've noticed me if I'd set myself on fire. Like other unfinished products of Mother Nature, I was an unloved acromegalic abomination with oversized feet, a reedy voice, and a complexion like a pepperoni pizza.

"Yucky," they'd have said as I melted into a loathsome pile. "Cooties!"

Pace's mother, when I refused more money, sighed: "All he wants to do is hunt."

"Let him," I said. "Maybe he'll get rich enough to stay out of jail and sire some pretty children."

Which is pretty much what Pace did.

It helps to know: Down here we give our kids first names from maiden surnames, like Beverly, Pace, and Flannery for matrilineal continuity. In turn, our infant children's premiere trials at speech nickname adults Pawpaw, Memaw, Bubba, Bumpy, Doodle, and Dingdaddy, appellations that stick for life and then some.

"You're jerking off!" Plumber calls to Patrick as another ceramic disk plops into the sparkle of the lake. The boys grin sheepishly, like acolytes caught red-handed drinking altar wine.

"Do what, Pawpaw?"

"Flinching," I translate. "You're jerking off the target."

"Oh."

"Pawpaw?" I smile.

Plumber ignores me, thick forearms resting on his knees. My son still called me Doe-Doe when I turned him over to Plumber. Too young to shoot, he stumbled after Plumber and a quadroon dog, establishing a debt in all these years I haven't paid the interest on.

"I've spoiled them and know it," Plumber says, lighting a cheroot Corinne won't let near her new lodge, "but I enjoy my grandchildren." Speaking around the cigar, he's as articulate as any Southerner. "I enjoyed my children, too," he reflects. "Hell, I even enjoyed your children."

While we watch the youngsters shoot, Beau, the overseer

and the Flanigans' oldest grandson, pulls up reporting that a backhoe patching a dam has run over a company truck.

"Lean into it, Gussie," Plumber calls out to his granddaughter. "And keep the shotgun swinging."

Augusta tilts, hind leg in elegant tiptoe, returning the clay pigeon to charcoal dust, it seems, before it gets out past the muzzle. She's a competitor like Aunt Lila, and her cousins love her for it. They'd rather see her beat them at a game than win one themselves.

Beau shrugs and smiles, returning to the work. It's Plumber's way to take things one on one and easy, skirting enterprises that require new clothes. I never know if he's broke or flush, and if he doesn't peek into Corinne's books he may not either. His work and play and life are fused into one seamless kinetic—the relentless, easy gait of who he is—a single, measured, perpetual motion that will go on while Plumber does.

When construction flat-lined, instead of laying off he brought his crew and backhoes out to make this place. For three years now they've carved dirt roads, dug fishing lakes, and groomed habitat from scrub and thicket. Corinne made them mark and spare a thousand native dogwood trees.

"All these years he plods along, looking too laid-back to suck air," says an employee since Old Man was running things. "Now he's done got rich as four foot up a bull's ass, and it couldn't happen no better." But it's clear in large part his success derives from monomatriarchy, the uninterrupted rule of one good woman. His bulk has settled some upon his bucket, but essentially, he's the same young man who kicked the fire and said, "I will." The thatch of hair he passed on to daughters, and they to the grandkids, has tarnished some with hoar and thinned through distribution, receding past the foremost cowlick of his youth, flaming hair of Gone Again having surfaced only once, in a great granddaughter.

"Well, Pawpaw, how'd you come to sire this pretty progeny?"

The mute answer: Corinne, strolling from the full-length porch of her lodge, checking on her grandchildren. Lila's boys, the twins, are shooting trap with Patrick out of Barbara's Jim and Beverly's Augusta.

*

After a safety DVD in the great room of the lodge, Plumber says, "Patrick, you're a big, fine boy, but if you shoot one of my dogs or grandchildren, I moan take my belt off and whip your ass. You understand me?"

"Yessir," Patrick grins.

"Or the guide!" adds Keith, the guide.

"The guide is CYOA, " says Plumber.

We leave the young hunters at the lodge to fetch the dogs and a hunting truck, like something out of Africa, with high bench seats mounted above dog boxes. At the kennels, two dozen pointers bounce on hind legs, hurling themselves against the chain-link gates, howling like they've treed us. Beau threatens them with the high-pressure water hose that cleans the pens, producing an immediate and uncanny silence, but as he drops the hose, the nozzle cracks open. We hoot louder than the dogs, jumping lashing loops and ducking icy spray.

"What y'all doing wet?" Augusta wants to know when we return.

*

From the high sway of the hunting truck, Gussie and I watch Patrick hunt beside his father. More birds fly to Jim. He kills them almost apologetically with a humpback Browning knob-grip passed down from his father.

For birds that come his way, Patrick errs on caution's

side—the right stuff—taking shots too late, about the time the quail shift gears from afterburn to sail, watching them angle through the pines among dogwoods, fanning down into the paisley hardwood and cypress bottoms of Muckalee Creek, doing Grandma proud. Finally, a single hooks to Patrick's side. He shoots a little late, but the bird drops a leg and wobbles down into the sedge for Jack. The boy's first quail, his daddy on the spot, the way things should go and almost never do.

"Well done!" Keith takes the bird, slaps Patrick's shoulder.

On the wagon, Augusta's knee is jerking up and down, her daddy's blood. To tame it she stands up. "Good shot, Pat!" she calls, sitting down, the knee cranking off again with a life of its own.

"If you believe in the hereafter," I whisper to Jim as he and Patrick climb up. "That there's what we came here after." With eyes glazed over, he stares out where a lot of birds escaped, beatific smile stamped in a face flushed red as his cap. A boy's first bird has some great sway upon a father.

Now comes Augusta, down with Blake and Jack. How can I help but follow? These are my students' kids: their daughter, sons, nephews, niece, and all. I'm kin enough. My own grandmother, like Corinne, was nicknamed Bud. She could find a blood connection to anyone in the South at will or scratch one out of the Bible. Down here, we're kin to who we want to be, to better know each other and ourselves.

"I want the 20 gauge," Augusta tells Keith as he hands her the .410.

"Pawpaw's orders," he says.

She loads red shells thinner than her granddaddy's pinkies. We stalk the dogs, Jack squirming through a millet patch. A warm wind bullies off the chill. I carry coats back to the truck. Over pale hills stacked against each other, a dark cloud moves in from the south, spilling rain. The light softens shadows, and the distance changes Gussie back into her mother. The bright orange cap against her hair recalls a black bird's epaulets, and I want this moment merging with forever—the smell of rain, dogwoods gone to berries bright as blood, the hickory's antique gold and piebald bark of sycamore, the hectic shimmer of burnished leaves blanched by backing gusts.

"You want a gun, O.V.?" Plumber shouts to me.

"No thanks, I'm having too much fun."

I catch back up to Gussie at the point—Jack, that beautiful bench-legged SOB, staunch as a bulldog doorstop at the edge of tall millet, the backing dog on shaky haunches, tail stiff as wire.

"Keep to the edge, Gussie." With Blake and Keith across the patch, anything up is hers. I place my palm between her shoulder blades and urge her to the dogs. The touch revives her mother, behind me on a ladder stand. I sat the footrest at her feet, my back against her knees to keep the gun out front. Beverly went with us but wouldn't shoot. Her younger sister, Lila, mother to the twins, would scramble a tree alone in predawn darkness carrying an iron sight .30-.30 with the bluing worn silver, and stay there till you came.

"I can't shoot this gun," Augusta whines.

"You have before."

"I know, but now I've got it in my head."

"Don't think about it, you'll forget it's there. Just get the stock against your cheek and do like Pawpaw said." I push her close against the wall of golden millet. A cock breaks loose that must've grazed Jack's nose, and Gussie, leaning into her shot, tumbles it, her back leg poised on tiptoe, suede boots trimmed in fur.

Suddenly a bat or a bobwhite quail behind her flushes in my face. I hit the dirt and roll and hold my ears. She breaks her gun and helps me up.

"You find a hole?" She smiles.

"Just giving you a shot," I mutter.

"We don't shoot the quail that break behind," says the girl who's never ever shot a quail but one.

Jack hasn't moved and won't until he's tapped. She chambers two. Before she locks the breech, a third bird flushes up in front. She kills it clean before it levels off—it's not a double, but close enough for kin. Down feathers ride the backing breeze. I tap Jack's head, reanimating him to snort around fetching her birds, grinning around them in his mouth, her cousins smiling wide as Jack.

"Can I please have the twenty now?" she begs.

"Ask Pawpaw."

She does. He says, "Climb back up, give Brett a turn." Plumber wants her moment to sink in, and mine. She wants another moment, but her pout, if it is that, is brief as youth, fleeting as a quail bird's flutter. She knows that hunting's not a game to win like shooting is but learning what you know is twice as hard—*the twins are on the ground, like, both of them at once. Jack's slinking through the sedge and...*

"Pawpaw!" she calls, her knee pumping faster than her heart, and he ignores her, lighting his cheroot. She takes her case to Keith and Beau, who shrug and smile. I climb back to the topmost seat and pat the restless knee her father gave her. On high seats, I am as aging monarchs are: the passing lords of all they know and see, a perfect moment in a perfect world, where everything in changing stays the same. Of fathers being heroes to their sons. Of all that is and all there's ever been. Of quail and dogs and boys becoming men, and by God, pretty women being who they are: root, branch, and bud.

Buzzard Luck

Contemplate the buzzards
Winding overhead.
If you think they circle you,
You're paranoid or dead.
Wiggle first your fingers
Then rotate your feet
Don't forget to make a fuss
Or you'll be buzzard meat. —O. Victor Miller

Cochise Pez and I grew up on the same body of water—he on the banks of Lake Chehaw at Turtle Hill north of Albany, Georgia, and I on the Flint River downstream four miles south of the power dam. Now we are old men—he in his sixth decade, I in my seventh. We hunt together because his wife and my significant other don't want us hunting the riverbank alone. It's easy enough to accommodate them.

Cochise and I've been trespassing these banks since we were teenagers.

Just before sunup we arrive by jon boat to a gas pipeline right of way on the riverbank, a long ribbon of grass that looks like a private landing strip with yellow caution signs down the middle and a tall chain-link fence on either side. With his longbow, Cochise is to stalk a half circle through the downstream side of the swamp and come out where a pig trail enters the pipeline through a gap in the fence across the easement from where I'll hunt from a climbing stand. We hope he'll get a shot at a feral hog or drive one out into the pipeline for my rifle, but we've tarried over coffee at camp and are running late. We'd planned to get set in the dark and to hunt only until sunrise, when we'd speed upstream to the boat ramp and across town to Turtle Hill,

Cochise's childhood home, where four generations of Pezes have lived and where the outdoor memorial for his beloved Aunt Jean is to be held that day. Her cremated remains are to join Uncle Jim's in Lake Chehaw.

    Yesterday we'd scouted out a hog trail crossing the easement about 200 yards from the riverbank. It doesn't take an accomplished woodsman to scout out a sounder of piney woods rooters. The grassy turf was uprooted in large patches. The trail had puddles of standing water laced with heart-shaped hoofprints, the largest cloudy with mud that hadn't had time to settle. Then there's the smell. Wild hogs don't stink so bad as domestic hogs, but downwind you can sometimes locate a sounder of them by their heady odor. A rutting boar hog is somewhat headier than a sow, and you better be downwind when you smell them or they'll smell you first. To get my scent above the hog trail, I've attached my climbing stand to the trunk of a loblolly pine above a hole in the chain-link fence hogs were passing through. They'd rubbed the base of the pine tree bare, the sap bleeding amber tears.

    I can still climb a tree if I go slow enough, stopping to rest every couple of yards. A sloth can outrun me climbing a pine tree, but we figure the security guard who patrols the easement on a four-wheeler isn't likely to scan the treetops for trespassers, and he'd never find the jon boat unless he dismounted and walked down the riverbank.

    This river and Lake Chehaw are sacred to us both. Cochise circled Turtle Hill with his son and nephew in a Cessna to scatter his father's cremated remains. On the ground we heard them sizzle through the live oak we stood beneath. He helped me scatter my own father's cremated remains from my jon boat off the bank of my childhood home four miles downstream, and he was there when my mother's ashes were strewn with camellia petals beneath a high bluff downstream of where we're hunting hogs. We figure our loved ones' ashes grandfather our hunting rights for life all the way to Apalachicola, Florida, and the Gulf of Mexico. Uncle Jim had said if my mother knew my father's ashes were in the same river, the water would boil.

We secure the johnboat and Cochise sets out for the river swamp beyond the fence. I top the bank, pausing to scan the long expanse of grassy right of way before heading for my climber.

Whoa!

The inky silhouette of a razorback boar appears at the edge of the grassy pipeline easement right beside my unoccupied stand a hundred yards away. If l were up the tree where I belonged, I could drop a brickbat on this hog, but as luck would have it, I'm caught out in the open with nothing to hide behind and nothing to brace my rifle on but a thin fringe of broomsedge. I stand my rifle on its butt and gingerly lower myself, squatting on my heels, arthritic knees popping loud enough for the hog to hear. This shooting position is one I remember from the army manual but one I'd hadn't practiced in 50 years. Soldiers didn't like it. They complained it presented a frontal exposure of their testicles, their asses hanging between their ankles. I figure the stance is okay for hogs; they can't shoot back. This homely squat was also the one prescribed for personal latrine use in the field. The military has training manuals for everything, but they weren't written for old farts 75 years old. Not only has that second cup of coffee made us late, but my bladder is uncomfortably full besides. I know the hog hasn't detected us yet or it would've scatted back through the gap in the fence the way it came.

The sun is just breaking on the horizon, sprinkling diamond dust across the frost.

If the hog ventures more than a few yards forward, the sun will flash into my scope to blind me. The hog raises its nose to snort the chill air. A vapor fume rises above its head like a cartoon balloon. *Runk, Ree!* it seems to say. *Runk, Ree!* A lone boar hog looking for love, it trots over to my empty stand. It can't rub its tree with the climber in the way. It takes an angry swipe with its tusks, rattling it. Then it roots up a divot at the edge of the grass, and stands broadside, looking both ways. This is the only shot I'm liable to get, but it's a perfect shot to pass up—too much green between me and my target, the rising sun in my eyes. I've never reckoned myself a crack marksman even in my prime, and I fear I'm some 40 years past making this shot, but we've been three days in the woods without bagging anything. No venison or pork for the freezer. We won't get a better chance than this one. It's already time to quit hunting and head out for Turtle Hill.

Cochise is watching me through the chain-link fence from the downstream edge of the pipeline, partially obscured by a live oak with a posted sign nailed to it. He's a tall, lanky hombre with shoulder-length blond hair and a Buffalo Bill mustache and goatee.

I take off my glasses and set them behind me in my shadow so they won't flash sunlight and spook the hog. I push my safety off and raise my rifle, the backs of my arms resting on my knees, the weight of the rifle tilting me forward. I've climbed the riverbank too fast as well as too late. My heart is thudding against my ribcage just this side of angina. The scope's fuzzy crosshairs palsy with my pulse, and I'm getting a cramp in my foot.

I take a deep breath, let half of it out, hold on the hog's shoulder as best I can.

The longer I aim, the shakier I become. I start squeezing the trigger. Splinters of sunlight flash into the scope. I squint and pray and the rifle fires—*Ka-woom!* The recoil, true to Newtonian physics, kicks me flat on my back in the frost. I feel my glasses crunch beneath my shoulder blades.

The boar hog takes off like a jackrabbit. Damn! Yonder

goes the pork! I watch despondently through the fork of my knees as it scats out across the pipeline. Buzzard luck, I think. I can't kill nothing, and nothing won't die.

Halfway across the pipeline, the speeding hog leaps high in the air, somersaults, landing flat on its back in the opposite way it was headed. I can hardly believe my eyes.

I don't get up so quick as I used to either. When I fall down, I lie still for a while and take inventory. Then I thank the Lord I'm still on this side of the grass. Above me buzzards circle in the high clean sky. By the time Cochise gets over here, I'm struggling to get back on my feet, using my rifle as a crutch.

"Good shot." He grins, taking my hand to pull me up. He knows damn well the shot was beyond my ability to make it, but he's a gentleman of sorts. Like a golfer's hole in one, it takes skill to hit the green, but going in the pen involves pure dumb luck. "Let's go get our hog and get the hell out of here," I say, scanning the horizon for a four- wheeler.

We are meat hunters, I might as well tell you right now. I'm carnivorous. Cochise not so much. He's a vegetarian who eats only meat we've harvested and processed.

We both figure the only good reason for killing any animal is to butcher, cook, and eat it. Usually, we bone out our quarry in the woods, leaving the viscera and skeleton for the buzzards. There are always buzzards around a lucky camp. Sometimes we brain tan the hides and carve small animals and peace pipes out of bones and antlers, but we won't have time for any of that today. We have a memorial service to get to.

We hike to the dead hog, down one hill and up another, printing boot tracks in the hoarfrost. All my geriatric handicaps—the pulse of my racing heart, my labored breath, my fuzzy eyesight, my palsy—have acted contrary to one another, synchronizing incredibly into a perfect heart shot just behind the shoulder. I'm a heap less proud of my skill than of my good fortune. If ever I wanted to hang a trophy on the wall, this would be the hog to mount. It's a prototypical razorback boar, long of head and lean of haunch, high-backed and bristled with a snarl of tusks and whetters hiking its upper lip. It could be a descendant of the hogs de Soto's army drove through here in the 16th century looking for gold, spreading pestilence, and murdering Indians. Or it could be a farm hog that reverted to type many generations ago.

We castrate and field dress our pork, raking the steaming viscera into a pile on a shadow of bright blood. By the time we finish, my knife is blunt as a spoon from the sand and grit embedded in the hide. Our hands and forearms are painted with dried gore up to the elbows. We each take a front hoof, dragging our prize down one hill and up the next to the riverbank. The drag is a time again farther than the shot. We rest whenever I start wheezing. Cochise, being in better shape, does most of the dragging while I catch my breath. Between our footprints we leave a snail track wide as a hog through the melting frost.

At the riverbank, we turn the hog around to lower it backwards down the embankment against the grain of its hair. We slide on our asses alongside it, braking with our heels. At the water's edge we nudge the johnboat's flat bow against the bank and drag the carcass into the boat. We rinse our hands and forearms as well as we can in river water. You can't field dress a boar hog without smelling like one. Despite my efforts to clean them, my fingernails are still framed in blood.

A couple of black buzzards have already found the mound of guts. They perch in the lowest limb of the pine my unused climber is attached to. When Cochise strolls over to retrieve the climber, they flap away, the hinges of their wings squeaking as they cross the pipeline.

The older I get, the more I admire buzzards. Their circular

flight suggests the cyclic nature of things—of wind and sea currents, of seasons, of history, karma, and life itself—what goes around comes around given time. Their patterns of flight also suggest that after a rich and adventurous life, it's appropriate that heaven has conspired to fetch me back with the buzzards to roost at my childhood home, to eat, sleep, and die on the bank of this same body of water where my parents' ashes are.

Bodies of water are favored by buzzards. Maybe they frequent rivers and lakes because they know wounded animals go to water to die. In any case, there are always buzzards above the Flint River and its backwaters. The redheaded turkey buzzards sniff out their carrion with their keen sense of smell, black buzzards eyeball theirs with sharp vision and will sometimes kill prey that ain't quite dead. Black and turkey buzzards flock together to cooperate.

The frost melts and the sun burns the mist off the river. It's going to be a warm day in Southwest Georgia, a perfect day for an outdoor memorial service, but we'll have to hustle. With 300 pounds of additional weight, the johnboat sits low in the water.

Cochise takes the helm, and we proceed slowly upstream to keep water from splashing over the bow. We're almost to the first curve when we see a four-wheeler pull up to the riverbank. Cochise waves and I do too.

A few turkey buzzards follow our slow progress upstream like gulls behind a garbage scow. I lean back to enjoy the scenery. We pass wide-hip cypress trees, their Gothic roots, their whiskers of Spanish moss. Bone-white sycamores slide by with river birch, bay, and tupelo. We flush a pair of gaudy wood ducks from a backwater eddy.

They splash into flight, trailing bright water beads—ear, ear, ear—and circle back over us: *ear, EAR, ear.* A kingfisher crosses the river, flashing blue. Above us circle the ubiquitous buzzards.

Yelling over the complaining outboard motor, I ask Cochise if he knows what animal William Faulkner wanted to be reincarnated into.

"Nope! What?" he shouts.

"A buzzard!" I say.

"Why?" he yells.

"They soar through the heavens, they're protected by the law, and they can eat anything!"

Cochise grins and nods.

The ride upriver to the boat ramp takes most of the morning. We pull out, unhitch the trailer, and lower the truck's tailgate. Cochise backs the truck over the tongue of the trailer flush with the bow of the boat. We drag the hog over the tailgate into the bed, leaving the trailer where it is. On the way to Turtle Hill we buy three bags of party ice to tuck inside the hog's body cavity, speeding across town to the service with no time to spare for cleaning up, changing clothes, or dealing with our prize boar hog.

We park at the bottom of Turtle Hill. It's a bluebird day after the morning frost, perfect for an outdoor service. I take off my coat to cover—don't ask me why—as much of the hog as a coat will cover. Its shaggy front hooves are bent reverently as if in prayer, the corners of its mouth turned up in a beatific smile. Between the lashes, I gaze into a wild, black eye. Past my own reflection, I can see all the way back to Eden, to the first swine lazily foraging acorns and forbidden fruit—a senior moment that speaks of the kinship of all living things and the infinitesimal insignificance of my own existence.

For one lost moment I forget who I am. I'm a part of everything I've ever killed, including this hog.

When I recover, I step in behind Cochise, climbing Turtle Hill with its grand lawn and stately live oaks, their thick low limbs thatched with resurrection fern. The folding chairs are filling up. This is a happy occasion, a touching celebration of the rich lives of Aunt Jean and Uncle Jim, who has predeceased her. The couple remained sweethearts all their lives. The mere mention of their names brings fond smiles. There's plenty of food and drink, plenty of funny stories, plenty of laughter and some tears. More and more it seems I have more dead friends than living.

I sit down on the back row so no one will notice the muddy stain on the seat of my pants. Cochise takes the empty chair beside me. We feel conspicuous in our hunting clothes, but nobody seems to mind. We know Jean and Jim wouldn't mind. The male Pezes and their in-laws are all outdoor sportsmen. Jean and Jim were sports. I close my fists to hide fingernails framed in blood, hoping I don't smell too much like a boar hog in rut.

Near the end of the formal part of the service, a buzzard sails down to perch in a dead gray tree at the water's edge. "That's Jim," somebody near me whispers, "coming back home to fetch Jean." As if to verify the notion, another buzzard flies down to light beside the first one. They huddle together like lovebirds on the dead limb, facing us mourners in their claw hammer coats, their hunched shoulders touching.

After the service there are handshakes, hugs and kisses. Some of the ladies, I noticed, step back with flared nostrils after I hug them, or maybe I imagine it. I hope I imagine it. Then we watch the pair of buzzards flap off together. They rise higher and higher, circling in the thermal over Lake Chehaw until they are winding specks against a cerulean sky.

Cochise and I walk back down Turtle Hill to the truck in silence. We have a hog to butcher, but we've been touched by the service and our minds are on the two vultures that sat in attendance.

"Buzzards mate for life," Cochise says suddenly.

"I know," I say. "I know they do."

Avarice

The avarice of mankind is insatiable. —Aristotle

𝓘t's the last afternoon of deer season, a Sunday. When I was a kid, there were blue laws against hunting on Sunday, and even though I haven't been a kid for a half century, I still feel a little pang of guilt hunting on the Sabbath. Having arrived by jon boat a couple of days before, I am camped downriver from my childhood home, where my sister and I are flat out of deer meat, and because I have coronary heart disease, I eat very little red meat besides venison. Also, at present, there are two more mouths to feed—my son's ex-girlfriend Melissa and her dog moved in with us after the romance went south. The dog, rescued from a Dempsey Dumpster, gave my two Boykin spaniels the mange, but we've learned to love Melissa like a daughter. From Wisconsin, Melissa is a pretty blond girl, strong, Nordic, and willing. She brought a gust of fresh air into our family home on the Flint River, a blessing in our 70s to have a youngster in the house again.

I absolutely do not mean to suggest that a bum ticker and an empty larder are acceptable excuses for killing three deer on one hunt. Reprobates can always employ hindsight to mitigate a deadly sin. There is nothing illegal about what I've done, but if my son or one of my young hunting protégés had done it, I'd have raised bloody hell. Such is my hypocrisy. I guess I just got carried away in the moment, got caught up in an urgency I should never have brought with me into the woods. Some sins cry out to be confessed even though I'll carry the brand of my sacrilege to my grave—a ruptured disc and a crooked back that suggests a more crooked soul. I only hope my confession will serve young hunters as an example of what not to do and that I'll be viewed hereafter as a penitent more sinned against than sinning. Pure and simple avarice accounts for my ruptured disc. I deserve to be crippled. It's my own damn fault. Listen up, dear reader. There's a moral lesson here.

*

I'm after a big buck, and I set up my climber near his primary scrape—a bare area the size of a beach umbrella on the forest floor. The cleared ground has been spattered with urine, and the heart-shaped hoofprint of a randy doe is imprinted dead center.

I climb the tree as quietly as I can. Almost before I get settled, a doe with a six- point in tow bounces out from behind a privet bush, close enough for neck shots. I kill them both. I have my work cut out for me. I sling my rifle across my chest, turn around to face the tree, and start down—when suddenly, the 10-point I've been hunting all season comes up behind me. Oblivious to my presence, it starts pawing its scrape. I know I'll never unsling my rifle without spooking it, so I draw my .44 magnum revolver from a shoulder holster, twist slowly around, aim behind the shoulder, and fire. The buck bolts in a tight circle and falls. It kicks a time or two and dies. Now what? I have three deer on the ground and no one to help me. I have no idea what I was doing with a pistol up that tree in the first place.

I attach my safety harness to the doe and drag it to the steep riverbank, lowering it with the safety strap to the water's edge. I do the same with the six-point with a little more difficulty on account of its larger size. When it comes to the 10-point, I harness it the same way, fixing its front hooves above its rack so they wonít drag. This makes a sort of sled runner of its chest. With the strap over my shoulder, I start dragging the buck. Ití' heavy as a horse. With its front hooves above its rack, it seems to be protecting its ears against some hideous noise—maybe the report of a .44 magnum. I'm able to drag it only inches at a time. I lean against the strap, pull and rest, pull and rest the 50 yards to the peak of the high riverbank.

I mean to balance the buck teetering on the edge of the steep incline. Then I'll go around behind it to lower it down to the river's edge as I've done the other two deer. I'm almost there. One more tug should do it, but one more tug is one too many. I feel a quick slack in the harness strap over my shoulder, and before I can get out of the way, the buck overruns me, riding my back down the steep bank.

"Whoa!" I cry, "Whoa!" Thorn vines switch us every which way. During the long slide downhill, we rake up about two bushels of briars. They tear my shirt and stitch my hide, but they slow our speed until the buck's antlers plow into the mud, stopping us from sliding into the river.

Of the tumbleweed of briar vines snagged comprehensively into my clothes and epidermis, the most formidable is a variety of smilax with black-tipped thorns colloquially and appropriately called whoa vine or dammit vine. According to myth, smilax was a wood nymph transformed into a whoa vine after an ill-advised love affair with a mortal.

Whoa vine derives its nomenclature from the sudden stop its snagged victims undertake. A smilax thorn had raked across my scalp, removing my ballcap. Plavix- thinned blood runs down my temple and drips off my chin. The buck and I are encysted in a nest of these diverse briars that include blackberry, Cherokee rose, and some other ornery invasive stickers I can't identify. Cherokee rose, native to China, is said to have sprung up from mothers' teardrops on the Trail of Tears. I'm scratched up and bleeding in my bondage, buried in briars and bound cheek to jowl with a dead deer, its sardonic tongue protruding, its sightless green eyes accusing and diabolical. I've narrowly missed being impaled. I'm fastened face down on the riverbank a foot from the water's edge. The smell of spearmint fills my nostrils. The tines have plowed through a patch of wild mint before pegging me to Mother Earth. A purple winter wildflower grows within inches of my nose.

  The abrupt stop and my headlong position must've sloshed some extra blood into my brain. My face flushes hot. My vision blurs. Tiny balls of fire bounce behind my eyelids, pyrotechnics. A fountain of sparkling floaters and a grand finale of starbursts drift by. A distant ding-dong of a church bell. A tightness in my chest warns the onset of angina. I lie there wondering if I'm dead or just dying.

  Perhaps it's proper here to assert, dear reader, that I'm no absolute stranger to death. In 1986, after my first heart attack and before a coronary bypass operation, an allergy to catheter dye stopped my clock. I was awake. I watched myself flatline on the life signs monitor. Compared with other near-death narratives, mine was unremarkable. I had an out-of-body experience, moving toward a tunnel of bright light. The sensation was not unpleasant. Dying was peaceful. I felt sad for the nurses who were frantically trying to shock my mortal coils back to life. Don't worry, sweethearts, I wanted to say. I still have a couple of things I need to do, like make a will, finish a novel, repent, but what the hell, everybody's got to die sooner or later, don't they?

  I didn't stay dead for very long. The cardiologist already had a line in my heart. He gave it a shot of adrenaline that brought me back to this vale of tears. The fact that the event was spiritually uplifting may have had something to do with the sedatives they'd administered for me to let them poke a catheter into my groin and run it up my femoral artery into my aorta. A couple of weeks out of the hospital from the bypass operation, I got bit on the thumb by a rattlesnake. On the way to the emergency room, my throbbing thumb swelled to the size of a golf ball and the bright world was bathed in a lovely amber. I thought I was dying then, but I wasn't. A few days later, I had a reaction to the antivenin, and my face and hands swelled up like catcher's mitts. I itched so bad I almost wished I were dead. That happened 30 years ago.

*

  Now, besides being buried under a dead deer and caught in a tangle of thorns bunched around and over me like hoops of concertina wire, I can lift only my shoulders and head. The rest of my torso is wedged under the deer. Reflected in the water is a confounded, gray-haired, sag-faced old man with a half rack of antlers growing out of the top of his head. A breeze sizzles through the trees. A cypress ball falls from the branches above me—*bloop*—shattering my reflection, centrifugal ripples spreading out to infinity. I can see open mussel shells on the sandy bottom, mother-of-pearl iridescent in the low sunlight. Water trickles by, spinning little silver whirlpools along the edge of the backwater eddy. The rising water might float the deer off me, but it would drown me first, wound and bound in brambles.

  "Things are only as bad as you make them," says my father's ghost. When you circle back home to live out your seniority, ghosts are just a natural part of the landscape. Both my parents' cremated remains have been committed to this river.

  "Well, right now," I answer, "I've made matters pretty bad." I mumble a prayer that a fisherman will happen by, which is unlikely. I haven't heard any boats in the two days I've been camped. My second prayer cancels out the first. After considering my predicament, I don't want anyone seeing me like this, mounted as I am by a swollen-necked buck from behind. Anybody arriving on the scene will have a smartphone.

  They'll take pictures before they rescue me and broadcast

it all over the internet. I'll be humiliated for the rest of my life. Even if I die, somebody might laugh. Of course, I carry no telephone. I left it at home as a symbol of my independence—O vanity! My sister and Melissa won't even expect me for another day. I've lied to them, adding an extra day to my planned sojourn to keep them from worrying. They won't think of sending someone after me until tomorrow or the next day. I can get mighty uncomfortable by then. I reckon I have to get out from under this deer before the power dam 10 miles upriver releases water through the turbines for the evening demand. As a matter of fact, in all probability, the water has been let go already. All it has to do is get down here.

A couple of anatomical events can occur when a dead buck is on top of you with both of you facing downhill: One, the inverted deer may exsanguinate from the bullet hole you shot into it, which in this case is .44 inches in diameter. Two, the slain deer's urinary bladder may shift so as to release its contents. Lukewarm blood drips between my shoulder blades and runs down to the back of my neck. Then I feel tepid water wetting the seat of my pants. Indignity of indignities, a trophy deer has mounted me, bled down my back, and pissed up my leg. However alluring the scent of buck urine may be to a doe in estrus, to a Homo sapiens, I can assure you, it is abominable.

*

Southeastern Indians had a taboo against what I'd done. Deer were to be apologized to after the kill. The spirit of Little Deer sent crippling rheumatism to hunters who failed to properly respect the deer and to thank it for sacrificing its life. The hunter then makes an offering of golden pine pollen over the slain deer before he moves it.

Sometimes he cuts the hamstrings of the slain deer to keep its spirit from following him home. Sometimes he lights a fire in his path.

My behavior lacked reverence. I'd climbed that bay tree to harvest venison with no more respect in my heart than if I'd gone to a meat market. The slide down the hill had rattled my bones. Already I can feel the little flames of arthritis igniting in my spine, shoulders, and hips. Maybe I'll die out here, deserving to. After that I'll be confined facedown and paralyzed in the fifth terrace of Dante's Purgatory, reserved for the greedy and avaricious. I've broken pagan and Christian laws. The 10-point wears an insolent garland of smilax vines.

As a matter of fact, my death upside down on the riverbank where I'd spent so much of my life is somehow fitting. It has a roundness to it. Surely no one could find a more beautiful place to cash in their chips. Maybe dying isn't such a bad idea, a satisfactory closure, and it will absolve me of all the labor ahead of me before I can go to sleep in a warm bed at home. I think of Tillie, the black saint who raised me and my sister. Tilley was afraid of four things: the Devil, snakes, the Flint River, and Studebakers—cars so aerodynamic you couldn't tell if they were coming or going. Every morning of my childhood, she warned us of all four. As soon as she got busy in the kitchen, I headed down to the riverbank, hunting snakes.

*

A lacy sycamore leaf falls into the tannin-stained water. Caught in a little whirlpool, it spins around and around, slinging kaleidoscopic tendrils of prismatic light across the sandy bottom. The network of capillary roots at the waterline suggests some grand and intricate order that surges its design throughout the cosmos. Minnows tug at a stringy blood clot. Everywhere we pause, the glory of creation asserts itself. I can't tell if this is a revelation, a stroke, a senior moment, or all of the above. Suddenly it dawns on me how very, very tired I am. My thighs are still burning from dragging three dead deer the 50 yards from my climber to the lip of the riverbank. I'm almost too tired to twitch. My trapped foot has gone to sleep, pin pricks all the way to my calf. I can barely wiggle my toes. An exhausted voice inside me says, "It's time to rest. All creatures must have sleep." I close my eyes and have already dozed off when the ghost spirit of Tillie, the tyrant of my childhood, speaks up:

"Vic, what you doing down there?" she snaps. "I told you ever day of your life, 'Don't you go near that river,' and here you is stuck in the mud and catclaws with the river fixing to rise."

"Oh, Tillie, I'm old and slap give out. Just let me rest my eyes for a minute."

"Do, and when that river come up, you drown."

I blink myself awake. I writhe and wallow until I can turn over on my back. Supine, I lift the rack out of the mud and push the buck's head aside. Bright heart blood, cooler now, drips on my flannel shirt over my own heart. I'm still bound by briars. Each wand I remove is replaced by two more that bite through my shirt into my hide. I swear I'll never again shoot more than one deer at a time, and to that deer I'll offer sincere thanks and heartfelt apologies.

ending sideways, I manage to reach my Swiss Army knife. I use the little scissors to snip through the blackberry wands, saw through the barbed smilax vines with the blade. Some of the thorns are still snagged in my clothing. Some are still snagged into various and sundry parts of my person. All of them are sharp and vengeful. I'm wet, muddy, and shivering cold.

It takes me until dusk to cut myself out of the basket of briars that have me entwined, but my foot remains wedged beneath the deer's haunches. Doubling over sideways, I find I can reach the top of my boot. Slowly and painfully, I unlace it, and after much tugging, I pull my foot free. My sock comes off inside my boot. The top of my narrow foot is cold and blue as ivory, an old man's foot.

Finally, inch by inch, I low crawl from beneath the 10-point, crabbing through the mud, cutting briars as I go. Finally, I'm free. Now all I have left to do is load up my three deer into the jon boat and head upriver for home. I'm comprehensively anointed with mud, blood, and deer piss. I begin to wish wholeheartedly I'd shot three squirrels instead of three deer. Then I begin to wish I'd missed the deer I shot at. Then I wish I'd never left home.

*

The boat is low in the water and the going upstream is slow. I ferry through the Vs of rapids where rushing water plaits silver moonlight over the rocks. Orion, the hunter, is visible overhead, as is Canis Major, his dog. It's late by the time I return to the boat ramp. I back my trailer down and pull out, too exhausted to notice the port side of the boat isn't snug on the trailer's runners. The imbalance of cargo tilts the johnboat to one side. I hit a pothole that slides the left side of the boat off the trailer, dumping the last deer I'd piled in—the 10-point—at the intersection of the public boat ramp and Radium Springs Road. By now I'm very close to crying. If I'd brought my telephone, I could call Melissa, who'd come to help me get the buck back into the jon boat. Vain pride has stumbled its way into hubris. I'm cold and alone in the dark. Bad karma has coiled back around to bite me on the ass.

I muster all the strength I have left, which is more than I expected. I heave and grunt the deer back into the jon boat. Only with great effort can I rock the boat back on its runners. These combined efforts rupture a lumbar disc, and a sawtooth stab of pain from the small of my back runs down my right leg. The spirit of Little Deer has overcome me with a vengeance, marking me for life. From this point until my death, I'll walk bent over at the waist like a broke-open shotgun, dragging a leg and rocking from side to side—a shuffling gait to remind me of thanklessness and the cardinal sins of pride and avarice.

At home I pull the boat into the backyard and wake up Melissa. We hang a gambrel hook over the cross-piece of the swing set and start butchering deer. I nurse my back and offer instructions as she does nearly all the work. It's after midnight by the time we get started on the last of the deer. I know for the next couple of days getting out of bed will be a challenge, but I don't yet know I'll limp for life.

Melissa, too much of a lady to mention my residual odor, holds a bloody knife. Brushing a blond strand of hair out of her eyes with the back of her hand, she sighs.

"So, how'd you manage to kill three deer at one time?" she says.

"Nothing to it," I reply.

"Well, how'd you get so scratched up and bloody?"

"Penance," I say, "but that's another story."

The Goodbye Bob

...jealousy! It is the green-eyed monster which doth mock the meat it feeds on. —Shakespeare

"Son of a bitch! That was the luckiest shot I ever saw!"

Karen, my editor and significant other, drives me behind the hunters in Clyde's new truck. Clyde, Jimmy, and Polly walk. I'm riding shotgun since I've gotten too lame to keep up with the dogs. Whenever there's a point near the wagon trail, they ask me to come up, but I don't want their charity.

The Browning sweet 16 that Clyde totes he inherited from his uncle Bob, who taught him to hunt quail about the same time my uncle Thad taught me. Uncle Thad sent a little Model 12 20-gauge back to Winchester to have the stock cut down for a growing boy. It had belonged to his only son, who was killed in England the year I was born. When either Clyde or I make a shot beyond the reckoned ability of the shooter, it's ascribed to the ghost of the previous owner, a gift from a higher power, which everybody who's ever quit drinking whiskey knows all about.

"Nice shot, Uncle Bob!" I bray.

"Be a good sport," Karen scolds.

I've been hunting with these guys for 25 years, I tell her. A quarter century is long enough to know what's luck and what ain't. That bird was flat gettin' it, corkscrewing through longleaf pines like a bat. Clyde's lucky shot folded it into an enchilada.

I used to outwalk everybody. Now I can't even keep up to my own dog, a gray mouth Boykin deaf and cripple as I am. He obeys hand signals when he wants to, pretending not to see me when he don't. I should've brought him along, but he'd bust a covey just to embarrass me. Plus, I'm not sure how Clyde would take to a dog in the cab of his new truck, which must've cost more than my first house.

  This is my last hunt. I'm only 75, but my friends are in better shape than I am, and more famous. Still, I think this new truck is a little too much, a double cab with automatic four-wheel drive. When it's parked next to mine, it's a lot too much. Infuriating bells chime reminding you to buckle your seatbelt from one point to the next. When there's a point, I get out just in case a stray single comes my way.

  When you can't keep up with the dogs, it's time to hang up your hat. I don't have a bit of trouble walking short distances, but once the gimp leg drags through blackberry briars, a collapsed disk in the small of my back cranks down on the sciatic nerve, dumping me on my ass like a puppet with cut strings, not a good thing on a quail hunt. Sometimes I get excited and think I can walk better than I actually can. If endorphins get to cracking, I can walk better than I did a few moments before. The smell of gunpowder and the company of old friends can make me move quicker than I ought to.

  Ike, the chestnut and white piebald Brittany spaniel, is busy finding Clyde's bird, its feathered tail swishing, Jimmy calls Jake, the black and white English setter, over to look for one he thinks he hit but didn't. Jake isn't as enthusiastic as Jimmy about it. Ike loves to hunt so much he sometimes gets carried away and goes off on his own. Jimmy keeps a shock collar on him. If he's gone too long, it usually means he's off pointed somewhere. When Jimmy can't find him, he has to jazz him and listen for the yelp. More often than not, the yelp flushes birds.

  His shooting eye blinded by a briar, Uncle Thad didn't actually show me how to shoot. He just told me when I was old enough to listen and had me dry firing around the house. I'd throw up on a picture or an antique vase and the gun would click as I shouldered it. All my practice made my high-strung mother more highly strung, but it was tolerated, even encouraged, because around our house, Uncle Thad and Aunt Maudelle were much revered.

Thad arranged my first quail. We rode the wagon behind hunters on horseback.

At sundown he chose the single to put me on, sent me up to the point alone with his son's 20 gauge, my heartbeat sizzling in my ears. Of course, I remember every detail to this day some 65 years later.

Clyde's Uncle Bob started him out in the Florida Panhandle about the same time. Our first hunting trip together was born of a mutual nostalgia sometime after Clyde's first or second novel. Now he has something like nine and a couple of nonfiction titles on flying and fatherhood. Over the years we've discovered our lives have run eerily parallel. He flew sorties over Cold War Korea while I was a grunt in a DMZ below. We were both jailed at different times for youthful excess in Myrtle Beach, South Carolina, and we both had beloved uncles who taught us to hunt quail and bequeathed us haunted shotguns. Now Clyde holds a creative writing chair at a big university, which trumps the hell out of my career as a freshman comp teacher at a community college.

Jimmy, Polly, and Karen are better writers than I am, too. I'm pretty sure our mutual friendship developed because I live slap in the middle of the bobwhite capital of Dixie. Over the years I suspect my friends have grown to like each other better than they like me, and it chaps my ass, especially in light of the fact that I've become progressively less likable. They keep me around like a bad habit, trailing them in a garish truck. Clyde, Jimmy, and I are old enough to be curmudgeons, but I'm the only one who is. More than anything I envy their ability to walk.

This year Catherine, mistress of Blue Springs Plantation, has put us up on the second floor of the big house, where we're guests, not clients. We've been coming here long before there were clients. Collin and Margie, dog trainers from Wisconsin, are staying up on the third floor. Margie brought newborn Brittany puppies down for us to see. She tried to hand me one, but I turned her down. I'm done raising birddog pups, though the mama bitch has the prettiest face I reckon I've ever seen on a dog.

My mother and I rode horseback on Blue Springs for the field trials back in the '50s, when Eisenhower came here to hunt. It's the plantation most like the quail plantations of my youth. I scattered her ashes with flower petals beneath a bluff where the sun sets on a wide slow bend on the Flint River. Catherine arranged for the choir from the black church on the place to sing spirituals. A few months later we put my father's ashes in a few miles upriver, where my sister and I were raised. I never hunt on Blue Springs without a presentment of ghosts.

"Those puppies were cute," Karen says. To women, baby rattlesnakes are cute.

But I'm too old to train a puppy. When you quit hunting, the last thing you want is a birddog pup around to remind you of what you used to do and don't anymore—almost as bad being surrounded by friends who outdistance you in every way and have laurels to prove it. Jimmy and Polly walked over 500 miles of Georgia wilderness trails to co-write a book about it. With his novel, that makes two books this year for Jimmy. Karen is editor of a regional magazine that publishes me only once in a while. I'm the lame duck on this bird hunt with the sparsest laurels under my ass. I might've spent too much time hunting when I should've been learning to write.

I killed my first quail with the 20 gauge in the seat beside me, and my son did, too. He once shot three wild birds with it on a covey rise, and I should've passed the gun on to him right then. But I wait too late to do the things I ought to do, and to him it's just a gun.

About the time I retired, Clyde remarried. Now he has a son old enough to hunt, but the boy elected at the last minute to stay home in North Carolina, which about crushed Clyde and me both. My grandson is way too young to appreciate a shotgun. By the time he's ready, wild bobwhites will be the name of a video game and my ashes will be in the Flint River with his great-grandparents'. These days it's hard to find a kid to inherit your guns. Over the generations, passed down guns stockpile in attics—the ghosts of previous owners fading away among Christmas decorations.

*

Polly gets on a single too quickly, hits it before the pattern spreads, the bird ruined for eating unless you like them cubed. She's far enough away that I see her blond ponytail swish before I hear the shot. At supper Clyde, the former jet jockey, will say the bird was traveling at about 40 miles an hour when it accelerated from its feathers at twice that speed, Mach something or other. It's not Polly's gender that intimidates me. I've got two daughters who can outshoot me when they put their minds to it. Truth is I don't like anybody shooting better than I do, and almost everybody I know does. After Uncle Thad died, I developed every shooting flaw that thinking about it causes.

What does it mean when you're too old to keep up with the dogs, and your friends and children exceed you in every way? It means you've got better friends and children than you deserve, that you should reconsider the blessings of friendship and paternity, that you are lucky to have more living friends than dead. I'd turn green with jealousy if I didn't love these people so much.

Karen doesn't believe I'm quitting. "You'll be right here next year," she says.

"No hell I won't."

Seems like I could appreciate what all I've got.

*

A good rain came through last night. This morning was windy, but the wind lay back at dinnertime, and now it's a bluebird afternoon, the ground damp enough for the dogs to smell, a chill in the air. I'm a guest on the prettiest quail plantation in Dixie, riding shotgun in a truck the size of a Hummer, closer to the action than I'd be without it. We declined Catherine's offer to hitch up the mules. The last time I rode the wagon, I had a heart attack on a covey rise, crippled a bird, and had to be taken to the ER in briar britches. Anybody with a brain would've quit then.

  Karen pulls up behind the hunters, splashes of DayGlo orange on a drab knoll. Jake, the setter, points. Ike backs. I haul myself out the door to chiming bells, load two shells, mostly for the hell of it. I'm leaning against the fender when the flushed covey swarms from the hillside. A single sails back my way over the treetops. The little 20 gauge goes up and fires a Hail Mary farewell, shunting all the bad habits learned by the adult brain. While I'm pumping for a second shot, a rotator cuff wimps out, leaving the slide at half-mast. Miraculously, the bird tumbles, falling in the firebreak with a slight bounce. Karen must've seen it if she wasn't texting. No use confessing I'd lost sight of the bird when the gun went off.

  When I galumph back to the truck, she's reading her smartphone. The smell of powder must've set a happy endorphin dancing. My backache has temporarily vanished. I've noticed that with friends around I'm sometimes not so crippled. For the moment I've forgotten all about a ruptured disk together with my occluded and multi-stinted heart. Now I can quit on a better note, an acceptable closure.

  "Clyde sent you a text," Karen says.

  "What?"

  "'Nice shot, Uncle Thad.'"

*

At supper, to seem polite, they'll ask about my work in progress. A lot of my work is in perpetual progress. I have trouble ending things. Clyde will ask if I shot that bird out of the tree, and I'll look to Karen to back me up. She must've seen the bird fall through the rearview mirror or maybe reflected in all that generous chrome. "I was texting," she'll say, keeping neutral.

Uncle Thad chose the first quail for me. We'd followed horseback hunters in the dog wagon, watching on. Near sundown, the muscular English pointer, a liver-spot with yellow, rattlesnake eyes, flowed like a wave down a fence row. Nearly overrunning the single, it suddenly froze into a rigid S—sure and shivering, head cocked, nose nudging a tuft of broomsedge. Thad sent me up. Don't aim, he said. When your bird levels off, kill it with your eye.

*

All three hunters raise their cellphones to snap the point, the dogs poised in a golden touch of a low sun on wiregrass and broomsedge, the lavender bark of longleaf pine, the silver splash of needles. Ike, who can't distinguish between the shock transmitter and a smartphone, tucks in his tail and scats. Smartphones are making a neurotic mess of Ike, just like dry firing in the living room made a mess of my pretty mother.

They want us to find Ike, Karen reads from her phone. We splash through deep puddles on the trail, dappling the fenders of Clyde's new truck with muddy water.

Eventually we find Ike pointed, low down and sleazy, in the scrub fringe between the road and the cypress swamp, his nose nudging a tuft of wiregrass.

"Here's y'all's dog!" I holler through the open window.

"What?" yells Polly.

"Text them Ike's pointed."

"They texted you take it." Karen says.

"They're hoping I'll miss."

"Well, don't then." She smiles.

The pressure's on. Friends with cellphones raised like crab claws, watching from the hill, Karen looking through the windshield. My chance to end things without a whimper. A second parting shot with the same haunted gun I started with 60 years ago.

I march through the briars like there aren't any, brace up behind the little Brittany. The lay is more than déjà vu. It's exactly the same—a tuft of grass, oak scrub, a cypress swamp beyond. It's the exact same point with a different dog, Ike down low, eyes rolling around, looking back for a smartphone, the faint ghost of that old liver-spot backing.

The single shatters gravity with a flatulent rattle, floating like a toy balloon, a family portrait on the wall. I've got plenty of time, just like that first quail all those years ago. Just fix it with your mind and let the gun go off when the stock is snug against your cheek. I know there ain't no way I'll miss the bird I've been killing all my life. But, what the hell, with my dead eye on the bird my arms and shoulders merely spasm, will dampened by reverie. Some frayed neuron between resolve and action shorts the system. Some pinched or worn-out nerve can't bridge the gap. The model 12 spasms at port arms and then discharges—Poom! Live oak leaves above my head rain down. My last quail sails happily into the dark yawn of cypress swamp, Uncle Thad lifting his hat in good-bye.

Back at supper nobody mentions my parting shot, a safe silence. I'll let them think I departed venery with a noble gesture, sparing one immortal bird to get away forever. Margie brings the puppies down again. This time I pick one up, scrub its head.

"How much y'all want for this pup?"

Circles Unbroken

Will the circle be unbroken By and by, Lord, by and by?
—Lyrics by Roy Acuff

When I first see Betsy Franck, I'm speechless, transfixed. My heart sloshes an extra beat. She's a hereditary composite of her father and grandparents, favoring a youthful Cher. Her long dark hair falls to her elbows. It's as though she has stepped enigmatically into the present from my childhood. I feel I've known her all her life.

An accomplished musician and songwriter, Betsy has an entertainer's charisma.

She has come from a gig in Statesboro—a tribute to Gregg Allman—to my childhood home on the Flint River in search of her father's boyhood, so her son can know something of his grandfather and to scatter his ashes in the places where as an adolescent he loved to roam. We were playmates, Bobby and me, wild boys, who loved the woods and springs. We hunted and fished along this riverbank, swam the swift currents, shot the rapids where the whitewater braids itself over the rocks.

We sit on the deck my son built overlooking the river. Much of what we'll say to each other will seem already said. We are silent, soaking in the view. I pick a pomegranate from its tree on the edge of the lawn, scoring the rind with my pocketknife, breaking the fruit in half. She holds out her palms to catch the ruby red arils. The fleshy seeds spill into her hands like bloody tears. We share the fruit as I try to recall details of her father's childhood 65 years ago, reviving memories that would've remained forgotten of a time when everything was green and possible, and we thought we'd live forever. Gazing downriver, we become aware of time as a vortex when all things past and present exist in the same eternal moment, when the best and happiest moments are immortal and bad karma can coil around and bite you on the ass. I believe the forbidden fruit was a pomegranate, that Mother Eve got caught red-handed with ruby juice dribbling down her chin.

In the dusk we watch migrating chimney swifts flitting like bats as they circle and dive to roost in the chimney of mother's Williamsburg cottage. The house is haunted by my mother, a poltergeist. The house remains much as she left it, a monument to herself and her exquisite taste. Nothing but 18th-century antiques suit the house. My father's ghost is a river spirit, haunting the corner of the lot where the deck now stands. Bobby spent almost as much time at my house as he did at his own home. For our nocturnal ramblings we snuck out the upstairs dormer window, dropping to the lawn like cats.

We'd meet our sidekick Marvin and set out on adventures preconceived by Betsy's father, like gigging eels.

"There's one," Bobby hisses in the dark, "dead ahead." Marvin and I stand up to see, rocking the rowboat we've borrowed without permission from Radium Springs Resort. Bobby's Boy Scout lantern spotlights a black and silver eel lying in an S on the bottom of the sandy channel of Radium Creek. He hands the lantern to Marvin and eases his bamboo gig pole into the water. Allowing for refraction, he jabs, leaning his weight on the gig. The eel is pinned, the pole quivering. He lifts it off the bottom and the eel goes ballistic. The pole bends and wobbles. Nothing fights like a three-foot eel on a bamboo pole. Bobby brings it up thrashing, slinging moonlight, but the eel wiggles free before he can boat it. "Son of a biscuit eater," declares Bobby. "Got dog!" Bobby is learning to cuss. He blames me for paddling too fast with the broom we've stolen from Tillie, the

saint responsible for my deportment and, by extension, for Bobby's. He blames us for rocking the boat.

It must be a trait of adolescent boys to want to gig something. Bobby, the oldest and closest to puberty, always got the first turn with the gig. His rules. Marvin went first if snatch-hooking was called for. He was by far the most accomplished snatch-hooker. He tossed his treble hook over a sleeping jack or into a school of flaring silver shad. At just the right time, he snatched and we ducked the barbed missile when he missed.

Generally, I was the kid in the back of the boat with Tillie's broom.

We missed more eels than we harvested, but one we've boated lashes around in the dark bilge against our bare ankles, causing more misses. These eels, we'd learn later, were born in the Sargasso Sea. Their mothers migrated from the spring creek over the little dam into the Flint River, which joins the Chattahoochee at the Florida line to form a third, the Apalachicola, before it flows into the Gulf of Mexico. The eels rounded the cape of Florida to the Atlantic and the Sargasso Sea, where they spawned and died. The elvers retraced their mothers' voyage back to the springs. Some nights we fished for bass in the creek, baitcasting a luminous Jitterbug plundered from my father's tackle box, which being retrieved wobbled webs of moonlight across the crystal water.

Our mothers would cook a bass but wouldn't come near an eel. They wouldn't even allow the metallic-smelling shad in the house. Bobby, a winsome maverick with blond hair unruly as a sandspur, could sweet-talk Tillie into frying an eel for us. He had sway over any woman regardless of age. My mother called him harum-scarum and didn't trust a word he said, but he was her favorite. She was as susceptible to his boyish charm as was everybody else. They rivaled each other on the piano. Bobby played well although he never practiced. "That boy full of the Debil." Tillie smiled, but he wooed her with his mischief and irrepressible energy. She was putty in his hands.

There are no longer eels in Radium, which in modern times dries up during the summer. Much of Bobby's old neighborhood was devastated by last January's tornado. Many houses were destroyed, his former home damaged. Riparian wetlands where Bobby and I hunted squirrels were demolished as well, great live oaks sucked up by the roots, longleaf pines twisted and splintered, strewn akimbo like fiddlesticks. I have to re-create much of our childhood geography as I recall our adolescent adventures. It's as if the setting of our boyhood has vanished with the eels. I find solace only in that our childhood venue was destroyed by natural forces and not by bulldozers.

The next morning my sister and I drive Betsy the quarter mile down the road to Radium Springs, the largest spring in Georgia and the heart of our childhood geography. From Bobby's house on the Radium golf course or my house on the river, you could hear the bass thump of dancehall music from a jukebox. When a formal ball was held in the grand casino, the live music wafted up the river and across the links until late at night. The grand casino, a white antebellum colossus, was destroyed by flood, then fire. Swimming in the springs is forbidden now, which in my mind is a sin. The water is surrounded by a metal fence of thick wire cables to protect folks from themselves. This was the nucleus of our childhood, where we went at least once a day all summer, the major setting of our youth and the best years of our lives. Now the springs are closed on Monday, the gates locked. Sneaking in from the creek, we have the old resort to ourselves. All my life I've known how to sneak into Radium Springs. We sit on the wall over the boil, the deep blue crater with a cave that is the artesian source of the swimming area and the creek. The water today is as uncharacteristically clear as it was in our childhood, although the rest of the lake is choked by hydrilla.

*

As a teenager, Bobby worked in the locker room and concession stand, the perfect summer job because all the high school kids came there to swim, sunbathe, and dance. Bobby got paid to be where he'd have been anyway, and for that reason he wasn't paid much. During our childhood the water boiled from its underground source at a thousand gallons a second. The flow has diminished in modern times, sometimes desiccating to a murky sump that doesn't produce enough water to feed the creek. As adolescents, we dived the 30 feet to the sandy bottom, finding lost coins, mastodon teeth, and Native American artifacts. It was a rite of passage to dive to the bottom of the boil, bringing up a fistful of white sand as proof. In the heat of summer nights before air-conditioning, we dived into the boil, cooled down enough to sleep. On New Year's Day, on double-dog dares, we dived into the 68-degree constant temperature of the spring water, which felt warm until we climbed the mossy steps into the chilly ambient air. Bobby could accomplish a full gainer off the high dive into the boil.

 Our first brush with mortality occurred at the springs when a navy frogman recovered the body of a lost scuba diver from the underwater cave. He described great caverns and many rooms deep inside the bowels of Radium Cave. Years later, when I was 18, I was called on to recover the corpse of another diver. The body was covered with eels, so I know there were still eels in Radium in 1960. Those eels and that body remain burned into my memory, illuminated against the pitch dark of Radium Cave.

 Now, gazing into the deep blue water, I'm overcome by synchronistic nostalgia.

 Some craving, some senior moment, some urgent thirst

for baptism and rebirth, or maybe just the proximity of a beautiful woman, moves me to strip down to my boxers, climb over the restraining fence, swinging a spindly leg over the NO SWIMMING sign. Maybe I seek some spiritual salvation where others have died. I attempt a swan dive, pointing my toes, but my legs splay and flop at the knees. I'm suddenly enveloped in the marrow-chilling shock of the exquisite and transcendent cold. To say the water temperature is 68 degrees is to miss the point. In the heat of summer, Radium Springs is icy cold. The frigid water, reputed to have healing properties, has focused me, swept the geriatric cobwebs from my brain, slapped me back to the 1950s. I swim toward the dark, ultramarine blue of the cave. When the pressure hurts my ears, I ascend in a galaxy of fizzing bubbles and climb the mossy steps a younger man. Betsy and Sister avert their eyes as I shiver back into my trousers. Then Betsy pours a milky cloud of ashes into the boil. Bluegills rise to it. One sucks in a fragment, spits it back out. A great blue heron lights on the lime-spattered concrete platform, where girls in bright bathing suits used to bask in the summer sun. Beneath the platform, Bobby, Marvin, and I speared fish in the gothic shadows and otherworldly gloom.

*

"Moan," says Bobby through his snorkel. We follow him under the fossil rock arches into the partial dark beneath the platform. In the noonday twilight, our suntanned bodies are sallow as cadavers. Bobby carries a homemade Hawaiian sling, a joint of bamboo with an inner tube rubber band attached. It works like a slingshot with a tube instead of a Y, but unlike a slingshot, we'll have to be careful not to pull the rubber back too far. For spears we've hammered flat the tips of coat hanger wires and rubbed them to a point on the concrete steps.

Our snorkels drag tendrils of scratchy hydrilla that floats in patches beneath the platform. A dead musk turtle with a sardonic smile bobs in the scum. As a rule, we miss the fish we shoot at, our spears trailing tiny tracer bubbles behind our darting prey, but once in a while we impale a bream, the coat hanger wire hanging from its side like a bandolier. Then the three of us, in mask, snorkel, and swim fins, try to chase it down.

Sometimes a stricken fish swims in circles and we capture it. More often our quarries shrug off our harpoons and get away.

"Hot tamale nose!" he squeaks. "Hot tamale nose!" It's a whopper, fanning the bottom, thick lips sucking detritus, barbels twitching. WOW! We've never shot a fish this big. Bobby stalks within range. The carp ignores him. It moves along, resting again on the bottom in a golden ray of light. Bobby gets set. He loads the sling, inserts the wire harpoon into the bamboo barrel, seats the butt of the spear into the crotch of the sling. He knows he'll have to pull the rubber way back to penetrate the carp's thick scales. We watch him aim, drawing the rubber back farther than he's ever drawn it before. It vibrates, the point of the harpoon overriding the breach, falling into the palm of his extended hand. In this penultimate moment, Marvin and I see what's fixing to happen. We bleat warnings through our snorkels. "Nu, nu!" Bobby lets fly, and to our adolescent horror, the spear enters the heel of his hand beside the ball of his thumb, running beneath the lifeline, tunneling under the tough hide of his palm, stopping halfway through, half in and half out.

Bobby's eyes widen to fill his face mask. ¡Arhoo!" he trumpets. We splash through the stone arch back into the full sunlight, meeting at the platform steps, ripping off our face masks. Bobby's palms are squeezed together between his knees, a gesture of an inverted prayer. "Got dog!" At first he doesn't want to show us, doesn't want to look, but

Marvin and I insist. Bobby pulls the black wire all the way through. "Hot tamale nose!" he squeaks.

"Hot tamale nose!" we echo sympathetically. We can't seek first aid from the lifeguard without revealing we've been spearfishing in the swimming area. We examine the wound, two punctures on either side of his palm. It bleeds hardly a trickle but leaves an indelible trace of tiny black flakes under the tough skin. Before the end of summer, Marvin and I will sport the same black lines. Our mothers will think we've been tattooed by some clandestine gang of juvenile delinquents.

*

From the springs, Sister and I take Betsy to Radium Dam, where the mile-long creek cascades turquoise water that marbles into the whiskey brown river where huge striped bass circled like gray ghosts in the deep clear pools. Above the dam Bobby and I dived for golf balls that we sold by the bucket to his father to practice chip shots. In the riprap beneath the dam, we found arrowheads the color of caramel, so thin you could see sunlight through them. In early spring we caught shellcrackers in the foaming tailwater, and one autumn Bobby killed a wild turkey here while hunting squirrels. At the time, he wasn't sure he hadn't shot a turkey buzzard. He took it to my house, where his elder brother, Duffy, identified it and Tillie baked it for us.

The Radium golf course, now abandoned, lies along the riverbank downstream from the dam. Golfers used to carry shotguns or fishing rods in their caddy carts.

Turkeys roosted along the river, and fish sought the clear spring water to spawn. When the Flint flooded the 18th hole, we bodysurfed the rushing water over the hilly fairways and elevated greens. My son has given me a Savannah River projectile point he found on this high bank. We give it to Betsy for a memento of her daddy's youth. We feel the arrowhead has passed through us to seek her out.

   Leaving the dam, we cross the railroad tracks where there was a dependable covey of bobwhite quail for Queenie, the Francks' aging black and white pointer, to find and flush, quivering like a tuning fork. We took turns missing the rattling covey rise with Bobby's .410 Mossberg bolt action. Across the tracks were a trap and skeet range and a log lodge where we had Boy Scout meetings. We played war among the trap bunkers and Capture the Flag. We had American and German helmets to reenact WWI I, tossing dirt clods for hand grenades until we graduated to Red Ryder BB guns. For the War Between the States, Confederates wore Levi's turned inside out, gray with a blue stripe down the outside leg. Nobody wanted to be a Yankee. For that, we had to draw the short straws.

*

   To retrace the riverbank we toured by automobile, we launch my jon boat.

   Reaching Radium Dam, we kill the outboard and drift with the current into the shoals adjacent to the golf course. A breeze sizzles through the ruddy brown cypress needles and rattles the golden leaves of a sycamore, swaying gray beards of Spanish moss, slinging diamonds of sunlight across the water. We flush a pair of wood ducks that lift off the water, trailing pearls. We commune with the river spirits and the ghosts of my childhood and wonder how our grandchildren will know what's holy when all the forests are gone. Where will the ghosts go when there is no wild? Where will God go? ,

   Betsy has told me she wants to learn to cast a flyrod. I assemble a 6-weight and tell her to pretend she's slinging paint off a paintbrush. It doesn't take long for her to catch on. Soon she's casting sassy loops and S's between 10 o'clock and 2. Tick, tock. There's kinetic magic in this vibrant woman casting a fly rod, poetry in motion, a symphony of life and death. It's as if she waves a magic wand that stirs the past into the omnipresent now, sunlight flashing from her hair. Yet she insists on casting toward the middle of the river instead of to the bank. "You won't catch a fish until you cast to the shore," I tell her.

"I don't want to catch a fish," she says, "until I learn to cast." Betsy's as hardheaded as her daddy was. She has his contagious energy for anything new. Before we return to the boat ramp, she inverts the urn, pouring the last of her daddy's ashes into the river. The breeze blows a wisp of gray dust back into the boat. The rest of Bobby is caught into a tiny whirlpool, spinning and spreading white ashes like a spiral galaxy in miniature. Betsy has finished what she came for, and I've discovered there's no joy greater than giving an old friend's daughter a new glimpse of her father. I go to wishing I had some words, some wisdom to pass on, but I realize I got old without becoming wise.

When it's time for her to drive home to Nashville—to her profession and to her husband and son—I ask her to sing a song on the riverbank. We return to the deck where we shared the pomegranate. She opens the battered case of her daddy's guitar and sings a requiem to her father in her full-throated womanly voice. The sweet music tumbles down the river, reviving memories and resurrecting ghosts. It carries to the Radium Dam and to its headwater springs, over the hills and greens of the vanished golf course, through the tornado devastation of our childhood forest. It mingles with the sizzling breeze, wafting and twisting over the currents and backwater eddies. It carries downriver to the golf course, the whitewater rapids, the vanished Radium casino, the boil, the concrete platform, and the ghosts of sunbathing girls in bright bathing suits:

*Will the circle
be unbroken,
By and by, Lord,
by and by?*

  It's as though, gazing down this river, we have entered a snag in the fabric of time. The past bonds with the present. The years between us have melted. We feel her daddy's childhood and other spirits that haunt the riverbank. The music wafts in the sweet acoustics over the water. Bobby's ashes will follow the path of eels, when there were eels, to the Gulf, around the cape of Florida, to the Sargasso Sea and to the oceans of the world.

*There's a better
home a waiting,
In the sky, Lord,
in the sky.*

Praise for *One Man's Junk*

As with the very best writers, Miller puts you so squarely into the action of his stories you forget they are written. You are there. And you get re-amazed at each of these strikingly different, strikingly alive stories, stories—as their teeth sink in—that leave you sucking in your breath, shaking your head, laughing out loud. *One Man's Junk* was this man's pleasure.

Clyde Edgerton

I read these stories with a blend of aristotelian pity and terror—the true signs of wonder in art. Also, I read with a joy at their author's skill, fierce tenderness and wit. I know that Mr. Miller is a black-water diver, which means he goes places the rest of us only suspect, cannot bear to experience for ourselves, and yet are only too glad to read about in headlines. Mr. Miller takes us farther than that; he dives deep, as one of his chracters says, into waters infested with who-knows-what reptiles. Below the surface he sees with his senses, as well as his eyes. He does not grope, he knows. He does not shrink from what he finds but rather enlarges us by his courage, and yes, it must be aadmitted, his hi-jinks. His comedy is dead serious. His ear is perfect, his dialogue breath-taking, his characters jaw-droppers. It well may be we'd rather not know some of these things, but I dare any reader to forget them or find one false word. His stories are full of sinkholes, black holes and fire, of dark and light reflections, shimmers, glares and glitters, like the young man who rescues the dead from Radium Cave, we don't entirely know what the message is, in that effervescent moment of revelation as we grapple with death, but we know the way out is up, and we rise if we are lucky, with eyes open, changed forever into life and awe.

Mary Hood

The stories in One Man's Junk are so crammed with such a variety of characters, moods, and surprises that they need to be read more than once. But there are four ways to read a Victor Miller story: fast, fast, because your worried about what's going to happen next to the wonderfully real poor wretches who people the stories; slow, because you want to chew each parenthetical aside and read it to your wife; fast slow, because you keep leaping ahead for the action and doubling back for a metaphor you might have missed; and slow slow, because you mistakenly think that by memorizing every word you can learn to talk something close to the way Victor Miller writes. Any way you read them, you are continually amazed to find yourself laughing at the horrible lives of human beings and delighted in the art that transforms your horror into love. And then you read them again.

John DuVal

Vic Miller is one of the most innovative, intuitive Southern writers since Faulkner—on par with Cormac McCarthy. Every word in *One Man's Junk* has been weighed.

Janice Daugharty

About the Author

Fans of O. Victor Miller's short stories will delight at this collection of articles published in *Gray's Sporting Journal* and several Georgia publications over the past 30 years. A retired English professor from South Georgia, he's both irreverent and imaginative as he shares his tales of adventure, hunting, fly fishing, river life and travel. Vic offers highly engaging outdoor tales with an elevated turn of phrase that reads like fine literature. You'll laugh out loud, share his stories with friends, and be amazed that he survived every one of these tales and is still alive at 80.